"The stewardship and focus of the Baylor Health Care System (BHCS) documented in *Achieving STEEEP Health Care* provides the multi-dimensional journey to sustainable quality improvement needed to address America's health system challenges. Under the clear direction of its board and senior leaders, BHCS has firmly addressed the vital components of culture, knowledge, teamwork, alignment of incentives, and change expectations to advance BHCS toward its vision. Embedding the Institute for Health Care Research and Improvement under the direction of BHCS Senior Vice President and Chief Quality Officer Dr. David Ballard and his team has provided the bench strength to implement and attain such needed change. Vision driving change to better care—an important read and roadmap to follow."

Arja P. Adair, Jr., MBA
President and Chief Executive Officer
Colorado Foundation for Medical Care

"Quality of care is the central tenet of the promise that every health care provider makes to the patient. This text is a must for all those who believe that a constant search for better ways to assure and improve quality is an important part of keeping that promise."

John Agwunobi, MD
Senior Vice President and President of Health and Wellness
Wal-Mart Stores, Inc.

"Inspiring, motivational, evidence-based, 'can do' blueprint for incorporating quality into the organizational DNA and culture of complex health care systems. Practical tips like making the chief financial officer a quality champion and creating infrastructure for sustaining quality through transforming the professional nurse practice environment make this volume a must read."

Linda H. Aiken, PhD, FAAN, FRCN, RN
Claire M. Fagin Leadership Professor of Nursing
Professor of Sociology
Director of the Center for Health Outcomes and Policy Research
University of Pennsylvania

"*Achieving STEEEP Health Care* is a compelling and comprehensive book on improving quality. Baylor Health Care System's commitment to better health care is unmatched, and in David Ballard they found a person who can not only lead change, but also capture and characterize the key insights that will help the rest of us get on the path to superb care."

Troyen A. Brennan, MD
Executive Vice President and Chief Medical Officer
CVS Caremark

"The International Society for Quality in Health Care has taken a number of initiatives in its quest to 'inspire, promote and support continuous improvement in the quality and safety of healthcare worldwide,' one of which is to seek to enhance the quality of the 'patient journey.' I was impressed therefore to reference in this excellent publication from Baylor Health Care System to meeting '...the needs of the individual patient across the continuum of care.'

Achieving STEEEP Health Care comprehensively guides us through the operationalizing of the delivery of safe, timely, effective, efficient, equitable and patient-centered care and as such it provides both a welcome focus and a useful practical guide to all who want the best for those in their care."

Peter Carter
Chief Executive Officer
International Society for Quality in Health Care

"The American health care system is undergoing much needed and dramatic change driven by the need to be more efficient and more effective in delivering high quality and safe care that improves the overall health of the population and does not bankrupt the country in the process. What will this health care system of the future look like? The Baylor Health Care System, which this book outlines in such detail that it could be a cookbook for how to create a future health care system. David Ballard is the architect, STEEEP is the foundation, and this book is a roadmap of how Baylor Health Care System has made the journey to this new destination. Any health care leader faced with this inevitable transformation of their organization will find this book an essential part of their survival guide in the rapidly changing landscape that is the American health care system."

David Classen, MD, MS
Chief Medical Information Officer
Pascal Metrics
Associate Professor of Medicine and Consultant in Infectious Diseases
University of Utah School of Medicine

"This book is a 'must read' for leaders in health care—Baylor Health Care System leaders have been wonderful national contributors and a catalytic force in the quality and safety arena. The practical strategies and tactics they put forth will save lives, save money, and create value in the communities we serve."

Charles Denham, MD
Founder and Chairman
Texas Medical Institute of Technology

"'Vision without execution is hallucination,' Thomas A. Edison said. Baylor Health Care System developed a vision and executed it. Ballard and his colleagues have led a terrific transformational process of the health care system in which they work. *Achieving STEEEP Health Care* documents this process and measures the results in terms of quality improvement and patient safety. This book is a very useful tool for those aiming to lead change, not only in U.S. health care organizations, but also in other health care systems worldwide."

Carlo Favaretti, MD
President and Founder
Italian Society of Health Technology Assessment
Former Chief Executive Officer
Udine University Hospital (Italy)

"Dr. Ballard and his colleagues strongly make the point that the journey to health care excellence requires a committed transformation of leadership, operations, and every aspect of the enterprise. Best care is not the result of a stand alone 'initiative.'"

Ziad Haydar, MD, MBA
Senior Vice President and Chief Medical Officer
Ascension Health

"While the journey may be STEEEP, Dr. Ballard's accomplishments demonstrate that higher quality is attainable. The roadmap provides inspiration to all those dedicated to achieving a better health care system."

Trent Haywood, MD, JD
Chief Medical Officer
Blue Cross and Blue Shield Association

"Transforming health care delivery in a large health system like the Baylor Health Care System is no mean feat. In this book, David Ballard and his team spell out their journey over the past decade to achieve such change based on STEEEP as a practical approach to high-quality care in its broadest sense. This book is a great basis for those less advanced on such a journey, and will accelerate the travels of those who read it."

J. Michael Henderson, MD
Chief Quality Officer
Cleveland Clinic

"Enhancing and ensuring the quality of health care delivery in the 21st century is the principal obligation of all health care executives and providers. *Achieving STEEEP Health Care* will greatly assist leaders in fulfilling that critical obligation."

Ira J. Isaacson, MD, MBA
Senior Vice President/Partner
Phillips, DiPisa, & Associates

"At the heart of quality improvement lies W. Edwards Deming's idea of fundamental knowledge—the concept that there is a difference between theory and reality. Theory is always an abstraction. Reality is the devil lurking in the details, down in the mud and weeds. Said another way, some talk about it; a relatively few actually do it.

You hold in your hands the detailed journey map of a group who has done it, with elegance and flair. It tracks the transformation as theory becomes functional reality. Those seeking to move to the safety of the high ground in an increasingly difficult health care delivery world will find it valuable beyond compare."

Brent James, MD, MStat
Chief Quality Officer
Executive Director of the Institute for Health Care Delivery Research
Intermountain Healthcare

"All too often, case studies of health care organizations that are actively involved in transforming their delivery of care focus on only a single element of that transformation, as if it were the 'magic bullet' that could solve all problems. By contrast, Ballard and his colleagues have set forth a comprehensive look at the multiple initiatives—from simple to quite complex—that are enabling the Baylor Health Care System to play a leading role in transforming health care in the U.S. Every leader who aspires to achieve safe, timely, effective, efficient, equitable, patient-centered care should read and learn from this book."

William F. Jessee, MD, FACMPE
Senior Vice President and Senior Advisor
Integrated Healthcare Strategies

"This book provides a lens into one organization's journey to safe, timely, effective, efficient, equitable and patient-centered care. Full of insights, strategies, lessons and resources, this is an important read for any health care organization striving for improvement."

Maulik Joshi, DrPH
President
Health Research & Educational Trust
Senior Vice President of Research
American Hospital Association

"This book represents a tremendous contribution by a highly respected organization that is fully grounded in the challenges and opportunities of American medicine. Table I.1 alone is worth many times the price of any book—it is essentially a playbook for forward-looking, progressive organizations, and one that meets them where they currently are, and takes them forward. David Ballard and Baylor Health Care System's national leadership reach a new level with this book's publication."

Thomas H. Lee, MD
Chief Medical Officer
Press Ganey Associates, Inc.

"In this monograph, Dr. David Ballard and colleagues describe how they have embedded the basic dimensions of the Institute of Medicine framework for quality (i.e., safe, timely, effective, efficient, equitable and patient-centered care), into a practical set of tools used by the Baylor Health Care System—but applicable to any other health care system in the country—into day-to-day operations designed to improve care. They describe the essential components that make their system work, including leadership commitment, use of standardized measurement and quality improvement tools, care coordination across the continuum and the creation of a safety culture. As a health care professional for 35 years, but also a stage IV cancer patient for the last 2 years, I can only hope all health care professionals read and take to heart the advice contained in this book."

Jerod M. Loeb, PhD
Executive Vice President
Division of Healthcare Quality Evaluation
The Joint Commission

"This book will find a permanent place within quick reach of anyone working to implement clinical quality and safety improvement in the real world. It is filled with in-the-trenches wisdom on topics ranging from effective leadership at the top to getting the details right in the front lines of care."

Michael L. Millenson
President
Health Quality Advisors LLC
Author, *Demanding Medical Excellence: Doctors and Accountability in the Information Age*

"*Achieving STEEEP Health Care* describes the Baylor Health Care System's bold experiment to align teams, evidence, systems, and a culture of caring in the unwavering pursuit of higher value health care. The result is a continuously learning health care system poised, along with new partners, to tackle one of the most urgent and significant challenges confronting our nation—optimizing the health of populations while maximizing increasingly finite resources. The valuable lessons from Baylor Health Care System's journey accelerate the capacity of health systems in all communities to assume a leadership role in addressing this challenge."

Mary D. Naylor, PhD, FAAN, RN
Marian S. Ware Professor in Gerontology
Director of New Courtland Center for Transitions and Health
University of Pennsylvania School of Nursing

"In today's health care world of swirling, conflicting reform pressures and 24/7 information overload, a book has to exceed a very high bar to merit executive attention. David Ballard and colleagues' *Achieving STEEEP Health Care* clears that bar with truly exceptional room to spare. This is the book that will explain why physician leadership is essential and possible, and how it can effectively align complex organizations and the larger health system culture to the triple aim vision of better care, better health, and lower cost. It represents a major contribution to the science of performance improvement precisely because it explains *how* it was institutionalized in a large and diverse Dallas, Texas institution in the last 14 years. This is the story of how American health care can reform and sustain itself, if it but will."

Len M. Nichols, PhD
Director
Center for Health Policy Research and Ethics
Professor of Health Policy
College of Health and Human Services
George Mason University

"Achieving STEEEP Health Care presents not only a roadmap but also a how-to manual for health systems striving to achieve the Triple Aim. Within these pages, those interested in improving America's health care will learn how to transform the elements of the Institute of Medicine's ideal state of American health care into action. This book should be read by all health care leaders on their journey to safe, quality health care."

Robert W. Pryor, MD, MBA, CPE, FAAP, FCCM, FCCP
President and Chief Executive Officer
Scott & White Healthcare

"Baylor Health Care System has been at the forefront of quality in health care for many years. Dr. Ballard and his colleagues, by describing the approach used at Baylor, have created a useful blueprint for others in health care that should speed their journey in quality improvement."

David B. Pryor, MD
Executive Vice President
Ascension Health
President and Chief Executive Officer
Ascension Clinical Holdings

"Like a basic scientist who takes a discovery from the bench to the bedside, Ballard and his colleagues at Baylor Health Care System (BHCS) have taken quality improvement from hypothesis testing to application in a large delivery system. Their description of the historical context of quality improvement at BHCS and 'lessons learned' is especially authentic for health care CEOs who attempt to walk the tightrope of performance improvement without a net. At the VCU Health System, we have used the STEEEP acronym for years in our own journey toward quality improvement. The experience at BHCS, as described in Ballard's book, is both illuminating and sobering—this is a race without a finish line. *Continuous* improvement is the only option."

Sheldon M. Retchin, MD, MSPH
Senior Vice President for Health Sciences
Virginia Commonwealth University
Chief Executive Officer
VCU Health System

"This book, by the Baylor Health Care System enterprise, should be a bellweather mark for our industry, as Baylor is *living* where health care needs to be in the near future. We must find a way to engage the industry to focus on quality and safety as the way to control costs and to effectively lower hospital expenses; rather than working on quality as separate from costs. This is an example of one system's approach and other models will follow. A great body of work, from a strong national example of high quality care."

Dan Stultz MD, FACHE, FACP
President and Chief Executive Officer
Texas Hospital Association

"The Institute of Medicine's six aims provide a sound framework for those dedicated to transforming the care we deliver to our patients and communities. David Ballard and his colleagues describe a remarkable journey operationalizing this framework across all six dimensions in a complex, growing health system. Their story is both instructive and inspirational. This book, with its detailed descriptions of approaches, lessons learned, and real-life examples, is a must-read for health care leaders and quality professionals."

Gary Yates, MD
President
Healthcare Performance Improvement, LLC
President
Sentara Healthcare Quality Care Network
Former Senior Vice President and Chief Medical Officer
Sentara Healthcare

Achieving STEEP Health Care

David J. Ballard, MD, PhD, Editor

Associate Editors:
Neil S. Fleming, PhD
Joel T. Allison, MHA
Paul B. Convery, MD, MMM
Rosemary Luquire, RN, PhD

Foreword by David B. Nash, MD, MBA

CRC Press
Taylor & Francis Group
Boca Raton   London   New York

CRC Press is an imprint of the
Taylor & Francis Group, an **informa** business

A PRODUCTIVITY PRESS BOOK

CRC Press
Taylor & Francis Group
6000 Broken Sound Parkway NW, Suite 300
Boca Raton, FL 33487-2742

Printed on acid-free paper
Version Date: 20130617

International Standard Book Number-13: 978-1-4665-6537-1 (Hardback)

Library of Congress Cataloging-in-Publication Data

Achieving STEEEP health care / editor, David J. Ballard.
   p. ; cm.
   Includes bibliographical references and index.
   ISBN 978-1-4665-6537-1 (hardcover : alk. paper)
   I. Ballard, David J., editor of compilation.
   [DNLM: 1. Baylor Health Care System. 2. Hospitals--standards. 3. Quality of Health Care. 4. Hospital Administration--methods. 5. Leadership. 6. Organizational Innovation. 7. Patient-Centered Care. 8. Quality Improvement. WX 153]

RA971
362.11068--dc23
                                                   2013023914

Visit the Taylor & Francis Web site at
http://www.taylorandfrancis.com

and the CRC Press Web site at
http://www.crcpress.com

Contents

SECTION I System Alignment for STEEEP Care

Foreword

It is no secret that our health care system is at a crossroads. We, as a nation, must decide how to implement the Patient Protection and Affordable Care Act (PPACA) signed into law in March 2010. Through its implementation, we hope to achieve the "Triple Aim" of improving the patient care experience (including quality, access, and reliability), improving the health of populations, and reducing the per capita cost of health care.

While many experts view the Triple Aim as the "organizing framework" for the PPACA, few organizations have created the infrastructure and, more importantly, established the organizational will to implement its important goals. Baylor Health Care System (BHCS) is one of those few.

The United States, then, needs to chart a course for implementing a health care system that simultaneously operates through management of population health and meets the needs of the individual patient across the continuum of care. We need a detailed roadmap for changing the very culture of the major health care delivery systems in our country and positioning them appropriately to accomplish the Triple Aim.

The good news is that Dr. Ballard and his team, I believe, have created such a roadmap. I hope the rest of the country is ready to accept the challenges and solutions they lay out.

Dr. Ballard's career mirrors the evolution of the field of quality measurement and improvement. For nearly 30 years and at leading organizations such as the Mayo Clinic and the University of North Carolina, he has demonstrated unwavering focus in his drive to measure and improve what we do each and every day at the bedside. His career trajectory is a symbol of the progress we have made in creating a bona fide science out of the theories linking industrial process improvement to health care quality and safety. His idea to align a health care system's long-term quality goals with the six domains of improvement outlined by the Institute of Medicine in 2001 was an inspired and galvanizing approach. This approach, encapsulated by the STEEEP acronym registered as a trademark by BHCS in 2007, not only provided an organizational framework for quality improvement within BHCS, but makes the organization's mission of providing care that is safe, timely, effective, efficient, equitable, and patient-centered clearly identifiable and accessible to all its members. By grasping the importance of these dimensions, the entire organization was motivated to move in the right direction.

Each of the principal sections of this book serves as a "deep dive" into the infrastructure and tools necessary to deliver STEEEP care. They provide a host of rich examples, even on a service-line basis, including care of patients with high priority conditions, such as cardiovascular disease, cancer, and diabetes.

Congratulations, then, to Dr. Ballard and his team for creating a roadmap for achieving the Triple Aim under the aegis of PPACA. My hunch is that other organizations will embrace the book and its underlying message that, although the organizational and cultural change required to achieve the Triple Aim is vast and at times disruptive, it is achievable.

Who should read this book? I fervently hope that all major health care organizations and their leaders will embrace the key tenets of STEEEP care. I also hope they will start now educating their executive, clinical, and administrative directors about the science of performance improvement, which lays the groundwork for implementation of the Triple Aim. Culture change is a decades-long journey, but, regrettably, we don't have that kind of time left. We must start immediately and this book will put us on the right track today.

David B. Nash, MD, MBA
Founding Dean, Jefferson School of Public Health, Thomas Jefferson University
Philadelphia, Pennsylvania

Preface

This book describes practical strategies and tactics Baylor Health Care System (BHCS) has used to operationalize the delivery of safe, timely, effective, efficient, equitable, patient-centered (STEEEP) care. BHCS has been committed to the delivery of high-quality health care since the organization was founded as Texas Baptist Memorial Sanitarium in 1903. My focus, since joining BHCS as the organization's first chief quality officer in 1999 and founding the Institute for Health Care Research and Improvement,[1,2] has been the development and implementation of strategies to improve health care quality across the system and the communities served by BHCS.

The origins of this book, as well as my health care quality improvement efforts, date back to the late 1970s, when I was an undergraduate economics student as a Morehead Scholar at the University of North Carolina at Chapel Hill (UNC) and developed a tool to detect inappropriate hospital admissions for the North Carolina Memorial Hospital Utilization Review Committee. In the 1980s, as a doctoral student in the UNC Schools of Medicine and Public Health, I collaborated with my faculty advisor and mentor, Ed Wagner, to characterize and develop interventions to improve the process and outcomes of medical care in the management of hypertension,[3–5] and then went on to shape, with Denis Cortese, the Chair of the Mayo Clinical Practice Committee, Mayo Clinic's health care quality improvement strategies and tactics.[6] The latter engagement included leading Mayo's participation in the Working Group of the Appropriateness Project of the Academic Medical Center Consortium, which was ahead of its time in terms of trying to address the overuse of care.[7–10]

In the 1990s, I served as president of the Kerr L. White Institute for Health Services Research, which focused on population-based health care quality and efficiency research. The institute included among its member organizations five state-level health care quality improvement organizations[11] (then called peer-review organizations (PROs)) created by Congress in 1984 to monitor the cost and quality of care received by Medicare beneficiaries. To do this, the Health Care Financing Administration engaged the PROs through a series of contracts. One of these contracts initiated the Health Care Quality Improvement Program in 1990 as an application of the principles of continuous quality improvement. My work with these five PROs provided me with valuable insight into leading quality improvement efforts and creating infrastructure to support quality improvement on a large scale.[12–21]

When I joined BHCS in 1999, I recognized that it was a complex organization and would require strong infrastructure, robust measurement tactics, leadership alignment, and other elements to enhance the delivery of high-quality health care. Around the time of my arrival at BHCS, the organization renewed its focus on organizational development. In early 2000, the chair of the BHCS Board of Trustees established an ad hoc committee, which I chaired, to develop the BHCS strategic plan to focus its efforts on the organization's goal "to deliver the best and safest care available, focusing on wellness, prevention, early detection, acute and subacute care, and supported at every point by education, research, and improvement."[1]

During this time, the Institute for Healthcare Improvement was seeking proposals for its Pursuing Perfection Initiative, which challenged hospitals and physician organizations to improve patient outcomes dramatically by "pursuing perfection" in all major care processes.[22] As BHCS developed a proposal for the initiative, we considered our approaches to health care quality improvement and realized we needed effective ways to communicate our quality improvement goals and strategies to internal stakeholders (employees) as well as external stakeholders and potential partners. As the Institute of Medicine (IOM) was then developing its report "Crossing the Quality Chasm,"[23] we considered the six IOM dimensions of high-quality health care (safety, timeliness, effectiveness, efficiency, equity, and patient centeredness) and their relationship to the transition of a state of ideal health care delivery. My BHCS colleague, John Anderson (then BHCS senior vice president for Clinical Integration), and I imagined the analogy of climbing a mountain and the acronym STEEEP was born.[2] Embracing the elements of STEEEP care lent BHCS the IOM's authority to convey to internal and external stakeholders the importance of improving health care quality, and also helped align our work with national health care priorities.

Meanwhile, the health care quality improvement strategic committee—especially committee member Bill Aston, who was then chair of the Baylor University Medical Center Board of Trustees—recognized that BHCS had a history of linking leader compensation to financial performance and suggested the organization extend that focus on performance to other areas.[24] Over the next several years, BHCS modified its performance award program to include the areas of People (employee retention); Quality (hospital-standardized inpatient mortality ratio, readmissions, and delivery of evidence-based processes of care); and Service (patient satisfaction) as well as Finance. Although many health care organizations have a culture that precludes linking compensation to performance, BHCS was able to implement a robust approach to designing incentives linked to quality improvement goals. Currently, BHCS has approximately 20,000 employees, all with their own goals in the areas of People, Quality, Service, and Finance, and annual performance reviews and associated annual merit compensation changes are based, in part, on the extent to which they have achieved these goals.

As an organization, BHCS recognized that, to build a culture of quality improvement that would extend to all its employees, a core group of leaders would need an in-depth understanding of quality improvement methods, tools, and language. From 2001 through 2003, BHCS sent 40 quality leaders to the Intermountain Healthcare mini-Advanced Training Program course led by Brent James.[25] James shared his educational templates with BHCS, and we adapted them, with his approval, to provide BHCS-based examples relevant to our employees. Over the past decade, more than 1,500 BHCS physicians and nursing and administrative leaders have received health care quality improvement training through the resulting "ABC Baylor" course (now, the STEEEP Academy), either in its full form or in one of the tailored adaptations designed to meet the specific needs of certain group leaders (e.g., those who needed a "Fast Track" course).[26,27]

BHCS leaders understood that, in addition to the STEEEP Academy training and the incentives provided by linking leader compensation to clinical quality performance, the organization would need structures to support a commitment to quality improvement. When I led quality efforts at the Mayo Clinic, I was impressed by how clinical, financial, and operational leaders came together through the Mayo Clinical Practice Committee to address approaches to high-quality health care delivery.[28] Over time at BHCS, we have crafted an approach that brings these leaders to a common table through the STEEEP Governance Council (SGC), which promotes improvement efforts that encompass and achieve synergy across all domains of STEEEP care. The SGC structure has enabled BHCS to apply clinical, financial, and operational frames of reference to organizational decisions about health care initiatives.

As our STEEEP journey evolves, many of these decisions will focus on the shift from volume-based to population-based health care. Berwick et al.[29] described the "Triple Aim" of health care delivery systems that seek to improve the overall health of populations while reducing costs: (1) improve the patient care experience (including quality, access, and reliability); (2) improve the health of populations; and (3) reduce the per capita cost of health care. The Triple Aim has become the organizing framework for the U.S. National Quality Strategy called for under the 2010 Patient Protection and Affordable Care Act[30] and for public and private health organizations around the world, including BHCS. Despite the acknowledged need for population-based care, tensions can arise when health care delivery organizations must make decisions that represent the right thing to do for patients, but that pose problems for organizational financial performance over the short term (e.g., the elimination of clinically unnecessary and/or inappropriate cardiovascular procedures[31]).

One current challenge BHCS faces involves its efforts to refocus its contracts with payers from volume-based to population-based care delivery. This is a particularly complicated task in the Dallas–Fort Worth Metroplex, which is less mature in terms of its focus on population health and the total cost of care than many other markets in the United States.

BHCS is addressing the shift toward population-based health care through several large-scale initiatives, including the founding of its accountable care organization, the Baylor Quality Alliance[32,33] and the formation of the Diabetes Health and Wellness Institute, both described in this book. BHCS is also broadening its quality improvement focus to address overuse of care, defined as the provision of health services for which the potential risks outweigh the potential benefits,[23] and to promote more widespread use of effective care. Such strategies will enable the system to more effectively and efficiently use scarce resources to optimize the health of a given population. In addition, BHCS enjoys collegial relationships with health care delivery systems in Texas that have historically had a strong population focus, such as Scott & White Healthcare, which has had a health care plan since 1982 and an impressive, more recent history in applying Lean thinking, culture, and tools to improve care. These strengths and strategies will help to support BHCS during the next segment of its quality journey, when, like many other health care delivery organizations, it will need to transition its work from volume-based to population-based care, and use health care resources as efficiently as possible.

David J. Ballard, MD, MSPH, PhD, FACP

REFERENCES

1. Ballard, D. J. 2003. Indicators to improve clinical quality across an integrated health care system. *International Journal for Quality in Health Care* 15 (Suppl 1): i13–23.
2. Ballard, D. J., B. Spreadbury, and R. S. Hopkins, III. 2004. Health care quality improvement across the Baylor Health Care System: The first century. *Proceedings* (Baylor University Medical Center) 17 (3): 277–288.
3. Ballard, D. J., D. S. Strogatz, E. H. Wagner, D. S. Siscovick, S. A. James, D. G. Kleinbaum, L. M. Cutchin, and M. A. Ibrahim. 1988. Hypertension control in a rural southern community: Medical care process and dropping out. *American Journal of Preventive Medicine* 4 (3): 133–139.
4. Ballard, D. J., D. S. Strogatz, E. H. Wagner, D. S. Siscovick, S. A. James, D. G. Kleinbaum, C. A. Williams, L. M. Cutchin, and M. A. Ibrahim. 1986. The Edgecombe County High Blood Pressure Control Program: The process of medical care and blood pressure control. *American Journal of Preventive Medicine* 2 (5): 278–284.
5. Siscovick, D. S., D. S. Strogatz, E. H. Wagner, D. J. Ballard, S. A. James, S. Beresford, D. G. Kleinbaum, L. M. Cutchin, and M. A. Ibrahim. 1987. Provider-oriented interventions and management of hypertension. *Medical Care* 25 (3): 254–258.

6. Ballard, D. J., S. C. Bryant, P. C. O'Brien, D. W. Smith, M. B. Pine, and D. A. Cortese. 1994. Referral selection bias in the Medicare hospital mortality prediction model: Are centers of referral for Medicare beneficiaries necessarily centers of excellence? *Health Services Research* 28 (6): 771–784.

7. Ballard, D. J., J. A. Etchason, L. H. Hilborne, M. E. Campion, C. Kamberg, D. Solomon, L. L. Leape, J. P. Kahan, R. E. Park, and R. H. Brook. 1992. *Abdominal aortic aneurysm surgery: A literature review and ratings of appropriateness and necessity.* Santa Monica, CA: RAND.

8. Nevitt, M. P., D. J. Ballard, and J. W. Hallett, Jr. 1989. Prognosis of abdominal aortic aneurysms. A population-based study. *New England Journal of Medicine* 321 (15): 1009–1014.

9. Herrin, J., J. A. Etchason, J. P. Kahan, R. H. Brook, and D. J. Ballard. 1997. Effect of panel composition on physician ratings of appropriateness of abdominal aortic aneurysm surgery: Elucidating differences between multispecialty panel results and specialty society recommendations. *Health Policy* 42 (1): 67–81.

10. Ballard, D. J. 1994. The RAND/AMA/AMCC Clinical Appropriateness Initiative: Insights for multi-site appropriateness studies derived from the abdominal aortic aneurysm surgery project. *International Journal for Quality in Health Care* 6 (2): 187–198.

11. Ballard, D. J. 1997. A little statistical compassion linked to an intense and creative look at healthcare evidence: The genius of Kerr White. *Health Services Research* 32 (1): 5–10.

12. Grant, J. B., R. P. Hayes, R. D. Pates, K. S. Elward, and D. J. Ballard. 1996. HCFA's health care quality improvement program: The medical informatics challenge. *Journal of the American Medical Informatics Association* 3 (1): 15–26.

13. Cangialose, C. B., A. E. Blair, J. S. Borchardt, T. B. Ades, C. L. Bennett, K. Dickersin, D. H. Gesme, Jr., et al. 2000. Purchasing oncology services. Kerr L. White Institute/American Cancer Society Task Force on Purchasing Oncology Services. *Cancer* 88 (12): 2876–2886.

14. Cook, S. S., C. B. Cangialose, D. M. Sieburg, S. M. Kieszak, R. Boudreau, L. H. Hoffman, K. S. Elward, and D. J. Ballard. 1999. Red blood cell transfusions for elective hip and knee arthroplasty: Opportunity to improve quality of care and documentation. *Clinical Performance and Quality Health Care* 7 (1): 5–16.

15. Elward, K. S., D. Martin, E. Merwin, R. P. Hayes, and D. J. Ballard. 1994. The role of the principal clinical coordinator in the Health Care Financing Administration's Health Care Quality Improvement Initiative. *Clinical Performance and Quality Health Care* 2 (2): 73–79.

16. Grant, J. B., R. P. Hayes, D. W. Baker, C. B. Cangialose, S. M. Kieszak, and D. J. Ballard. 1997. Informatics, imaging, and healthcare quality management: Imaging quality improvement opportunities and lessons learned from HCFA's Health Care Quality Improvement Program. *Clinical Performance and Quality Health Care* 5 (3): 133–139.

17. Hayes, R., D. Bratzler, B. Armour, L. Moore, C. Murray, B. R. Stevens, M. Radford, et al. 2001. Comparison of an enhanced versus a written feedback model on the management of Medicare inpatients with venous thrombosis. *The Joint Commission Journal on Quality Improvement* 27 (3): 155–168.

18. Hayes, R. P., and D. J. Ballard. 1995. Review: Feedback about practice patterns for measurable improvements in quality of care—a challenge for PROs under the Health Care Quality Improvement Program. *Clinical Performance and Quality Health Care* 3 (1): 15–22.

19. Hayes, R. P., M. T. Lundberg, and D. J. Ballard. 1994. Peer review organizations: Scientific challenges in HCFA's health care quality improvement initiative. *Medical Care Review* 51 (1): 39–60.

20. Meehan, T. P., J. Hennen, M. J. Radford, M. K. Petrillo, P. Elstein, and D. J. Ballard. 1995. Process and outcome of care for acute myocardial infarction among Medicare beneficiaries in Connecticut: A quality improvement demonstration project. *Annals of Internal Medicine* 122 (12): 928–936.

21. Hayes, R. P., D. W. Baker, J. C. Luthi, R. L. Baggett, W. McClellan, D. Fitzgerald, F. R. Abrams, D. Bratzler, and D. J. Ballard. 2002. The effect of external feedback on the management of Medicare inpatients with congestive heart failure. *American Journal of Medical Quality* 17 (6): 225–235.

22. Institute for Healthcare Improvement. Pursuing perfection: Raising the Bar for Health Care Performance. Online at http://www.ihi.org/offerings/Initiatives/PastStrategicInitiatives/PursuingPerfection/Pages/default.aspx (accessed March 20, 2013).

23. Corrigan, J. M., M. S. Donaldson, L. T. Kohn, S. K. Maguire, and K. C. Pike. 2001. *Crossing the quality chasm: A new health system for the 21st century.* Washington, DC: National Academy Press.

24. Herrin, J., D. Nicewander, and D. J. Ballard. 2008. The effect of health care system administrator pay-for-performance on quality of care. *The Joint Commission Journal for Quality Patient Safety* 34 (11): 646–654.

25. Intermountain Healthcare. 20-day course for executives & QI leaders—Advanced Training Program (ATP). Online at http://intermountainhealthcare.org/qualityand-research/institute/courses/atp/Pages/home.aspx (accessed March 21, 2013).

26. Haydar, Z., M. Cox, P. Stafford, V. Rodriguez, and D. J. Ballard. 2009. Accelerating best care at Baylor Dallas. *Proceedings* (Baylor University Medical Center) 22 (4): 311–315.

27. Haydar, Z., J. Gunderson, D. J. Ballard, A. Skoufalos, B. Berman, and D. B. Nash. 2008. Accelerating Best Care in Pennsylvania: Adapting a large academic system's quality improvement process to rural community hospitals. *American Journal of Medical Quality* 23 (4): 252–528.

28. Berry, L., and K. Seltman. 2008. *Management lessons from Mayo Clinic: Inside one of the world's most admired service organizations.* New York: McGraw-Hill.

29. Berwick, D. M., T. W. Nolan, and J. Whittington. 2008. The triple aim: Care, health, and cost. *Health Affairs* (Millwood) 27 (3): 759–769.

30. Patient Protection and Affordable Care Act. Public Law 111–148—March 23, 2010. 124 Stat. 119. Online at http://www.gpo.gov/fdsys/pkg/PLAW-111publ148/pdf/PLAW-111publ148.pdf

31. Ballard, D. J., and B. M. Leonard. 2011. National priorities partnership focus on eliminating overuse: Applications to cardiac revascularization. *American Journal of Medical Quality* 26 (6): 485–490.

32. Ballard, D. J. 2012. The potential of Medicare accountable care organizations to transform the American health care marketplace: Rhetoric and reality. *Mayo Clinic Proceedings* 87 (8): 707–709.

33. Couch, C. E. 2012. Why Baylor Health Care System would like to file for Medicare Shared Savings accountable care organization designation but cannot. *Mayo Clinic Proceedings* 87 (8): 723–726.

Acknowledgments

A book of this kind is a collaboration among many individuals. I am appreciative of the efforts of my associate editors, Neil Fleming, Joel Allison, Paul Convery, and Rosemary Luquire, as well as the contributions of the book's authors. I am also grateful to Kathleen Richter, Tara Marathe, Kelli Trungale, and Briget da Graca, who provided editorial support during the production of the book; and to Scott Ranson of the University of North Texas Health Science Center and Arja P. Adair, Jr. of CFMC for their careful review of earlier drafts.

The story of the Baylor Health Care System (BHCS) quality journey could not have been told without the contribution of John Anderson, former BHCS senior vice president for Clinical Integration, who first coined the acronym "STEEEP" in a discussion we had in 2000. Over a decade ago, he and I envisioned the analogy of climbing a mountain to represent the transition from the current state of health care delivery to one that could be characterized by the Institute of Medicine's six domains of ideal care: safety, timeliness, effectiveness, efficiency, equity, and patient centeredness.

I also am appreciative of the vision of the late Bill Aston, former chair of the Baylor University Medical Center Board of Trustees, who in 2000 drafted the board resolution to prioritize quality throughout BHCS. This resolution has been the basis for quality improvement at BHCS for the past 13 years. In addition, I am grateful to the late Dale Jones, former chair of the BHCS Board of Trustees, who in 2000 gave me the charter to develop a quality improvement plan for BHCS that has provided the framework for the organization's journey to STEEEP care.

As I complete the final editing of the book galleys on the occasion of my mother's 94th birthday, I want to recognize the role modeling of a commitment to STEEEP health care by my parents, Margaret S. Ballard, RN, and the late Joseph A. Ballard, MD, who began their health care careers in the throes of World War II serving for the U.S. Army, long before the founding of the Institute of Medicine and its landmark publication, Crossing the Quality

Chasm. Finally, I want to thank my wife, Michela Caruso, MD, a Texas Oncology radiation oncologist, who has been a sounding board and source of support throughout my health care quality journey since we first met in 1985 as residents at the Mayo Clinic.

David J. Ballard, MD, MSPH, PhD, FACP

Introduction

Baylor Health Care System (BHCS) has been guided by its commitment to providing high-quality health care to all of the residents of Dallas–Fort Worth since its original founding over 100 years ago. This dedicated focus is reflected in the question that the Rev. George W. Truett, pastor of the First Baptist Church of Dallas, asked of the city's business leaders and citizens in 1903: "Is it not now time to begin the erection of a great humanitarian hospital, one to which men of all creeds and those of none may come with equal confidence?"

Later that year, the Texas Baptist Memorial Sanitarium was established with 25 beds in a 14-room renovated house. This modest community hospital developed during the twentieth century into Baylor University Medical Center, and then the multifacility BHCS. The BHCS network now includes more than 300 multiprovider access points of care, including

- 30 hospitals that are owned, operated, joint ventured, or affiliated with BHCS
- 28 ambulatory surgery/endoscopy centers
- 209 locations for the HealthTexas Provider Network (the BHCS-affiliated ambulatory care physician network) with 60 primary care medical homes
- 91 satellite outpatient facilities for imaging, rehabilitation, and pain
- 3 senior health centers
- 6 retail pharmacies
- 3 Baylor Research Institute locations
- 1 accountable care organization

During the past century, BHCS has developed into a complex system whose facilities, departments, and employees are all aligned toward a common vision (to be trusted as the best place to give and receive safe, quality, compassionate health care); mission (founded as a Christian ministry of healing, Baylor exists to serve all people through exemplary health care, education, research, and community service); and values (integrity, servanthood, quality,

FIGURE I.1 The Baylor Health Care System Circle of Care.

innovation, and stewardship) (Figure I.1). In contrast to its modest beginnings as a small community hospital, by July 2013, BHCS had grown to include

- 21,388 employees
- 4,735 medical staff members
- 3,420 active physicians
- 3,653 licensed beds

and annually:

- $5.3 billion in total assets
- $4.1 billion in total operating revenue
- 2.8 million patient encounters
- 122,007 inpatient admissions
- 20,094 babies born
- 409,375 emergency department visits
- 603,155 outpatient registrations

TIMELINE: HEALTH CARE QUALITY JOURNEY

The timeline at http://www.baylorhealth.com/about/Pages/Timeline.aspx describes in more depth some of the important events and milestones in the BHCS quality journey.[1,2]

Operationalizing the Delivery of STEEEP Care

BHCS's century of growth has required an unwavering commitment to health care quality. To continually improve health care quality, BHCS has operationalized the delivery of safe, timely, effective, efficient, equitable, patient-centered (STEEEP) care. According the Institute of Medicine (IOM),[1] STEEEP care is care that is

- Safe—avoiding injury to patients from care that is intended to help them, without accidental error or inadvertent exposures;
- Timely—reducing waits and harmful delays impacting smooth flow of care;
- Effective—providing services based on scientific knowledge to all who could benefit and refraining from providing services to those not likely to benefit (avoiding overuse and underuse);
- Efficient—using resources to achieve best value by reducing waste and reducing production and administrative costs;
- Equitable—providing care that does not vary in quality according to personal characteristics, such as gender, income, ethnicity, location; and
- Patient-centered—providing care that is respectful of and responsive to individual patient preferences, needs, and values.

Originally improvised at BHCS in 2000, the STEEEP acronym was trademarked by BHCS to communicate the challenge of achieving its objective to provide ideal care in terms of the IOM call for care that is safe, timely, effective, efficient, equitable, and patient-centered.[1]

This book presents the evidence-based strategies and tactics BHCS has used to operationalize the delivery of STEEEP care, and describes its contribution to the improvements achieved in patient, clinical, and organization operational outcomes.

Recently, Scott & White Healthcare and BHCS announced their intent to merge, which will create the largest not-for-profit health system in the state of Texas.[3] Scott & White, unlike BHCS, includes an owned and operated health care plan in its operations, and is farther along its journey in applying Lean thinking to the quality improvement journey. As collaboration between the organizations is growing while the merger discussions move forward, we asked Scott & White authors to contribute chapters on these topics to provide a more complete picture of the quality improvement tools and strategies that can contribute to achieving STEEEP care. We anticipate that the two organizations will benefit from each other's respective experience with implementing STEEEP and Lean principles following the merger, facilitating more rapid spread across the newly created entity as well as greater gains in quality and efficiency stemming from the complementary nature of these improvement and management approaches.

To place our quality improvement work in the broader context of the initiatives playing out at the national and international levels, we have framed the first three sections around the Institute for Healthcare Improvement's (IHI's) Seven Leadership Leverage Points for Organization-Level Improvement in Health Care.[4]

Section I: System Alignment for STEEEP Care

Ultimately, health care quality improvement at BHCS stands on the foundation of strong leadership and a commitment across the entire organization to deliver STEEEP care. Leaders at all levels throughout BHCS continue to build on the efforts of those who embraced the original challenge of achieving BHCS's goal of ideal care. The first section of the book focuses on the elements of governance; leadership; organizational structures; alignment, goal setting, and incentives; financial leadership; physician leadership; and nurse leadership; and how these components align to drive STEEEP care across the system (Chapter 1 to Chapter 7).

Section II: Infrastructure and Tools for STEEEP Care

Aligning a complex health care system to achieve STEEEP care requires not only a commitment to quality, but also a variety of specific tools and infrastructure elements. The second section of the book describes the infrastructure BHCS has established to improve health care quality, including the STEEEP Academy's rapid-cycle quality improvement course; applications of Lean to STEEEP care improvement; the STEEEP Analytics department, which guides and supports data-driven improvement; and the STEEEP Care Operations department, which operationalizes quality improvement and patient safety initiatives. It also discusses methods BHCS has used to evaluate clinical and financial outcomes to determine best practices, techniques it has used to drive STEEEP care across its multiple hospitals, and methods to drive STEEEP care across a physician provider network (Chapter 8 to Chapter 14).

Section III: Achieving STEEEP Care

The third section of the book provides real-world examples of strategies and tactics BHCS has used to improve care in the areas of safety, clinical excellence (timeliness and effectiveness), efficiency, equity, and patient centeredness. It describes successes as well as residual challenges associated with these approaches. The chapters in this section also present lessons BHCS has learned as it has applied and evaluated various strategies and tactics to improve its quality across the six domains of STEEEP care (Chapter 15 to Chapter 19).

Section IV: STEEEP Care in Practice:
Service Lines and Other Lines of Business

Driving STEEEP care across a large, complex health care system requires the application of STEEEP care improvement principles to a variety of service lines and other lines of business. The fourth section of the book describes concrete approaches and methods associated with improving STEEEP care in the areas of cardiovascular care, emergency services, critical care, oncology, surgical services, orthopedic services, the accountable care organization, and the Diabetes Health and Wellness Institute. This section of the book also discusses application of quality improvement methods by Scott & White Healthcare to drive STEEEP care through a health care delivery system-owned and -operated health care plan (Chapter 20 to Chapter 28).

Elements of the Quality Journey

If the BHCS vision and mission comprise the compass guiding BHCS on its quality journey, the STEEEP framework is the map to which this compass is applied. Table I.1 highlights key components of effective health care delivery systems—including administration and governance, physician and nurse leadership, quality improvement programs and expertise, data and analytics, and reputation and accreditation—and how these components must evolve along the quality journey. Readers who are interested in improving health care quality in their own organizations can identify the book chapters that are most relevant to their needs and goals based on the stage their organization has reached on the quality journey: initiation, foundation building, operationalizing, or continuous quality improvement.

David J. Ballard and Neil S. Fleming

REFERENCES

1. Corrigan, J. M., M. S. Donaldson, L. T. Kohn, S. K. Maguire, and K. C. Pike. 2001. *Crossing the quality chasm: A new health system for the 21st century.* Washington, DC: National Academy Press.
2. Wilsey, H. L. 2004. *How we care: Centennial history of Baylor University Medical Center and Baylor Health Care System, 1903–2003.* Dallas, TX: Baylor Health Care System.
3. Scott & White Health Care Fact Sheet. January 2013. Online at: www.sw.org (accessed April 9, 2013).
4. Reinertsen, J. L., M. Bisognano, and M. D. Pugh. 2008. *Seven leadership leverage points for organization-level improvement in health care*, 2nd ed. Cambridge, MA: Institute for Healthcare Improvement.

TABLE I.1 Achieving STEEEP health care is a journey that requires a commitment to quality improvement (QI) from the highest levels of leadership combined with the interdependent development of several key components of health care delivery: administration and governance, clinical leadership, program development, data analytics, and accreditation. Book chapters most relevant to organizations based on their stage of development in the STEEEP quality journey (initiation, foundation building, operationalizing, or continuous QI) are indicated.

Organizational Component	STAGE			
	Initiation	Foundation Building	Operationalizing	Continuous QI
Administration and Governance	• Often unaware of potential benefits of QI • Often do not view QI as their responsibility and instead delegate to clinicians **Ch. 1**	• Understand the necessity of becoming involved in and providing leadership in QI • Become engaged in QI initiatives **Ch. 2, 3**	• Directly involved in driving the organization to a culture of QI • Actively measure and reward improvement **Ch. 4**	• Fully engaged in, and see themselves as accountable for driving QI • Quality is an integral part of their, and the organization's incentive program **Ch. 5**
Physician and Nurse Leadership	• Often have marginal involvement in QI initiatives • Focus is primarily on clinical delivery and organizational issues **Ch. 2**	• Active engagement in some QI initiatives • Represent the clinicians *and* the patient in QI discussions and decisions **Ch. 6, 7**	• Work together to identify and lead QI initiatives • Become the voice of the patient as well as the clinician **Ch. 6, 7**	• Fully engaged in QI and drive innovation within their disciplines • Often responsible for engaging their professional communities in QI efforts **Ch. 6, 7, 20–28**

Quality Improvement Programs and Expertise	• Limited QI knowledge • Few formally established QI measurement tools and methodologies • Limited or basic safety programs in place **Ch. 3, 15–19**	• Pockets of QI expertise • Formal QI structure in place with limited measureable impact • Quality and safety programs across some disciplines and/or facilities • Some best practice initiatives **Ch. 8, 9, 15–19**	• Deeper expertise shared across disciplines and/or facilities • Formal structure in place with moderate QI • Organization-wide quality and safety programs **Ch. 11, 12, 15–28**	• Established governance and infrastructure for managing and coordinating QI • Formalized QI training for staff at multiple levels • Fully integrated processes, practices, data and analysis • Decision support drives innovation **Ch. 13, 14, 20–28**
Data and Analytics	• Little or no ability to extract relevant data and report on quality measures • Data integrity often an issue and a point of debate **Ch. 3**	• Outcomes/quality measurement and reporting in some areas • Infrastructure capable of extracting data but with little or no analysis or potential for organizational impact • Quality of data improving and slowing becoming accepted in a number of areas of the organization **Ch. 10**	• Ability to extract and analyze data to drive QI initiatives • Data integrity no longer an issue and accepted in most areas of the organization **Ch. 10, 12**	• Established procedures and timelines for data collection and analysis • Development and implementation of data-driven, clinical and operational best practices • Data is used to drive the incentive system for the organization **Ch. 12**
Reputation/ Accreditation	• Basic/minimal accreditation **Ch. 3, 15–19**	• Local reputation • Some advanced accreditation **Ch. 20–28**	• Regional reputation • Advanced accreditation in several areas **Ch. 20–28**	• Nationally recognized as a leader in quality, safety and innovation **Ch. 20–28**

The Editors

Editor

David J. Ballard, MD, MSPH, PhD, FACP, is senior vice president and chief quality officer for the Baylor Health Care System (BHCS), Dallas, Texas; executive director of the BHCS Institute for Health Care Research and Improvement; and president and founder of the BHCS STEEEP (safe, timely, effective, efficient, equitable, and patient centered) Global Institute. Dr. Ballard is responsible for leading health care quality across BHCS. Under his leadership, BHCS has received many awards for health care quality improvement, including the 2010 Medical Group Preeminence Award of the American Medical Group Association, the 2008 National Quality Healthcare Award of the National Quality Forum, and the 2007 Leapfrog Patient-Centered Care Award.

Prior to joining BHCS in 1999, Dr. Ballard held progressive academic appointments as assistant and then associate professor at the Mayo Medical School, associate professor with tenure at the University of Virginia School of Medicine, professor of medicine in the Emory University School of Medicine, and professor of epidemiology in the Rollins School of Public Health at Emory University. He also served as founding head of the Mayo Section of Health Services Evaluation, founding president of the Kerr L. White Institute for Health Services Research (1991–1999), president (2001–2003) of the International Society for Quality in Health Care, and chair of the Agency for Healthcare Research and Quality (AHRQ) Health Care Quality and Effectiveness Research study section (2006–2010). He currently chairs the AHRQ's Centers for Education and Research on Therapeutics Steering Committee (2013–2014).

Dr. Ballard serves on several editorial boards of peer-reviewed medical journals, including *Health Services Research,* the *Journal of Comparative Effectiveness Research,* and the *Mayo Clinic Proceedings* (for which he serves as Health Policy section editor). He has published more than 200 articles and was the 1995 recipient of the AcademyHealth New Investigator Award, given annually to the outstanding health services research scholar in the United States younger than 40 years of age. His research also received the 2012 John M. Eisenberg Article-of-the-Year award from *Health Services Research*. He is a member of the UNC School of Public Health Foundation Board and a past member of the Board of Trustees of the Texas Hospital Association.

A board-certified internist, Dr. Ballard trained at the Mayo Graduate School of Medicine following completion of his MD, MSPH, and PhD in epidemiology, and BA in chemistry and economics from the University of North Carolina, where he was a Morehead Scholar, North Carolina Fellow, and junior year Phi Beta Kappa inductee. In 2008, Dr. Ballard received the Distinguished Service Award from the UNC School of Medicine.

Associate Editors

Neil S. Fleming, PhD, ASQ CQE, is vice president and chief operating officer of the BHCS STEEEP Global Institute, which capitalizes on the health care system's successful strategies, tactics, and tools in health care quality improvement to enable other health care organizations to improve care while reducing costs. He previously served seven years as the BHCS vice president for health care research, evaluating clinical and financial outcomes of BHCS initiatives with a major focus on health information technology, work in which he collaborated closely with Dr. Ballard.

Before joining BHCS, Dr. Fleming was a consultant for over 20 years for organizations involved in the health care, energy, financial services, and telecommunications industries. His work included reviewing health maintenance organizations (HMOs) for federal qualification and compliance from financial (including actuarial) and marketing perspectives for the Health Care Financing Administration (now the Centers for Medicare and Medicaid Services), and creating a claims-based actuarial reporting system for the U.S. Department of Defense's CHAMPUS (Civilian Health and Medical Program of the Uniformed Services) Reform Initiative. Dr. Fleming began his professional career as a statistician at the Centers for Disease Control National Center for Health Statistics, followed by two years as a medical consultant with Electronic Data Systems (EDS) on the Texas Medicaid Program, where he conducted utilization and costs studies. He is a senior member of the American Society for Quality and has been a Certified Quality Engineer for 20 years.

Dr. Fleming received his PhD in medical sociology with minors in economics and biostatistics from Vanderbilt University under a fellowship of the U.S. Department of Health & Human Services' National Center for Health Services Research, and his BS in mathematics from Bucknell University.

Joel T. Allison, MHA, FACHE, is president and chief executive officer of BHCS. In this role, his primary responsibility is to lead the organization in attaining its vision "to be trusted as the best place to give and receive safe, compassionate, quality health care." To do so, Mr. Allison continues developing BHCS as a patient-focused health care delivery system and clinical enterprise that emphasizes quality, safe patient care, measurable outcomes and improvement initiatives, as well as continuous medical education and health care research.

Mr. Allison's career includes more than three decades of experience in health care management. He joined BHCS in 1993, and served as senior executive vice president and chief operating officer before being promoted to president and CEO in 2000. He is a Fellow of the American College of Healthcare Executives and serves on several national boards including the Healthcare Leadership Council, The Joint Commission Board of Commissioners, and the United Surgical Partners International Board. He also serves on numerous state and local boards, including the Texas Association of Voluntary Hospitals, Healthcare Coalition of Texas, Dallas Citizens Council, Dallas Education Foundation, and the Denison Forum on Truth and Culture. In 2012, Mr. Allison was named among the top 20 of *Modern Healthcare*'s 100 Most Influential People in Health Care.

He holds a master's degree in health administration from Trinity University (San Antonio, Texas) and a bachelor's degree in journalism and religion from Baylor University. He is also a graduate of the Advanced Management Program at Harvard Business School and, in 2004, received an Honorary Doctor of Humanities degree from Dallas Baptist University.

Paul Convery, MD, MMM, is a senior consultant for the STEEEP Global Institute. He served as senior vice president and the first chief medical officer for BHCS from 2006 until his retirement in July 2013. Under his direction, BHCS was recognized with several important quality awards, including the 2008 National Quality Forum National Quality Healthcare Award and the 2007 Leapfrog Patient-Centered Care Award.

Dr. Convery has over 20 years of medical management and health care leadership experience across multiple health care organizations. Prior to joining BHCS, Dr. Convery served as executive vice president and chief medical officer for SSM Health Care in St. Louis, Missouri, from 1999 to 2006. Under his leadership, SSM became the first health care organization to win the distinguished National Institute of Standards and Technology's Malcolm Baldrige National Quality Award. Dr. Convery also served as chairman of the St. Louis Medical Group and president and medical director of Southwest Medical Center, both of which are large multispecialty groups in St. Louis. He has chaired the Provider Council and the Leadership Network of the National Quality Forum and served on boards of several hospitals, health systems, and nonprofits including the Institute for Clinical Quality and Value and the Education and Research Foundation Board of the Dallas–Fort Worth Hospital Council. While at BHCS, he developed the curriculum for the advanced BHCS physician leadership programs offered in collaboration with the Southern Methodist University's Cox School of Business. He also has appeared on *Modern Healthcare*'s list of the 50 Most Influential Physician Executives multiple times.

Dr. Convery is a board-certified internist who practiced internal medicine for over 20 years. He is a graduate of the University of Illinois College of Medicine, and received his master's degree in medical management from Tulane University, and his BS from St. Louis University.

Rosemary Luquire, RN, PhD, NEA-BC, FAAN, is senior vice president and chief nursing officer for BHCS. She joined BHCS as senior vice president and corporate chief nursing officer in 2007, the first nurse to serve in that organizational capacity. She is responsible for overseeing both strategic and operational issues that impact nursing practice and patient care across 16 facilities.

Dr. Luquire came to BHCS from St. Luke's Episcopal Health System in Houston, where she served as senior vice president, chief nursing officer, and chief quality officer, and was responsible for overseeing the health care system's professional nursing practice and quality improvement program. In her 20 years at St. Luke's, Dr. Luquire earned a reputation for research-based practice, minimal staff turnover, and an unfailing commitment to cost-effective operations and patient care. She holds joint faculty appointments at Baylor University's Louise Herrington School of Nursing, Texas Women's University, and University of Texas. She is a fellow of the American Academy of Nursing, serves as vice president of the board of managers for the American Nurses Credentialing Center, and sits on several hospital boards. She is a member of the American Nurses Association, American Association of Critical-Care Nurses, and the national and local chapters of the American College of Healthcare Executives. Dr. Luquire served as a Magnet Commissioner from 2002 through 2010 and helped to implement standards by which nursing is evaluated internationally.

Dr. Luquire earned her PhD in nursing from Texas Woman's University, MS in nursing from The University of Texas Health Science Center at Houston, and BS in nursing from Emory University.

Contributors

Robert W. Baird, MD
Medical Director of Critical Care
  Services
Baylor Health Care System
and
Co-Director of Critical Care Services
Baylor University Medical Center
Dallas, Texas

Charles E. Bell, MD, MS
President
Diabetes Health and Wellness Institute
Juanita J. Craft Recreation Center
Dallas, Texas

Gary Brock, MPH
Executive Vice President and
  Chief Operating Officer
Baylor Health Care System
Dallas, Texas

**David L. Brown, MD, FACC,
FACP, FSCAI**
President and Chairman of the
  Medical Staff
Director of Interventional Cardiology
Co-Director Cardiovascular Research
  & Structural Heart Program
The Heart Hospital Baylor Plano
Plano, Texas

**Jan Compton, RN, BSN, MS,
CPHQ**
Vice President of Patient Safety and
  Chief Patient Safety Officer
Baylor Health Care System
Dallas, Texas

William B. Cooksey, RN, MBA
Corporate Director of Quality
  Improvement
Cardiovascular Service Line
Baylor Health Care System
Dallas, Texas

Carl E. Couch, MD, MMM
President
Baylor Quality Alliance
Dallas, Texas

Marsha C. Cox, PhD, RN
Director of Health Care
  Improvement
Baylor Health Care System
Dallas, Texas

Ed de Vol, PhD, MBA
Vice President of Quantitative Sciences
Baylor Health Care System
Dallas, Texas

J. Paul Dieckert, MD, MBA
Chief Quality Officer
Scott & White Healthcare
Temple, Texas

Ernest W. Franklin, IV, MD, MBA
Vice President
Surgical and Ancillary Services
Baylor Health Care System
Dallas, Texas

Clifford T. Fullerton, MD, MSc
Chief Medical Officer
Baylor Quality Alliance
and
Vice President of Chronic Disease
    and Care Redesign
Baylor Health Care System
Dallas, Texas

Jerri J. Garison, BSN, MSHA, FACHE
President East Region
Baylor Health Care System
Dallas, Texas
and
President
Baylor Regional Medical Center
Plano, Texas

Robert T. Green, FACHE, MBA, CPA
Formerly Senior Vice President
Strategic Financial Services
Baylor Health Care System
Dallas, Texas
and
Executive Vice President and CFO
Centegra Health System
McHenry, Illinois

Margaret Henry, CCAM
Associate Vice President
Systems Improvement
Scott & White Healthcare
Temple, Texas

Keith Holtz, CPA, CCP
Senior Vice President and
    Chief Human Resources Officer
Baylor Health Care System
Dallas, Texas

Alan Jones, MD
Program Director
Orthopaedic Trauma Surgery
    Fellowship
Baylor University Medical Center
Dallas, Texas

JaNeene L. Jones, RN, MHA, FACHE
Chief Operating Officer
Baylor T. Boone Pickens Cancer
    Hospital/Charles A. Sammons
    Cancer Center at Dallas
and
Vice President of Oncology
Baylor Health Care System
Dallas, Texas

Donald Kennerly, MD, PhD
Vice President and Associate Chief
    Quality Officer
Baylor Health Care System
Dallas, Texas

Bradley M. Leonard, MD, MBA, FACC
Chief Medical Officer
STEEEP Global Institute
Baylor Health Care System
Dallas, Texas

Jay D. Mabrey, MD, MBA
Chief
Department of Orthopaedics
Baylor University Medical Center
Dallas, Texas

Michael J. Mack, MD, FACC
Chairman
Cardiovascular Governance Council
Baylor Health Care System
Dallas, Texas

Andrew Masica, MD, MSCI
Vice President of Clinical Innovation
Baylor Health Care System
Dallas, Texas

Ian McCarthy, PhD
Director of Health Economics
Baylor Health Care System
Dallas, Texas

John B. McWhorter, III, DSc
Senior Vice President
Baylor Health Care System
and
President
Baylor University Medical Center
Dallas, Texas

Alan M. Miller, MD, PhD
Medical Director
Baylor Charles A. Sammons Cancer
  Center at Dallas
and
Chief of Oncology
Baylor Health Care System
Dallas, Texas

David Nicewander, MS
Director of STEEEP Analytics
Baylor Health Care System
Dallas, Texas

Terri Dyksterhouse Nuss, MS, MBA
Vice President of Patient Centeredness
Baylor Health Care System
Dallas, Texas

Fabian E. Polo, PhD, MBA
Chief Operating Officer
Baylor Institute for Rehabilitation
and
Director of Orthopaedic Service Line
Baylor University Medical Center
Dallas, Texas

**Kristine K. Powell, MSN, RN, CEN,
NEA-BC**
Director of Emergency Services
Baylor Health Care System
Dallas, Texas

William L. Roberts, MHA, CPA
Senior Vice President and Chief
  Strategy Development Officer
Baylor Health Care System
Dallas, Texas

J. James Rohack MD, FACC, FACP
Director, Scott & White Center for
  Healthcare Policy
Medical Director for
  System Improvement,
  Scott & White Health Plan
Senior Vice President,
  Scott & White Health
Temple, Texas

**Michael D. Sanborn, MS, RPH,
FASHP, FACHE**
President
Baylor Medical Center at Carrollton
Carrollton, Texas

Fred Savelsbergh
Senior Vice President and Chief
    Financial Officer
Baylor Health Care System
Dallas, Texas

Christopher Shutts, MBA, CSSBB
Director of STEEEP Academy
Baylor Health Care System
Dallas, Texas

Marvin J. Stone, MD, MACP
Director, Oncology Medical Education
Associate Medical Director, Baylor
    Charles A. Sammons Cancer
    Center at Dallas
Dallas, Texas

Marisa Valdes, RN, MSN, CPHQ
Director of Performance
    Measurement and Reporting
Baylor Health Care System
Dallas, Texas

Mark Valentine, MBA
President
The Heart Hospital Baylor Plano
Plano, Texas

**Nancy Vish, PhD, RN, NEA-BC,
FACHE**
President and Chief Nursing Officer
Baylor Heart and Vascular Hospital
Dallas, Texas

**Kevin R. Wheelan, MD, FACC,
FHRS**
Chief of Staff, Baylor Heart and
    Vascular Hospital
and
Chief of Cardiology, Baylor
    University Medical Center
and
Co-Medical Director of Cardiology,
    Baylor Health Care System
Dallas, Texas

F. David Winter, MD, MSc, MACP
President, Chairman, and
    Chief Clinical Officer
HealthTexas Provider Network
Dallas, Texas

Nestor R. Zenarosa, MD, FACEP
Medical Director of Emergency
    Services
Baylor Health Care System
and
Executive Vice President
Baylor/JPS Division
EmCare Inc.
Dallas, Texas

Abbreviations

AADE: American Association of Diabetes Educators
ABC: Accelerating best care
ACC: Ambulatory care coordinator or American College of Cardiology
ACO: Accountable care organization
ACS: American College of Surgeons
AE: Adverse event
AHRQ: Agency for Healthcare Research and Quality
AIDET: Acknowledge, Introduce, Duration, Explanation, Thank
AJRR: American Joint Replacement Registry
AMGA: American Medical Group Association
AMI: Acute myocardial infarction
ANCC: American Nurses Credentialing Center
APR DRG: All Patient Refined Diagnosis Related Group
ASPIRE: Achieving Synergy in Practice through Impact, Relationships and Evidence
BAEMT: Baylor Adverse Event Measurement Tool
BHCS: Baylor Health Care System
BHVH: Baylor Heart and Vascular Hospital
BHVI: Baylor Heart and Vascular Institute
BQA: Baylor Quality Alliance
BUMC: Baylor University Medical Center
CEO: Chief executive officer
CFO: Chief financial officer
CHW: Community health worker
CLIP: Continuous Learning and Improvement Program
CMO: Chief medical officer
CMS: Centers for Medicare and Medicaid Services
CNO: Chief nursing officer
COC: Commission on Cancer
CUSP: Comprehensive Unit-Based Safety Program

DEP: Diabetes Equity Program
DHWI: Diabetes Health and Wellness Institute
ED: Emergency department
EHR: Electronic health record
FACT: Foundation for the Accreditation of Cellular Therapy
HCAHPS: Hospital Consumer Assessment of Healthcare Providers and Systems
HEDIS: Healthcare Effectiveness Data and Information Set
HF: Heart failure
HIE: Health Information Exchange
HIPAA: Health Insurance Portability and Accountability Act
HMO: Health maintenance organization
HSMR: Hospital standardized mortality ratio
HTPN: HealthTexas Provider Network
HVHC: High Value Healthcare Collaborative
ICU: Intensive care unit
IHCRI: Institute for Health Care Research and Improvement
IHI: Institute for Healthcare Improvement
IOM: Institute of Medicine
LBP: Low back pain
LDI: Leadership Development Institute
NCQA: National Committee for Quality Assurance
NICU: Neonatal intensive care unit
NIH: National Institutes of Health
NSQIP: National Surgical Quality Improvement Program
OCN: Oncology Certified Nurses
OETC: Oncology Evaluation and Treatment Center
OPS: Office of Patient Safety
PABD: Preoperative autologous blood donation
PAD: Project Access Dallas
PCMH: Patient-centered medical home
PDCA: Plan–Do–Check–Act
PEERS: Prevention, empowerment, education, resources, support
POCMA: Phase of Care Mortality Analysis
PPACA: Patient Protection and Affordable Care Act
PRO: Peer review organization
QI: Quality improvement
RMA: Rapid medical assessment
RRT: Rapid response team
SBAR: Situation–background–assessment–recommendation
SCIP: Surgical Care Improvement Project
SCPC: Society of Cardiovascular Patient Care
SGC: STEEEP Governance Council
SIP: Surgical infection prevention
SMART: Specific, measureable, actionable, realistic, and time dependent

SMU: Southern Methodist University
SSC: Surviving Sepsis Campaign
SSHI: Southern Sector Health Initiative
SSSL: Safe surgery saves lives
STEEEP: Safe, timely, effective, efficient, equitable, patient centered
STS: Society of Thoracic Surgeons
THHBP: The Heart Hospital Baylor Plano
VBP: Value-based purchasing
VPMA: Vice president of medical affairs
WHO: World Health Organization

Section I

System Alignment for STEEEP Care

Chapter 1

Governance

Joel T. Allison and David J. Ballard

CONTENTS

INTRODUCTION

While many of Baylor Health Care System's (BHCS's) efforts predate the 2008 publication of the Institute for Healthcare Improvement (IHI) Seven Leadership Leverage Points for Organizational-Level Improvement in Health Care, they follow a similar framework:

1. Establish and oversee specific system-level aims at the highest governance level.
2. Develop an executable strategy to achieve the system-level aims and oversee their execution at the highest governance level.
3. Channel leadership attention to system-level improvement: personal leadership, leadership systems, and transparency.
4. Put patients and families on the improvement team.
5. Make the chief financial officer a quality champion.
6. Engage physicians.
7. Build improvement capacity.[1]

The first two points, like other recommendations from national groups for health care quality improvement,[1-3] call for quality improvement to begin with governance and be supported by the establishment of system-level goals and strategies. For meaningful and sustainable quality improvement to occur in a health care organization, the governing board must commit to such change as a system-wide strategic priority.

AFFIRMING AN ORGANIZATIONAL COMMITMENT TO QUALITY

The first of the IHI Seven Leadership Leverage Points is to establish and oversee specific system-level aims at the highest governance level. Boards need to commit to a quality aim, establish measures of system-level performance, and adopt aims for improving performance on those measures.[1]

The BHCS Board of Trustees has ensured that quality is "part of the fabric" of BHCS. Over a decade ago, the then-chair of our flagship hospital's Board of Trustees drafted a resolution that publicly affirmed the Board's commitment to improving quality throughout BHCS. The resolution, which was reaffirmed in 2010, stated:

> Whereas, maintaining the status quo or achieving quality and safety levels only equal to or slightly better than national, regional, or local norms is not compatible with the BHCS Vision and Mission Statements; and
> Whereas, regulatory and legislative changes and a growing number of more informed patients support better quality patient care and safety;
> Therefore, be it resolved, that the Board of Trustees of Baylor Health Care System hereby challenges itself and everyone involved in providing health care throughout the system to give patient safety and continuous improvement in the quality of patient care the highest priority in the planning, budgeting, and execution of all activities in order to achieve significant, demonstrable, and measurable positive improvement in the quality of patient care and safety.[4]

HEALTH CARE QUALITY IMPROVEMENT STRATEGIC PLANNING

Leverage Point Two of the IHI Seven Leadership Leverage Points is to develop an executable strategy to achieve the system-level aims and oversee their execution at the highest governance level. This strategy must be of an appropriate scale and pace, and must involve leaders with the necessary power and influence.[1]

In 2000, following the adoption of the Quality Resolution, the BHCS Board of Trustees established a Health Care Quality Improvement Strategic Committee to identify key health care quality indicators and to make recommendations to measure and improve the quality of care. The committee laid out a health care improvement strategic plan based on three critical elements: (1) the alignment of every board member across BHCS, as well as the BHCS senior administrative and medical leadership and frontline employees, toward making quality of care a priority; (2) the introduction of performance management incentives linked to clinical indicators; and (3) the creation of a multidisciplinary health care improvement operations team across all BHCS operating units for all hospitals.[4]

The committee examined the BHCS annual performance award program and proposed establishing annual incentives to encourage the adoption of ideal care objectives by linking management compensation to specific clinical indicators (see Chapter 4).[5]

APPROACHES TO ORGANIZING AND MANAGING SYSTEM-WIDE QUALITY INITIATIVES

The third of the IHI Seven Leadership Leverage Points is to channel leadership attention to system-level improvement: personal leadership, leadership systems, and transparency.[5] Similarly, the third recommendation of the 2000 BHCS health care quality improvement strategic committee was for the creation of a multidisciplinary BHCS leadership group to focus on system-wide implementation of health care improvement initiatives. This led to the formation in 2001 of the system-wide Best Care Committee to advance and report on STEEEP aims. Although health care quality improvement would involve a "steep climb," the Board recognized that focusing organizational efforts around STEEEP aims was the right thing to do.

In 2012, BHCS transformed the Best Care Committee into the STEEEP Governance Council (SGC), a fully aligned group for system-wide improvement efforts. This transformation engaged the fifth of IHI's Seven Leadership Leverage Points: "Make the chief financial officer a quality champion,"[1] to accelerate progress in the Efficiency domain of STEEEP care. The SGC's voting members include the system chief quality officer (who chairs the committee), the system chief operating officer, the system chief medical officer, the system chief nursing officer, the system chief financial officer, the chair of the board and president of the system-employed physician group, and the senior vice president with oversight of all of the system hospitals. The BHCS clinical service lines dock into the SGC, as do the five STEEEP subcommittees (Safety, Clinical Excellence, Efficiency, Equity, and Patient Centeredness). The SGC represents the consolidated efforts of clinical, operational, and financial leadership and ensures that improvement efforts encompass all domains of STEEEP care.

The SGC is charged with developing improvement initiatives and related resource allocations, coordinating the implementation of quality improvement projects throughout BHCS, and holding itself and others across BHCS accountable for results. The SGC focuses on prioritizing and committing the resources necessary to enable the successful implementation of system-wide health care improvement initiatives by assimilating the efforts of administrative, nursing, and physician leadership.[4,6]

The quality initiatives passed by the SGC have been guided by the STEEEP framework, as laid out by the Institute of Medicine (IOM).[3] Both for quality improvement purposes and to support the BHCS commitment to transparency in health care, the SGC reviews dozens of performance indicators across the STEEEP domains. A "snapshot" of performance on and trend status of these indicators is reported monthly to the Board of Trustees, chief executive officer, senior leadership, frontline health care providers, and, eventually, to all employees via the BHCS intranet Web site in the STEEEP Care Report. This report tracks BHCS's performance related to its annual Quality and Service goals. The SGC's work, therefore, also closely aligns with the first foundational element of the IOM Checklist for High-Value Health Care: Governance priority and the need for senior executive leaders and board members to provide visible and determined leadership on quality goals and progress.[2]

COMMITMENT TO PATIENT-CENTERED CARE

Patients need to be actively invited by every care giver at every interface with the health care system to participate in their own care and their own treatment decisions by communicating their needs and priorities, and by understanding all their options and the related risks and benefits. This is the only way in which truly shared and informed decision-making can occur. Patients likewise need to be actively engaged in the broader design and governance of the health care system and its ongoing efforts at improvement. The fourth IHI Leadership Leverage Point is to put patients and families on the improvement team, recognizing that organizations that achieve high levels of improvement often ask patients and families to be directly involved in the improvement process, putting them in positions of real influence.[1]

BHCS engages patient advisors to help motivate employees and catalyze change. An advisor may be a patient or a supporting family member or friend of a patient. Patient advisors serve on councils or participate in focus groups or workgroups. As of 2013, BHCS has 8 hospitals with active advisors, 13 hospitals with groups approved to add advisors, and 40 total advisors who provide input and recommendations on a variety of projects. For example, when the Andrews Women's Hospital, associated with Baylor All Saints Medical Center, was built, 20 advisors made recommendations about the design and flow of the facility. Patient advisors also provide input for patient safety and infection control work at Baylor University Medical Center.

In addition to its work with patient advisors, over the past several years, BHCS has worked to ensure that its patients and families remain together for inpatient stays, that they are included in bedside shift report and hand-offs, and that nursing and other clinical leaders regularly meet with them face-to-face during the hospital encounter.

ENGAGING PHYSICIAN LEADERSHIP

Leverage Point Six of the IHI Seven Leadership Leverage Points is to engage physicians. While physicians alone cannot bring about system-level performance improvement, their engagement is critical. Organizations are not likely to achieve improvement without the knowledge and leadership of physicians.[1] BHCS engages physicians through the Physician Leadership Council (see Chapter 6).

Additionally, a key component of the 2005–2009 BHCS financial plan was support for BHCS physician champions, who provide intellectual capital and leadership for quality efforts throughout BHCS. These physicians, many of whom now have expanded roles as BHCS clinical service line leaders, provide the motivation, encouragement, and medical and process expertise to collaboratively design solutions to address the challenges to quality improvement.

BUILDING QUALITY IMPROVEMENT CAPACITY

The seventh IHI Leadership Leverage Point is to build improvement capacity. A health care delivery organization must be technically capable of making, sustaining, and spreading improvements. This technical capability depends partly on the infrastructure dedicated to quality improvement efforts.[1]

One of BHCS's early explicit approaches to quality improvement was supported by the 1994 formation of its first system-wide clinical committee, the Quality Council, which offered a vision to incorporate quality measurement and improvement into BHCS on an organizational and process level. The Council created a quality improvement plan intended to provide a systematic, integrated, continuous quality improvement program to design, measure, evaluate, and improve performance of integrated clinical quality processes, outcomes, and the effective use of resources for the benefit of patients and health care system members.[4]

The Council's quality improvement plan resulted in the creation of multidisciplinary task forces driven by continuous process improvement methodology. Under this Plan-Do-Check-Act (PDCA) strategy, the need to improve a process was identified; next, an expert team examined the process and selected one or more improvement strategies to implement (P); then, after the change was in place (D), the team studied the new process (C) and used this analysis to redesign and implement an even more effective care delivery approach (A).

As a result of the quality improvement plan, the continuous quality improvement leaders noted in their 1996 annual report that there were 19 clinical teams, 10 new clinical carepaths or guidelines, and 18 carepaths or guidelines in development or pending approval. There were 98 physician members focusing on reducing variation and costs related to cardiovascular care, vascular surgery, orthopedics, internal medicine, and primary care.[4] The report concluded by noting: "Total estimated reduction in direct costs = $4,042,834. No reduction in quality based on indicators measured."[7]

In beginning to build the BHCS capacity for improvement, the Board reaffirmed its commitment to quality in 1999 by authorizing the hiring of BHCS's first chief quality officer, and focused a new strategic planning effort around the explicitly stated vision to "become the most trusted source of comprehensive health services." Currently, each BHCS hospital has an advisory board and a STEEEP Care Committee that inform and make decisions related to health care quality initiatives, striving to help BHCS realize its vision.

COMMITMENT TO NATIONAL 100,000 LIVES CAMPAIGN

In 2005, the IHI began its 100,000 Lives Campaign to save 100,000 lives over 18 months through 6 patient safety interventions:

- Deploy rapid response teams (RRTs) at the first sign of patient decline.
- Deliver reliable, evidence-based care for acute myocardial infarction to prevent deaths from heart attack.
- Prevent adverse drug events by implementing medication reconciliation.
- Prevent central line infections by implementing a series of interdependent, scientifically grounded steps called the "Central Line Bundle."
- Prevent surgical site infections by reliably delivering the correct perioperative antibiotics at the proper time.
- Prevent ventilator-associated pneumonia by implementing a series of interdependent, scientifically grounded steps including the "Ventilator Bundle."[8]

Recognizing the importance of this initiative to health care quality, the BHCS Board of Trustees passed a resolution committing BHCS to "rapidly implement" these six programs, and establishing a target of reducing the inpatient mortality rate by at least 4% from fiscal year 2005 to fiscal year 2006, both at the individual hospital levels and in aggregate across the system.

In addition to being an early adopter of the IHI 100,000 Lives Campaign, BHCS continued and expanded its work to improve patient safety by establishing the Office of Patient Safety to provide system-wide performance measurement and coordination for a broad portfolio of improvement activities to reduce risk-adjusted inpatient mortality. In addition, standardized trigger tools have been deployed and refined to measure the incidence of adverse events in inpatient and primary care settings, and to provide information on the nature of these events, which is needed to develop improvement tactics to prevent them.

The Board unanimously approved BHCS's participation in the IHI's 5 Million Lives Campaign on January 25, 2007. This campaign expanded the focus from preventing in-hospital deaths to preventing incidents of medical harm, including medication errors and adverse drug events.

ALIGNMENT WITH NATIONAL HEALTH CARE PRIORITIES

The BHCS Board's commitment to quality aligns with the recommendations of the 2008 IHI "Boards on Board" guide.[3] According to this guide, boards should focus on six major actions to improve health care quality and patient safety.

1. Setting Aims: Set a specific aim to reduce harm this year. Make an explicit public commitment to measurable quality improvement (e.g., reduction in unnecessary mortality and harm), establishing a clear aim for the facility or system.

    The BHCS Board sets system-wide goals related to quality (including mortality reduction and Centers for Medicare and Medicaid (CMS) process-of-care measures), service (including patient satisfaction), people (including employee satisfaction), and finance. These goals are cascaded to all employees and progress toward the goals is shared through transparency boards displayed throughout facilities.

2. Getting Data and Hearing Stories: Select and review progress toward safer care as the first agenda item at every Board meeting, grounded in transparency, and putting a "human face" on harm data.

    The BHCS Board receives patient safety data provided by the SGC in the monthly report, and from the CEO Dashboard, which is available on the Trustees portal and displays financial, quality, and patient satisfaction data at the system and facility levels. The Board hears and communicates stories from individual patients to drive improvement; for example, in 2006, the Board viewed BHCS's RRT video, which presents the story of a grateful patient and her husband, who describe how her life was saved by an RRT implemented by BHCS as part of its participation in the IHI 100,000 Lives Campaign.

3. Establishing and Monitoring System-Level Measures: Identify a small group of organization-wide "roll up" measures of patient safety (e.g., facility-wide harm, risk-adjusted mortality); update the measures continually and make them transparent to the entire organization and all of its customers.

    The BHCS Board sets system-wide goals related to inpatient mortality reduction, compliance with CMS process of care measures, readmission reduction, and performance on measures of patient experience, such as the Hospital Consumer Assessment of Healthcare Providers and Systems (HCAHPS) survey, and monitors progress toward these goals. Goal setting begins with recommendations from clinical leadership, who establish areas of focus and levels based on input from participation in organizations, such as the National Quality Forum. This participation by clinical leadership helps BHCS stay "ahead of the curve." The goals and current performance are displayed on transparency boards throughout each facility and are in the periodic system-wide STEEEP/Best Care Report.

4. Changing the Environment, Policies, and Culture: Commit to establish and maintain an environment that is respectful, fair, and just for all who experience the pain and loss resulting from avoidable harm and adverse outcomes: the patients, their families, and the staff at the sharp end of error.

The BHCS Board adopted five BHCS core values to establish a respectful and fair culture: Quality, Servanthood, Integrity, Stewardship, and Innovation (Introduction, Figure I-1). The Board's commitment to error disclosure is reflected in BHCS's disclosure policy, which defines a recommended process for disclosing errors to patients.

BHCS uses a common electronic system for personnel to voluntarily report patient safety events and near misses, such as falls, medication errors, adverse drug reactions, testing and treatment errors, hazardous material spills, operating room-related events, patient complaints, and employee injuries.

The BHCS Office of Patient Safety has also implemented a more objective tool for identifying and measuring hospital care-based harm, the Baylor Adverse Event Measurement Tool, which is an expanded version of the IHI's Global Trigger Tool.[9–11] This tool uses monthly audits of randomly selected inpatient charts to estimate adverse event rates in BHCS hospitals. In collecting and communicating performance data related to adverse event (AE) rates, BHCS emphasizes that its purposes are not related to disciplinary action for physicians or staff, but rather to assist in identifying patterns of AEs that might indicate system failures that hospitals/departments can then develop targeted improvement interventions to address.

5. Learning ... Starting with the Board: Develop your capability as a Board. Learn about how "best in the world" Boards work with executive and physician leaders to reduce harm. Set an expectation for similar levels of education and training for all staff.

The Board has encouraged the continued development of senior BHCS leaders by supporting their study of management and business administration. BHCS also brings leading experts to speak on health care and business from across the country to educate its leaders at the senior vice president, vice president, director, and manager levels during one-day Leadership Development Institute biannual meetings.

6. Establishing Executive Accountability: Oversee the effective execution of a plan to achieve your aims to reduce harm, including executive team accountability for clear quality improvement targets.

The Board drives the BHCS Performance Award Program.[5] Under this program, annual financial performance awards for BHCS leaders (manager level and above) are linked to Finance (fiscal operating margin); Quality (inpatient mortality, performance across CMS Core Measures, readmissions); Service (patient satisfaction survey scores); and People (employee retention). The program places a portion of leaders' compensation "at risk," with the specific amount being determined as a percentage of the employee's base salary, ranging from 5 percent for clinical managers to 40 percent for the chief executive officer. This incentive approach creates an environment in which leaders are explicitly accountable for health care quality.

CONCLUSION

The IHI has identified Seven Leadership Leverage Points for Organizational-Level Improvement in Health Care, with which the BHCS quality improvement efforts closely align.

Getting the "Board on Board" is the first step toward ensuring a commitment to quality throughout an organization. BHCS recognized this imperative early in its journey and the BHCS Board responded by formalizing its commitment to quality, establishing and overseeing specific system-level quality improvement aims, linking management compensation to clinical indicators, creating a multidisciplinary leadership group to focus on system-wide implementation of health care improvement, and adopting the IOM STEEEP framework. The Board's longstanding recognition that quality is integral to BHCS's business exemplifies the observation of Donald Berwick, IHI founder and former head of CMS, that "the buck stops in the boardroom."[12]

REFERENCES

1. Reinertsen, J. L., M. Bisognano, and M. D. Pugh. 2008. *Seven leadership leverage points for organization-level improvement in health care*, 2nd ed. Cambridge, MA: Institute for Healthcare Improvement.
2. Cosgrove, D., M. Fisher, P. Gabow, G. Gottlieb, G. Halvorson, B. James, G. Kaplan, et al. 2012. *A CEO checklist for high-value health care*. Washington, D.C.: Institute of Medicine, June.
3. Institute for Healthcare Improvement. 2008. 5 Million Lives Campaign. Getting started kit: Governance leadership "Boards on Board" how-to guide. Online at: http://www.ihi.org/knowledge/Pages/Tools/HowtoGuideGovernanceLeadership.aspx (accessed May 15, 2013).

4. Ballard, D. J., B. Spreadbury, and R. S. Hopkins, 3rd. 2004. Health care quality improvement across the Baylor Health Care System: The first century. *Proceedings* (Baylor University Medical Center) 17 (3): 277–288.
5. Herrin, J., D. Nicewander, and D. J. Ballard, The effect of health care system administrator pay-for-performance on quality of care. *The Joint Commission Journal on Quality and Patient Safety* 34 (11): 646–654.
6. Ballard, D. J. 2003. Indicators to improve clinical quality across an integrated health care system. *International Journal for Quality in Health Care* 15 (Suppl 1): i13–23.
7. *Executive summary, Annual report of the clinical CQI teams.*1996. Dallas: Baylor University Medical Center.
8. Institute for Healthcare Improvement. Protecting 5 million lives from harm. Online at: http://www.ihi.org/offerings/Initiatives/PastStrategicInitiatives/5MillionLivesCampaign/Pages/default.aspx (accessed December 12, 2012).
9. Good, V. S., M. Saldana, R. Gilder, D. Nicewander, and D. A. Kennerly. 2010. Large-scale deployment of the Global Trigger Tool across a large hospital system: Refinements for the characterisation of adverse events to support patient safety learning opportunities. *BMJ Quality and Safety* 20 (1): 25–30.
10. Kennerly, D. A., M. Saldaña, R. Kudyakov, B. da Graca, D. Nicewander, and J. Compton. 2013. Description and evaluation of adaptations to the Global Trigger Tool to enhance value to adverse event reduction efforts. *Journal of Patient Safety* 9 (2): 87–95.
11. Griffin, F. A., and R. K. Resar. 2007. *IHI Global Trigger Tool for measuring adverse events.* Cambridge, MA: Institute for Healthcare Improvement.
12. Berwick, D. M. 2006. An interview with Donald Berwick. Interview by Paul M Schyve. *The Joint Commission Journal on Quality and Patient Safety* 32 (12): 661–666.

Chapter 2

Leadership

Joel T. Allison and David J. Ballard

CONTENTS

INTRODUCTION

While an organizational commitment to quality begins at the highest governance level, organizational leadership at all levels is integral to executing and implementing this commitment. This is reflected in the third of the Institute of Healthcare Improvement (IHI) Seven Leadership Leverage Points, which calls for leadership attention to be focused on system-level quality improvement by channeling attention to personal leadership, leadership systems, and transparency.[1] BHCS has implemented numerous initiatives to develop personal leadership, leadership systems, and transparency throughout its facilities with the goal of improving health care quality for its patients.

LEADERSHIP COMMITMENT TO QUALITY

For leaders to successfully drive organizational-level improvement, they need to be committed to the BHCS vision, mission, and values (see Introduction, Figure I.1). An early effort to ensure this commitment was the Leadership Center, which was formed in 1991. Initially, the Leadership Center oversaw organizational improvements based on total quality management principles, and a clinical continuous quality improvement task force was initiated through the Center in 1992. In 1994, BHCS formed its first system-wide clinical committee, the Quality Council, and, in 2000, a health care quality improvement strategic committee was established to make recommendations regarding the measurement and improvement of the quality of care (see Chapter 1).[2-4]

COMMUNICATION BOARDS TO DRIVE ORGANIZATIONAL TRANSPARENCY

Organizational goals and BHCS's current progress toward meeting them are made transparent to employees on the organization's intranet Web site and on communication boards placed throughout the BHCS facilities, demonstrating our commitment to transparency. Communication boards publicly display quality improvement goals and actual performance at the system, facility, and department levels on the four system-wide areas of focus: people, quality, service, and finance. Many of these boards are visible not only to employees, but also to patients, families, and hospital or facility visitors. BHCS also uses regular departmental Town Hall meetings to communicate system, facility, department, and individual goals and performance to employees.

LEADERSHIP DEVELOPMENT MEETINGS

BHCS develops leaders through its Leadership Development Institute (LDI). Quarterly LDI meetings, which began in 2006, convene executives (including the chief executive officer and chief operating officer), directors, and managers. LDI meetings aim to:

- Develop leader skills so BHCS can achieve its goals;
- Align leader competencies with BHCS's values and focus areas;
- Improve individual leadership performance;
- Rekindle leader passion and commitment;
- Raise leadership accountability and consistency;
- Enhance employee satisfaction; and
- Change behavior, which in turn advances the BHCS Circle of Care (Figure I.1) and continues to move the culture to one of excellence.

At LDI meetings, leaders learn about current BHCS performance goals and progress toward meeting those goals. LDI meetings also bring nationally renowned experts, such as Quint Studer, John Kitzhaber, Mark McClellan, John Kotter, Jim Collins, Morten Hansen, Len Nichols, and Tom Morris, from outside the organization to teach and discuss business, leadership, and health care with the intent of providing attendees with a broader perspective of quality improvement and performance measures. LDI meetings also provide the opportunity for BHCS leaders to network and share ideas, strategies, and tools related to health care quality and other important considerations.

CONCLUSION

For meaningful and sustainable organizational-level health care quality improvement to occur, leadership attention must be committed to and focused on this improvement, specifically through personal leadership, leadership systems, and transparency.[1] BHCS recognized this early in its quality journey and has deployed extensive resources to develop and empower its leaders. From the early days of the Leadership Center and the Quality Council, BHCS has ensured that strong organization-wide leadership systems are in place. BHCS develops its leaders through LDI meetings to enhance leadership skills and raise accountability. With its commitment to consistent, accountable, quality-focused leadership that supports the organization's vision, mission, and values, BHCS advances its commitment to deliver STEEEP care to its patients.

REFERENCES

1. Reinertsen, J. L., M. Bisognano, and M. D. Pugh. 2008. *Seven leadership leverage points for organization-level improvement in health care*, 2nd ed. Cambridge, MA: Institute for Healthcare Improvement.
2. Ballard, D. J. 2003. Indicators to improve clinical quality across an integrated health care system. *International Journal for Quality in Health Care* 15 (Suppl 1): i13–23.
3. Ballard, D. J., B. Spreadbury, and R. S. Hopkins, 3rd. 2004. Health care quality improvement across the Baylor Health Care System: The first century. *Proceedings (Baylor University Medical Center)* 17 (3): 277–288.
4. Herrin, J., D. Nicewander, and D. J. Ballard, The effect of health care system administrator pay-for-performance on quality of care. *The Joint Commission Journal on Quality and Patient Safety* 34 (11): 646–654.

Chapter 3

Organizational Structures

David J. Ballard, Paul Convery, and Gary Brock

CONTENTS

INTRODUCTION

The seventh Institute for Healthcare Improvement (IHI) Leadership Leverage Point is to build improvement capacity.[1] A health care delivery organization must be technically capable of making, sustaining, and spreading improvements, and this technical capability depends partly on the infrastructure dedicated to quality improvement efforts. BHCS leaders recognized early in the quality journey that delivery of STEEEP care requires robust structural support within the organization.[2] In light of this imperative, they began to develop the infrastructure required to help the organization realize its vision to be "trusted as the best place to give and receive safe, quality, compassionate health care."[3] Through a variety of teams, councils, committees, and departments, BHCS has aligned its goals and activities with national priorities articulated by organizations, such as the Institute of Medicine[2,4] and the National Quality Forum.[5] BHCS has also brought its diverse hospitals and facilities together in service of its mission to "serve all people through exemplary health care, education, research, and community service." This chapter provides examples of important structural elements that have facilitated STEEEP care throughout BHCS.

STRATEGIES FOR SYSTEM ALIGNMENT

An early tactic to achieve greater system alignment through organizational structures was the System Integration Action Team, created in the late 1990s by Joel Allison, BHCS president and chief executive officer. Prior to 2000, the BHCS corporate governance structure focused on Baylor University Medical Center (BUMC); the BHCS and BUMC Boards of Trustees were identical. In 2000, the BHCS and BUMC boards began to function separately with little overlap of trustee membership. With the help of the System Integration Action Team, BHCS adopted a stronger corporate model, with a system-wide Board of Trustees functioning alongside an operating board for each hospital, which was fully implemented by 2007.

COORDINATION OF QUALITY IMPROVEMENT INITIATIVES

A significant evolution toward providing measurable improvement of clinical improvement efforts took place in 1998, when BHCS formed a Quality Management Coordinating Council, later renamed the Quality Improvement Coordinating Council. The Council served as the managing authority for the operational and organizational decisions related to coordinating, communicating, integrating, and providing education on BHCS quality initiatives. The Council included the quality directors from each BHCS hospital as well as medical directors from BUMC and other hospitals. The Quality Improvement Coordinating Council was supported by a Quality Improvement Communication Forum, which was responsible for communicating with and educating BHCS personnel about the integration of quality, resource, and outcomes management.[6]

The BHCS history of aligning organizational structures to support STEEEP care reached another important milestone on January 27, 2000, when the Board of Trustees established a Health Care Quality Improvement Strategic Committee (see Chapter 1). This was followed by the Best Care Committee in 2001 (transformed into the STEEEP Governance Council (SGC) in 2012; Chapter 1) to address the need for a multidisciplinary BHCS leadership group to focus on system-wide implementation of health care improvement initiatives. The reporting structure for the SGC is depicted in Figure 3.1.

SYSTEM-WIDE RESOURCE
FOR HEALTH CARE RESEARCH AND IMPROVEMENT

As BHCS enhanced its focus on STEEEP care, organizational leaders recognized the need to create a core resource to develop, implement, and measure the effect of quality initiatives across the system. In 1999, BHCS established

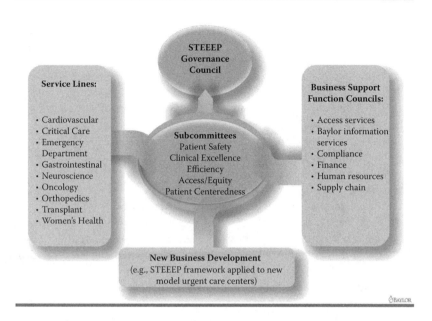

FIGURE 3.1 Reporting structure for the STEEEP Governance Council.

the Institute for Health Care Research and Improvement (IHCRI) to improve health care across BHCS and to conduct and support research related to quality throughout BHCS. Under the direction of BHCS's chief quality officer, IHCRI advances BHCS's health care improvement operational priorities. Its departments include the Center for Clinical Innovation, Epidemiology, Office of Patient Centeredness, Office of Patient Safety, Performance Measurement and Reporting, and STEEEP Analytics. IHCRI employs epidemiologists, health services researchers (including health economists and decision scientists), biostatisticians, data managers and programmers, and medical writers and editors. IHCRI improvement efforts are supported through BHCS operational budgets, while specific research projects are funded through external sources, such as the National Institutes of Health (NIH), the Agency for Healthcare Research and Quality (AHRQ), and foundation and private-sector research grants.

ENGAGING PHYSICIAN LEADERSHIP

Leverage Point Six of the IHI Seven Leadership Leverage Points is to engage physicians.[1] Aligning medical staff with organizational priorities is integral to ensuring delivery of STEEEP care, and is facilitated within BHCS through the Physician Leadership Council (see Chapter 6).

PHYSICIAN INTEGRATION AND ALIGNMENT

BHCS formed HealthTexas Provider Network (HTPN) in 1994 to integrate ambulatory primary care and specialty care physicians into the overall organization, creating an effective physician–hospital alliance within the strictures created by Texas laws prohibiting the corporate practice of medicine (see Chapter 14). The HTPN organizational structure is an important component of the BHCS approach to quality and STEEEP care delivery. Headquartered in Dallas, HTPN is a multispecialty medical group that employs over 590 physicians practicing in 191 care delivery sites in the North Texas area. The medical group practice comprises 66 primary care centers, 122 specialty care centers, 7 hospitalist programs, 3 pulmonary critical care units, 13 liver disease outreach clinics, 3 advanced heart failure clinics, 3 senior health centers, as well as 31 cardiovascular care sites and a family practice residency program.[7]

In fiscal year 2012, HTPN reported more than 1.7 million patient visits that year and $615 million in gross charges, making it one of the largest medical groups in the nation. HTPN was selected as an American Medical Group Association (AMGA) Acclaim Award Honoree in both 2011 and 2012, and received the AMGA's Medical Group Preeminence Award in 2010.[7]

In alignment with the BHCS mission and vision, HTPN is dedicated to quality and to fulfilling its mission "to achieve excellence in the delivery of accessible, cost-effective, quality health care and demonstrated customer satisfaction that delivers value to patients, payers, and the community."[7]

HTPN contracts with physicians, manages and operates primary care and specialty care practices, and pursues managed care arrangements with employers, insurers, and other payers. HTPN also expands patient access to quality health care service, expands the number of physicians serving Medicare and Medicaid patients, and expands the number of physicians available to serve the medically indigent.[8]

Through its economic alignment of physicians, its committee structures, and its model of distributed resources, decision making, and accountability, HTPN has achieved substantial success in creating a physician-led health care improvement culture across its ambulatory care centers and hospitalist groups.

ACCOUNTABLE CARE ORGANIZATION

The major health care challenges currently facing the United States include high pricing, unsustainable cost increases, less than ideal quality, and poor access for many Americans. BHCS leaders recognize that health care reform is needed, and that an important aspect of reform is greater accountability for both quality and cost. Baylor Quality Alliance (BQA) is developing an accountable care organization of physicians who recognize the nation's health care system is moving away from the current fragmented approach of payment for volume of services rendered toward payment for value that centers around the patient across the continuum of care.[9]

The Patient Protection and Affordable Care Act provides the legal context for BQA's development.[10] BQA is owned by BHCS through its controlled affiliates and has a 19-person Board of Managers, including 14 practicing physicians, 3 BHCS executives, a community representative, and a BHCS Board member. The BQA Board chairman is a practicing physician, and all the physician Board members (representing all parts of the BHCS system) were selected by their respective hospital medical staff communities.[11]

BQA represents a commitment to deliver the highest quality health care possible, in an efficient, integrated manner for the patients and communities it serves. It is the embodiment of the BHCS leadership's belief that accountable, evidence-based, collective, proactive, value-driven efforts will lead to a better health care system for the future, and that clinical integration around these principles offers the best solution to the health care system issues facing the nation. [12]

LESSONS LEARNED

BHCS learned early in its quality journey that standardization of protocols, processes, tools, supplies, and metrics is an integral component of STEEEP care. System-wide strategies for clinical and administrative standardization are needed, not just strategies that apply to a single facility or a single service line. The structure of the organization—starting with centralized governance—is foundational to driving quality improvement. Many health care delivery systems have the will to drive certain initiatives for quality, but struggle because they do not have the proper organizational structures in place.

BHCS also has learned that establishing and maintaining corporate infrastructures is essential to delivering STEEEP care. From the early days of the Quality Improvement Coordination Council to the creation of the IHCRI and, more recently, the establishment of BQA, BHCS has been committed to developing the foundation that is the basis for requisite resources and intellectual capital necessary to improve health care quality for its patients. This commitment aligns with a dedication to national health care improvement priorities as well as BHCS's organizational vision and mission.

CONCLUSION

BHCS made an early and major commitment to delivering high-quality, STEEEP care, establishing the infrastucture to fulfill this commitment by investing in the requisite structures and resources, including human capital. BHCS has sought to develop and continue, through its organizational structure, that commitment to deliver STEEEP care as part of the "fabric" of the system. BHCS's infrastructure helps to ensure that the organization is technically capable of making, sustaining, and spreading quality improvements, as called for by the IHI Seven Leadership Leverage Points for Organizational-Level Improvement in Health Care.[1] The BHCS providers of care—its hospitals, facilities, and controlled affiliates—not only support national priorities for health care quality, but are strongly aligned in their efforts to support BHCS's goal of providing the best possible care to all members of the communities it serves.

REFERENCES

1. Reinertsen, J. L., M. Bisognano, and M. D. Pugh. 2008. *Seven leadership leverage points for organization-level improvement in health care*, 2nd ed. Cambridge, MA: Institute for Healthcare Improvement.
2. Corrigan, J. M., M. S. Donaldson, L. T. Kohn, S. K. Maguire, and K. C. Pike. 2001. *Crossing the quality chasm: A new health system for the 21st century.* Washington, DC: National Academy Press.
3. Ballard, D. J. 2003. Indicators to improve clinical quality across an integrated health care system. *International Journal for Quality in Health Care* 15 (Suppl 1): i13–23.
4. Kohn, L. T., J. M. Corrigan, and M. S. Donaldson. 1999. *To err is human: Building a safer health system.* Washington, DC: National Academy Press.
5. National Quality Forum. Online at: http://www.qualityforum.org/Home.aspx (accessed January 21, 2013).
6. Ballard, D. J., B. Spreadbury, and R. S. Hopkins, 3rd. 2004. Health care quality improvement across the Baylor Health Care System: The first century. *Proceedings (Baylor University Medical Center)* 17 (3): 277–288.
7. HealthTexas Provider Network. Online at: https://www.dfwdoctorjobs.com/Pages/Index.aspx (accessed January 8, 2013).
8. Wilsey, H. L. 2004. *How we care: Centennial history of Baylor University Medical Center and Baylor Health Care System, 1903–2003.* Dallas: Baylor Health Care System.
9. Ballard, D. J., The potential of Medicare accountable care organizations to transform the American health care marketplace: Rhetoric and reality. *Mayo Clinic Proceedings* 87 (8): 707–709.
10. Patient Protection and Affordable Care Act. Public Law 111–148—March 23, 2010. 124 Stat. 119. Online at: http://www.gpo.gov/fdsys/pkg/PLAW-111publ148/pdf/PLAW-111publ148.pdf
11. Baylor Quality Alliance. Online at: http://www.baylorqualityalliance.com/Pages/home.aspx (accessed January 8, 2013).
12. Couch, C. E. 2012. Why Baylor Health Care System would like to file for Medicare Shared Savings accountable care organization designation but cannot. *Mayo Clinic Proceedings* 87 (8): 723–726.

Chapter 4

Alignment, Goal Setting, and Incentives

Keith Holtz and Ed de Vol

CONTENTS

INTRODUCTION

BHCS approaches the process of setting organizational goals and compensating leaders based on achievement of these goals in line with the Institute for Healthcare Improvement's (IHI) recommendation for establishing measures of system-level performance, adopting specific aims for improvement of these measures, and establishing oversight of these aims at the highest leadership levels under the first of Seven Leadership Leverage Points.[1] BHCS began linking performance management incentives to specific clinical indicators of health care quality in 2001. In the ensuing years, BHCS has more clearly defined its goal setting and incentives initiatives to focus on the four areas that guide the organization's goals (people, quality, finance, and service). System-wide goals in each of the four areas cascade to employees at all levels, and a performance award program places a proportion of executive pay "at risk" depending on achievement of the goals. Aligning incentives and goals in these ways has encouraged the adoption of quality care objectives throughout the organization.

PERFORMANCE MANAGEMENT INCENTIVES LINKED TO CLINICAL INDICATORS

When BHCS first added clinical indicators to its performance award program, the incentives were linked to meeting or exceeding performance targets for the five Centers for Medicare and Medicaid Services (CMS)/Joint Commission process of care "Core Measures" for acute myocardial infarction care.[2] This was the first time in the nearly 20-year history of the BHCS performance award program that senior leaders and managers were evaluated not just on fiscal indicators, but also on their ability to fulfill quality improvement expectations.[2-4] In the following year, the measures included in the clinical quality index of the incentive program were expanded to include the Core Measures for community-acquired pneumonia, and, in 2004 and 2005 respectively, the Core Measures for heart failure and surgical infection prevention were added.[2] In subsequent years, the measures included in the clinical quality index have changed to reflect the evolving focus of BHCS improvement efforts; for example, requiring that specified reductions in measures of in-hospital mortality be achieved.

IDENTIFICATION OF ORGANIZATIONAL STRATEGIC OBJECTIVES

In 2007, BHCS made another important change in its strategic objectives when, on the basis of both national and local needs, it identified four focus areas it needed to address to realize its vision of being trusted as the best place to give and receive safe, quality, compassionate health care:

- People: Be the best place to work
- Quality: Deliver STEEEP care, supported by education and research
- Finance: Be responsible financial stewards
- Service: Serve both our patients and our community

DEVELOPMENT OF SYSTEM-WIDE CARE GOALS

Guided by the four focus areas, BHCS developed 10 system-wide goals. *People* goals focused on employee retention, *Quality* goals were related to inpatient mortality and performance on CMS Core Measures, *Finance* goals were based on fiscal operating margin, and *Service* goals focused on patient satisfaction survey scores. These goals "cascade" down throughout BHCS so that all facilities, departments, and leaders are required to define goals that align with the system goals. The system-level goals were also incorporated into the performance award program, making leaders' compensation dependent on attaining the goals they set. The weight applied to each focus area in the performance award program varies, depending on which areas BHCS identifies as being the highest priorities for improvement each year. For example, in fiscal year 2013, 70 percent of the weight was placed on the Quality and Service goals. This enhanced focus on quality and service was driven by the Board's strong sentiment that financial success will follow from excellent quality and patient satisfaction scores.

Progress toward the system-level goals is presented to the Board of Trustees and Senior Leadership Council in the monthly STEEEP Care Report. Both groups and their commitment to quality improvement and the use of financial incentives to drive nonfinancial goals have been major driving forces behind BHCS's successful implementation and alignment of goal setting and performance incentive initiatives. Another secret to the successful implementation of the goal-setting program at BHCS is its transparency to employees. Organizational goals and BHCS's current progress toward meeting them are communicated to employees on the organization's intranet Web site and on communication boards placed throughout BHCS facilities (see Chapter 1).

CONTINUED EXPANSION OF GOAL-SETTING PROGRAM

The goal-setting program related to performance management expanded in 2008 to include all employees, and annual performance evaluations were then based on achievement of the goals organized by the four areas of focus. All employees are required to develop goals that are SMART (specific, measureable, actionable, realistic, and time-dependent) to align their work with and support the organization's goals.

STRUCTURAL SUPPORT FOR GOAL SETTING

A multidisciplinary Goal Setting Subcommittee was established in 2009, composed of BHCS stakeholders in each of the four areas of focus. The subcommittee identifies the goals to be included in the performance award program for any given year and makes recommendations to senior leaders and the Board about goals and metrics. For example, with the introduction of the CMS Hospital Value-Based Purchasing program[5]—which uses HCAHPS (Hospital Consumer Assessment of Healthcare Providers and Systems) patient satisfaction surveys to determine which providers should be rewarded and which penalized for their performance—the subcommittee recommended adopting the HCAHPS patient survey measures for the BHCS goals, to better align them with the national performance metrics.

PHILOSOPHY OF VARIABLE PAY

BHCS offers competitive base salaries for executives that approximate the 50th percentile of salary ranges for similar positions in similar organizations. With the additional compensation associated with the performance award program, when BHCS meets its target-level goals in the areas of People, Quality, Service, and Finance, BHCS executive salaries stand at the 75th percentile or above, depending on whether the target goal is met or exceeded. The Board's philosophy is to reward employees when the organization meets its goals while maintaining executive salaries as a variable cost if the organization fails to achieve its goals. This approach to compensation has helped BHCS to better allocate its cost for salaries and reward higher performance while challenging itself to appropriately evaluate goal achievement.

An additional strength of the BHCS approach to variable executive compensation is that incentives are discretionary rather than entitlement-based. The Board understands that pay needs to be results-based; otherwise the organization is just spending extra money without results. One challenge BHCS faces in the future relates to how the organization, in an increasingly cost-conscious environment, can broaden its variable pay philosophy to include more employees.

A QUANTITATIVE APPROACH TO GOAL SETTING

Setting organizational goals requires a strong commitment to performance measurement. Appropriate measures must be defined and used to drive goal setting. Although measures are often chosen based on the existence of good benchmark data, measure selection may also be driven by financial priorities and how CMS calculates reimbursement.

To ensure credibility and feasibility for its goals, BHCS takes an objective approach to goal setting. Statistical modeling/prediction, based on historical performance data, is used to set the performance targets for each goal, operating within constraints set by the Board (e.g., that the target level be at least as high as the previous year's performance). Targets are usually determined by modeling using a normal distribution, identifying a "threshold" performance (at which leaders will receive 25 percent of the portion of their compensation placed at risk), an "intermediate target" performance (corresponding to a 50 percent award), a "target" performance (at which they receive 100 percent of the portion of compensation placed at risk), and a "stretch" performance (which will result in leaders receiving 150 percent of the amount of compensation placed at risk). As an example of these performance levels, Table 4.1 shows the fiscal year 2013 performance levels for the HCAHPS Composite Score (one of the Service goals).

TABLE 4.1 Performance levels for HCAHPS composite score
for fiscal year 2013

Performance Level	HCAHPS Composite Score (Average of the top box averages of all eight domains[a])
Threshold	74.8
Intermediate Target	75.5
Target	76.1
Stretch	77.3

[a] Communication with doctors, communication with nurses, responsiveness of hospital staff, pain management, communication about medicines, discharge information, cleanliness of the hospital environment, and quietness of the hospital environment.[6]

One challenge associated with goal setting is predicting what performance should be in the future. Performance levels higher and lower than predicted must be defined and—for the purposes of the performance award program—appropriate awards must be associated with each performance level. One way in which prediction can be used to set performance levels is through examining the opportunity for improvement captured in a year. For example, if the average patient satisfaction score improved from the 80th to 90th percentile in the previous year, then half of the improvement opportunity (the distance between the 80th and 100th percentiles) was captured. In the following year, if half the improvement opportunity is again captured, the average satisfaction score will move from the 90th to 95th percentile.

BHCS applies probabilistic rules to its goal setting: the target performance level should have a 50 percent probability of being achieved, and a stretch goal should have a 10 percent probability. If a performance level has a 90 percent probability of being achieved, it is too easily attainable and a more challenging goal must be set.

CONCLUSION

Point One of the IHI Seven Leadership Leverage Points requires establishing and overseeing aims at the highest governance and leadership levels.[1] BHCS has aligned performance incentives for organizational leaders with performance on system-wide goals within its four areas of focus (Quality, Service, People, and Finance) through a performance award program that places a proportion of their compensation "at risk" depending on whether the goals are met. System goals are transparent throughout the organization and cascade to employees at all levels. In this way, BHCS establishes and oversees system-level aims at the highest governance and leadership level and helps ensure high-quality care for all of its patients.

REFERENCES

1. Reinertsen, J. L., M. Bisognano, and M. D. Pugh. 2008. *Seven leadership leverage points for organization-level improvement in health care*, 2nd ed. Cambridge, MA: Institute for Healthcare Improvement.
2. Herrin, J., D. Nicewander, and D. J. Ballard, The effect of health care system administrator pay-for-performance on quality of care. *The Joint Commission Journal on Quality and Patient Safety* 34 (11): 646–654.
3. Ballard, D. J. 2003. Indicators to improve clinical quality across an integrated health care system. *International Journal for Quality in Health Care* 15 (Suppl 1): i13–23.
4. Ballard, D. J., B. Spreadbury, and R. S. Hopkins, 3rd. 2004. Health care quality improvement across the Baylor Health Care System: The first century. *Proceedings (Baylor University Medical Center)* 17 (3): 277–288.
5. Centers for Medicare and Medicaid Services. Hospital value-based purchasing. Online at: http://www.cms.gov/Medicare/Quality-Initiatives-Patient-Assessment-Instruments/hospital-value-based-purchasing/index.html (accessed November 27, 2012).
6. HCAHPS: Hospital care quality information from the consumer perspective. Online at: http://www.hcahpsonline.org/home.aspx (accessed February 4, 2013).

Chapter 5

Financial Leadership

Fred Savelsbergh, Robert T. Green, and David J. Ballard

CONTENTS

INTRODUCTION

The fifth of the Institute for Healthcare Improvement (IHI) Seven Leadership Leverage Points recommends making the chief financial officer (CFO) a quality champion.[2] Connecting quality improvement and business performance is increasingly important for health care organizations. Pay-for-performance programs, changes to the Medicare payment system, and the elimination of payment for "never events" (i.e., "particularly shocking medical errors … that should never occur")[1] are examples of the increased visibility of quality and payment for many health care CFOs. Similarly, organizations are beginning to evaluate and understand the financial impact of harm events, such as falls, medication errors, and delayed care.[2] Health care improvement initiatives, therefore, require a collaborative effort between quality and financial executives. BHCS quality and financial leaders have long understood the need to work together to promote STEEEP care.

COLLABORATIVE EFFORTS BETWEEN QUALITY AND FINANCIAL LEADERS

An early collaborative effort between BHCS quality and financial leaders involved the Health Care Quality Improvement Strategic Committee established in 2000 (see Chapter 1). One of its recommendations was to link management compensation to specific clinical indicators to encourage the adoption of STEEEP care objectives, (see Chapter 4), making leaders accountable for health care quality.[3]

BHCS has also fostered collaboration between quality and financial leaders through the formation of the interdisciplinary STEEEP Governance Council (SGC), connecting efforts and investments to achieve integration across the domains of STEEEP (see Chapter 1). Other less formal collaboration includes routine monthly meetings between the associate chief quality officer and the CFO to remain abreast of changes, issues, and progress in their respective spheres within BHCS.

An additional factor supporting collaboration between leaders from these diverse disciplines is that many of them have training in both a clinical discipline (medicine or nursing) and business or administration (master's in business administration, health administration, or medical management). BHCS has both recruited leaders with these dual qualifications (e.g., former CMO Paul Convery held a master's in medical management in addition to his medical doctorate when he joined BHCS) and supported their pursuit of such qualifications (e.g., Terri Nuss, vice president for patient centeredness, completed the executive MBA program at Southern Methodist University (SMU) in 2011 while serving BHCS in this capacity). Other clinical quality leaders have likewise received support from BHCS to obtain certificates/degrees in medical management, healthcare management, and business administration. In addition, the Advanced Physician Leadership training course BHCS developed in conjunction with the SMU Cox School of Business specifically for BHCS physicians (see Chapter 6) incorporates a module on corporate finance to help physician leaders understand and use financial data in decision making, which also aids communication and understanding between these clinical leaders and BHCS's financial departments.

COMMITMENT TO TRANSPARENCY

As the IHI recommends in the third of its Seven Leadership Leverage Points ("channel leadership attention to system-level improvement, including personal leadership, leadership systems, and transparency"[2]), BHCS is committed to financial transparency across the organization. Performance on finance goals (related to net margin) (see Chapter 4) is routinely provided in monthly reports sent to all leaders of the director level and above, showing both system performance and performance of relevant locations/entities. While not all leaders routinely see data for all locations/entities, these are transparent within certain groupings in the system. Thus, for example, all the hospital presidents can see not only their own performance toward their particular hospital's financial goal, but also the goals and performances of each of the other hospitals. Likewise, within the corporate entities, leaders of each entity that report up to a single senior leader are able to see each others' entities' performance. System and location performance on these financial goals, in turn, is communicated to employees through communication boards and town hall meetings (see Chapter 2).

In addition to this transparency on performance toward the financial goals, the quality improvement/research and financial departments within BHCS share the necessary data to quantify and report the fiscal impact of quality initiatives. BHCS uses a data warehousing/decision support system that provides a clinical/financial database (loaded using a patient accounting interface, and containing such data as DRGs (diagnosis-related groups), diagnoses, procedures, charge codes and charges by date of service, actual payments, insurance plan codes, and many other patient data) and a financial/statistical/labor database oriented toward cost centers, job classes, and accounts (loaded monthly from the general ledger and payroll system). Access to these clinically-linked financial data enables analysis of the financial impact of specific quality improvement initiatives. Decisions regarding when this needs to be part of the evaluation of an initiative rests with leaders within the SGC, based on such factors as whether the initiative in question is intended (or expected) to impact factors like length of stay, readmissions, or use of particular products or services that impact costs of care. Examples of quality improvement initiatives for which the financial impact has been evaluated include an advanced practice nurse led transitional care program for elderly patients with heart failure that BHCS tested in 2009 and 2010, comparing outcomes and costs (pre- and postimplementation) for patients discharged with heart failure. Following adjustment for patient age, sex, race, and severity of illness, a statistically significant 48 percent reduction in 30-day readmissions for heart failure patients was observed at the BHCS hospital that implemented this program. During the same period, readmissions for heart failure patients at other BHCS hospitals decreased by only 11 percent. While the intervention had little effect on length of stay or total 60-day direct costs, it was found to reduce the hospital financial contribution margin by $227 per patient under the Medicare reimbursement system in place at the time.[4] Its financial effects would need to be reevaluated in light of the advent of the CMS Readmissions Reduction Program[5] and the planned addition of patient outcome measures to the Value-Base Purchasing Program.[6]

Other quality initiatives for which BHCS has quantified and published the financial and nonfinancial effects include implementation of standardized order sets for pneumonia and heart failure,[7-9] and of electronic health records in primary care practices.[10]

In addition to being published in peer-reviewed medical journals, these data were provided to physician, nursing, and quality leaders in the BHCS hospitals for use in their efforts to encourage adoption of the standardized order sets. These efforts included academic detailing-type discussions with physicians (particularly targeting hospitalists in the case of the heart failure order set, as they treat more patients admitted for this condition than any other single specialty) and monthly presentations to the hospital Medical Executive Committees and to hospitalist groups.

LESSONS LEARNED

The need to create an environment of transparency is one of the most important lessons BHCS has learned through the collaboration between its quality and finance departments. For the organization to succeed, everyone needs access to data. BHCS leadership has embraced the IHI tenet that "perhaps the most powerful method of channeling leadership attention is to harness the power of transparency,"[2] creating opportunities for the meaningful examination of the financial effects of health care quality improvement initiatives and recognizing that actions undertaken with one goal in mind may have unintended effects (positive or negative) on other aspect of the organization's operations.

Another lesson BHCS has learned through the collaboration between its quality and finance leaders is the significant language barrier that exists between these domains, and the importance of each group understanding the other's vocabulary and perspective. The currency of BHCS is relationships. Quality and financial leaders have worked to establish informal as well as formal relationships, and this enables leaders to take a balanced approach to the opportunities and challenges that arise, and to collaborate successfully.

Finally, BHCS has learned that connecting quality and finance strengthens its pursuit of its organizational vision, mission, and values (see Introduction, Figure I.1). While financial performance is important to BHCS's continued ability to serve its community, its ultimate focus must be on stewardship toward its patients. The strong alignment and collaboration between quality and finance leaders facilitates this stewardship as well as the delivery of STEEEP care across the organization.

CONCLUSION

BHCS has long understood the importance of connecting finance and quality in health care that the IHI recognized in making one of its Seven Leadership Leverage Points "to make the CFO a quality champion."[2] BHCS quality and finance leaders are committed to transparent sharing of data, which enables them to quantify the fiscal impact of quality initiatives throughout the organization. Anticipating and monitoring the financial impacts of quality initiatives is important, because health care organizations may need to identify new areas for cost saving when quality improvements lead to decreased contribution margins. Aligning the quality and financial aims of an organization facilitates alignment along all dimensions of providing STEEEP care.

REFERENCES

1. AHRQ Patient Safety Network. Patient Safety Primers: Never Events. Available at http://psnet.ahrq.gov/primer.aspx?primerID=3 (accessed July 15, 2013).
2. Reinertsen, J. L., M. Bisognano, and M. D. Pugh. 2008. *Seven leadership leverage points for organization-level improvement in health care*, 2nd ed. Cambridge, MA: Institute for Healthcare Improvement.
3. Ballard, D. J. 2003. Indicators to improve clinical quality across an integrated health care system. *International Journal for Quality in Health Care* 15 (Suppl 1): i13–23.
4. Stauffer, B. D., C. Fullerton, N. Fleming, G. Ogola, J. Herrin, P. M. Stafford, and D. J. Ballard. 2011. Effectiveness and cost of a transitional care program for heart failure: A prospective study with concurrent controls. *Archive of Internal Medicine* 171 (14): 1238–1243.
5. Centers for Medicare and Medicaid Services. Readmissions Reduction Program. Online at: https://www.cms.gov/Medicare/Medicare-Fee-for-Service-Payment/AcuteInpatientPPS/Readmissions-Reduction-Program.html (accessed May 17, 2012).
6. Centers for Medicare and Medicaid Services and H. H. S. 2011. Medicare and Medicaid programs: Hospital outpatient prospective payment; ambulatory surgical center payment; hospital value-based purchasing program; physician self-referral; and patient notification requirements in provider agreements. Final rule with comment period. *Federal Register* 76 (230): 74122, 74535–74536.
7. Fleming, N. S., G. Ogola, and D. J. Ballard. 2009. Implementing a standardized order set for community-acquired pneumonia: Impact on mortality and cost. *The Joint Commission Journal on Quality and Patient Safety* 35 (8): 414–421.
8. Ballard, D. J., G. Ogola, N. S. Fleming, B. D. Stauffer, B. M. Leonard, R. Khetan, and C. W. Yancy. 2010. Impact of a standardized heart failure order set on mortality, readmission, and quality and costs of care. *International Journal for Quality in Health Care* 22 (6): 437–444.
9. Ballard, D. J., G. Ogola, N. S. Fleming, D. Heck, J. Gunderson, R. Mehta, R. Khetan, and J. D. Kerr. 2008. The impact of standardized order sets on quality and financial outcomes. In *Advances in patient safety: New directions and alternative approaches,* eds. K. Henriksen, et al. Rockville, MD: AHRQ Publications, nos. 08-0034 (1–4).
10. Fleming, N. S., S. D. Culler, R. McCorkle, E. R. Becker, and D. J. Ballard. 2011. The financial and nonfinancial costs of implementing electronic health records in primary care practices. *Health Affairs* (Millwood) 30 (3): 481–489.

Chapter 6

Physician Leadership

Paul Convery and Carl E. Couch

CONTENTS

INTRODUCTION

Physician leadership is essential for health care organizations to adapt and excel in a continually evolving health care environment. Recognizing this, the Institute for Healthcare Improvement (IHI) identified physician engagement as one of its Seven Leadership Leverage Points.[1] The combination of medical expertise and leadership ability enables physician champions to improve health care organizations' capacity to address many of the challenges they face, particularly the need to improve access, affordability, and quality of health care.[2,3]

This chapter discusses the alignment and training of physician leaders as well as the ways in which they have been integral to success at BHCS, and the role they will continue to play as the organization addresses the challenges that lie ahead.

PHYSICIAN INTEGRATION AND ALIGNMENT

While physicians possess a number of leadership strengths (e.g., intelligence, rapid learning, and strong decision-making skills), their leadership weaknesses tend to lie in the areas of consensus building, team work, systems thinking and personnel-related decision making.[4,5] Physicians are trained to be autonomous and are often independent by nature. Much of their clinical training occurs one-on-one, and their most basic work is performed in a room with a single patient.[6] Additionally, in the traditional hospital–medical staff model, physicians are credentialled but voluntary members of the medical staff rather than direct employees. This can lead to a culture of independence and a conflict of perspectives between medical and administrative staff.[7] As concluded by Berwick, Godfrey, and Roessner in the National Demonstration Project on Quality Improvement in Health Care, physicians do not see themselves as part of the overall process of care.[8] While physicians can make major contributions to quality improvement when they are involved as quality defenders, many barriers exist to their participation, particularly the inability to connect their own benefit and self interest with the interests of the overall organization. Quality improvement often calls for independent physicians to engage in organizational issues that are not clearly connected to their own time and financial needs. Additionally, when systems and physicians interact, physicians often fail to appreciate how critical their leadership is to the success of the organization, and, even when they do, are seldom equipped with the necessary skills because leadership training is typically not included in their education. As such, a crucial part of physician alignment is education and mentorship.

Core leadership competencies that physicians need and that can be developed through formal leadership training include:

- Technical knowledge and skills (of operations, finance and accounting, information technology and systems, human resources, strategic planning, legal issues in health care, and public policy)
- Knowledge of health care delivery (reimbursement strategies, legislation and regulation, quality improvement)
- Problem-solving ability related to nonclinical issues (around organizational strategy, team work, and project management)
- Emotional intelligence (the ability to evaluate oneself and others and to manage oneself in the context of a group)
- Communication (in leading change in groups and in individual encounters, such as in negotiation) and conflict resolution
- Commitment to lifelong learning[2,5]

PHYSICIAN TRAINING FOR LEADERSHIP AND QUALITY IMPROVEMENT

Earnest efforts to engage and align physician leaders at BHCS began in 2000 with the recognition that a greater focus on quality improvement education was needed. Without providing medical staff with the skills they need to improve processes or outcomes of care, requests to do so are just instructions to work harder, and are unlikely to have the desired effect. Physicians at BHCS needed knowledge, skills, and techniques that would enable them to succeed as leaders. These were provided through the STEEEP Academy rapid-cycle quality improvement training program (see Chapter 8), which approximately 300 physicians completed between 2005 and 2012. The principle behind this training is that physician leaders, who are accustomed to putting the patient first, are ideally placed to promote team-based clinical quality and patient safety initiatives, and are critical to creating high-reliability organizations.[9] Without physician engagement, most quality improvement initiatives cannot attain their full potential.

In 2006, BHCS accelerated placement of physicians in leadership positions. At that time, BHCS offered no formalized physician leadership training program. Once the need for such training was recognized, BHCS resolved to begin providing more pragmatic (i.e., "real world") leadership training focused on communication, leadership styles and responsibilities, and conflict resolution. BHCS performed a needs assessment that (1) nominated multiple independent and employed physicians for training, based on their leadership potential; (2) obtained physicians' opinions on what type of training they wanted; and (3) obtained physicians' estimates of how much time they could commit to this training. From this information, BHCS designed a training curriculum and sent requests for proposals to several organizations to explore ways to structure this training. Ultimately, the nearby Southern Methodist University (SMU) Cox School of Business in Dallas was selected to provide the training, and the six-day Baylor Advanced Physician Leadership Program (teaching physicians skills in leadership, corporate finance, and strategy) was born. A one-day program for emerging physician leaders was developed as well.

Introductory Physician Leadership Course

Each year, BHCS senior leaders identify approximately 70 physicians with leadership potential to attend a one-day leadership course taught by senior BHCS physician leaders, a physician from the American College of Physician Executives, and the Greeley Company, an external consulting firm. The program introduces physicians to topics such as "Moving from an Effective Clinician to an Effective Leader," "Medical Staff Management and the Board," "Managing Disruptive Physicians," and "The Importance of Physician Leadership to Baylor." This course helps physicians behave collaboratively and understand their organizational roles in medical staff leadership and within the health care system.[5]

Advanced Physician Leadership Development

For more experienced physician leaders, BHCS and the SMU Cox School of Business offer a course taught in six full-day sessions spread out over

TABLE 6.1 Key curriculum elements in the Baylor Health
Care System Advanced Physician Leadership Course
(with Southern Methodist University)[5]

Area	Elements
Leadership	Analyze their leadership style and develop a plan for improving management effectiveness
	Develop personal awareness and effectiveness in dealing with conflicts and adverse behavior
	Lead effective organizational change initiatives
	Manage through influence, creating more productive and more enjoyable relationships
	Practice the art of leadership
Corporate Finance	Use financial information to make better business decisions through health care cost and financial management
	Utilize managerial accounting to improve planning, controlling, and decision making
	Employ financial analysis to better select projects and investments
Strategy	Apply strategic management to compete on the leading edge of turning ideas into business opportunities
	Apply corporate strategy to organizational planning
	Apply human capital strategy in managing performance to evaluate and develop employees

two years. Fifty physician leaders participate in these courses. The core elements of the Baylor Advanced Physician Leadership Training are described in Table 6.1.

Features of Effective Physician Leadership Courses

In the BHCS experience, successful physician leadership courses have certain characteristics. They are not typically taught in the hospital auditorium, because holding the course outside of the hospital reinforces its focus on leadership rather than hospital administration. Offsite immersion courses that last for at least three or four days can be effective. Holding the Advanced Physician Leadership Course at the SMU Cox School of Business has helped physicians to understand that the message is about leadership in a broad sense, rather than hospital management and health care delivery.

In addition to the location of the physician leadership training, the subject matter expertise of faculty is important. The Baylor Advanced Physician Leadership Program is taught by nonphysicians to physicians, which helps students appreciate that the skills taught are fundamental to business, and that they should not expect to have attained them through their clinical education or experience. At the same time, senior physician leaders from BHCS participate in the course, teaching some segments and engaging in the intraclass dialog to demonstrate the relevance and application of the skills taught to specific health care context. When multiple physicians attend along with senior physician mentors, such as the chief medical officer, conversations both inside and outside the classroom tend to focus on leadership and application of the skills learned.

Another important feature of the physician leadership training that BHCS developed is structured time for participants to meet for an informal dinner and "journal club" to discuss a health care business case. BHCS offers this as part of the program, one month after each formal classroom session. The dinner sessions are held at the homes of six senior physician leaders and the case study reflects and reinforces the material covered in the previous classroom session. Eight to 10 physicians from the class typically attend each session. Past participants have provided positive feedback on these meetings, particularly noting that it encouraged them to discuss nonclinical issues. Attempts to replicate the sessions online using social media (i.e., a Facebook page) were less productive; the face-to-face aspect was critical to its success.

Successful physician leadership courses also require organizational accountability and commitment. To be selected for the Advanced Physician Leadership Training Program, physicians must be nominated by an administrative leader and senior clinical leaders who have recognized their leadership potential. Following nomination, BHCS sends the physician an invitation to apply. The application is required for acceptance into the program and failure to submit it disqualifies the physician from participation. This is a basic, but important, step that requires physicians to acknowledge their commitment to a leadership role and to fulfilling the course requirements. It also holds them accountable for their actions.

Success of Physician Leadership Training

Approximately 150 physicians have completed the Advanced Physician Leadership Training, and 400 to 500 have completed the Introductory Physician Leadership course and/or the STEEEP Academy rapid-cycle improvement training.

Many positive results have grown out of the BHCS physician leadership training, including strengthened Medical Executive Committee leadership in each of the BHCS hospitals, nationally recognized achievement by HealthTexas Provider Network (HTPN), and formation of an accountable care organization. All of these achievements draw heavily on the cadre of physicians trained in leadership.

BHCS measures the success of the Baylor Advanced Physician Leadership Program with formal feedback surveys. According to these, 70 percent of course participants have advanced to a higher level of leadership after taking the course, and graduates have been particularly instrumental in BHCS initiatives related to implementing health information technology and clinical decision support. Furthermore, physician leadership has been an important component in the recognition BHCS has received nationally for its quality achievements, including the National Quality Healthcare Award and HTPN's American Medical Group Association Preeminence Award. Looking at a more specific example of the impact of physician leaders, many of BHCS's quality improvement efforts rely heavily on a physician champion model for implementation (see Chapter 1). Physician leaders who have taken on these roles, at the hospital, service line, or system levels, have been instrumental in driving adoption of tools that promote the practice of standardized, evidence-based medicine across the BHCS hospitals; for example, increasing use of the pneumonia and heart failure order sets from starting points of less than 50 percent of eligible patients to approximately 75 percent use within two years of the order set being released, which, in turn decreased patient mortality and costs of care for these two conditions.[10,11]

Evolution in Response to Physician Leadership Training

As more physicians acquire leadership training and skills, the BHCS infrastructure is evolving to provide the opportunity for them to apply what they have learned. For example, seven years ago, BHCS had one vice president of Medical Affairs (VPMA) in one hospital; now every BHCS hospital has a chief medical officer VPMA. These physicians lead operational work related to clinical practice, quality, and safety improvement, and drive change. All have graduated from the Baylor Advanced Physician Leadership Training Program.

Senior administrative leaders at BHCS are recognizing the importance of physician leadership and have made the organizational commitment to develop that capacity. To date, BHCS has financially assisted several physician leaders in obtaining their MBA degrees. Each of these leaders has advanced to the next level and made substantial contributions to the organization. BHCS recognizes that there is always risk that physicians may leave after the organization has invested in their business leadership training. Nevertheless, BHCS has decided to continue making this investment, while also developing physician leadership opportunities that should encourage these physicians to remain with and pursue their careers as leaders at BHCS.

CONCLUSION

Formal physician leadership training is an integral part of any strategy for health care organizations to anticipate and respond to the myriad changes facing the industry. Physician leadership has been an important contributor to BHCS's success in providing high-quality care. To be successful, physician leaders need formal training in administrative and leadership skills to supplement their clinical expertise and enable them to successfully address the complexities of the health care environment. Because physicians do not typically receive such business training during their clinical education, BHCS provides formal leadership training courses at various levels of intensity and time commitment.

Donald Berwick has suggested that the "barriers to physician involvement may turn out to be the most important single issue impeding the success of quality improvement in medical care."[8] Through its historical and ongoing investment in building physician leadership, BHCS has encouraged the involvement of its physicians. This is an important factor in BHCS's continued endeavors to position itself as a leader among health care organizations in the quality of care that it provides to the patients it serves.

REFERENCES

1. Reinertsen, J. L., M. Bisognano, and M. D. Pugh. 2008. *Seven leadership leverage points for organization-level improvement in health care*, 2nd ed. Cambridge, MA: Institute for Healthcare Improvement.
2. Stoller, J. K. 2008. Developing physician-leaders: Key competencies and available programs. *Journal of Health Administration Education* 25 (4): 307–328.
3. Stoller, J. K. 2009. Developing physician-leaders: A call to action. *Journal of General Internal Medicine* 24 (7): 876–878.
4. Huff, C. 2010. Are your docs management ready? *Hospitals & Health Networks* 84 (4): 20–23, 2.
5. Convery, P., C. E. Couch, and R. Luquire. 2012. Training physician and nursing leaders for performance improvement. In *From front office to front line: Essential issues for health care leaders*, ed. S. Berman, pp. 59–85. Oakbrook Terrace, IL: The Joint Commission.
6. Weisbord, M. R. 1978. *Organizational diagnosis: A workbook of theory and practice*. New York City: Perseus Books.
7. Starr, P. 1982. *The social transformation of American medicine*. New York: Basic Books.
8. Berwick, D. M., A. B. Godfrey, and J. Roessner. 1990. *Curing health care: New strategies for quality improvement*. San Fransisco: Jossey-Bass.
9. Sinclair, D. G., C. Carruthers, and J. Swettenham. 2011. Healthcare and physician leadership. *Healthcare Quarterly* 14 (1): 6–8.
10. Fleming, N. S., G. Ogola, and D. J. Ballard. 2009. Implementing a standardized order set for community-acquired pneumonia: Impact on mortality and cost. *The Joint Commission Journal on Quality and Patient Safety* 35 (8): 414–421.
11. Ballard, D. J., G. Ogola, N. S. Fleming, B. D. Stauffer, B. M. Leonard, R. Khetan, and C. W. Yancy. 2010. Impact of a standardized heart failure order set on mortality, readmission, and quality and costs of care. *International Journal for Quality in Health Care* 22 (6): 437–444.

Chapter 7

Nurse Leadership

Rosemary Luquire

CONTENTS

INTRODUCTION

Nurse leadership has been an integral focus for BHCS since its precursor, the Texas Baptist Memorial Sanitarium, opened its doors in 1909. Then-superintendent of nurses, May Marr, established a training school for student nurses to prepare them for serving patients in the 250-bed hospital. A reputation for nursing quality developed further at the organization in 1912, when Johns Hopkins-trained Helen Holliday Lehman became superintendent of nurses and enhanced the organization's focus on nurse education.[1] Today, nurse leadership at BHCS continues to be characterized by a strong focus on education, development, and professionalism, as well as structural empowerment, standardization, evidence-based practice, research, empirical outcomes, and community outreach. Through its commitment to nurse leadership, BHCS aligns with the Institute of Medicine's (IOM) call for nurses "to take more leadership roles and collaborate fully with other professionals in providing essential health care to a growing number of people."[2] BHCS uses the five Magnet domains (transformational leadership; structural empowerment; exemplary professional practice; new knowledge, innovation, and improvement; and empirical outcomes) as a blueprint for how the nursing organization should function. Magnet principles are embedded in all areas of work and design.[3,4]

THE FIVE AREAS OF FOCUS

Nurse leaders at BHCS have five overall areas of focus:

1. Transformational leadership—including the Shared Governance Model, planning and strategy, promotion of evidence-based practices, education and development, and achieving Magnet status for BHCS hospitals.[4]
2. Structural empowerment—including the Professional Nursing Practice Model, nursing councils across BHCS, the Advancing Nursing Excellence Scholarship program, the Achieving Synergy in Practice through Impact, Relationships and Evidence (ASPIRE) program, and nurses practicing community outreach.
3. Exemplary professional practice—BHCS strives to continually improve practice and patient outcomes. The Professional Nursing Practice Model (Figure 7.1) illustrates how BHCS achieves synergy through nursing practice based on clinical excellence, evidence-based practice, optimal patient outcomes, a culture of inquiry, and nursing research. Goals are routinely established to achieve the top quartile or top decile result.
4. New knowledge, innovation, and improvement—including research, evidence-based practice, technology with care, and electronic health records.
5. Empirical outcomes—including patient outcomes, nurse outcomes, organizational outcomes, and consumer outcomes.[5]

SHARED GOVERNANCE MODEL

Shared governance is a model of co-leadership in which hospital management structures and processes are redesigned to engage all staff in providing care to improve quality and efficiency.[6] The BHCS Shared Governance Model incorporates the concepts of equity, partnership, accountability, ownership, STEEEP, best care, decision making, patient safety, and evidence-based practice.[5] It is implemented through a council structure, stretching from Unit Practice Councils through Service Line, Central Partnership, Staff Nurse Advisory, and Nurse Manager Councils to the Nurse Executive Council, and gives nurses a voice as patient advocates, emphasizing the link between responsibility and authority. It also serves as a reminder that it is incumbent upon nurses, both individually and in their council work, to develop strategies and plans for the future of nursing practice at the unit, service line, hospital, and system levels. Participation in shared governance is a responsibility of the professional nurse and is not optional at BHCS.

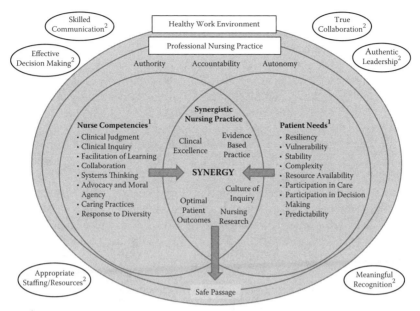

Skilled Communication[2]

Healthy Work Environment

True Collaboration[2]

Effective Decision Making[2]

Professional Nursing Practice

Authority   Accountability   Autonomy

Authentic Leadership[2]

Synergistic Nursing Practice

Nurse Competencies[1]
- Clinical Judgment
- Clinical Inquiry
- Facilitation of Learning
- Collaboration
- Systems Thinking
- Advocacy and Moral Agency
- Caring Practices
- Response to Diversity

Clinical Excellence   Evidence Based Practice

SYNERGY

Culture of Inquiry

Optimal Patient Outcomes   Nursing Research

Patient Needs[1]
- Resiliency
- Vulnerability
- Stability
- Complexity
- Resource Availability
- Participation in Care
- Participation in Decision Making
- Predictability

Appropriate Staffing/Resources[2]

Safe Passage

Meaningful Recognition[2]

[1]Nurse Competencies and Patient Needs from the AACN Synergy Model for Patient Care. American Association of Critical-Care Nurses, 1998.
[2]American Association of Critical-Care Nurses. AACN Standards for Establishing and Sustaining Healthy Work Environments, 2005.

FIGURE 7.1 Baylor Health Care System professional nursing practice model. (Data from Nurse Competencies and Patient Needs from the AACN Synergy Model for Patient Care. American Association of Critical-Care Nurses. AACN Standards for Establishing and Sustaining Healthy Work Environments, 2005.)

NURSE EDUCATION AND DEVELOPMENT

Education and development play a pivotal role in nurse leadership. The 2010 IOM Future of Nursing report called for nurses to:

- Practice to the full extent of their education and training;
- Achieve higher levels of education and training through an improved education system that promotes seamless academic progression; and
- Be full partners with physicians and other health care professionals in redesigning health care in the United States.[2]

Based on these recommendations, BHCS has focused on promoting education and development of its nursing staff since 2010 with many nurses pursuing their bachelor of science in nursing or advanced degrees. In 2007, BHCS had 4 nurses holding doctoral degrees; today, it has 30, with an emphasis on application of evidence-based practices and translational research. By 2015, BHCS seeks to attain a level of 80 percent of its nurses with baccalaureate degrees, five years in advance of the IOM goal for the United States.

To encourage nurses to pursue their academic degrees, BHCS offers the Advancing Nursing Excellence Scholarship program (sponsored by the Nursing Advocacy Group of the BHCS Foundation), as well as a generous tuition reimbursement program. Nursing scholars receive full-time salary and benefits while working part-time. Several nurses are selected to participate in the program each year. Unique partnerships have also been developed with nursing schools to promote education at reduced tuition rates. At any point in time, several hundred BHCS nurses are enrolled in academic programs to advance their knowledge base.

In addition to helping nurses earn advanced degrees, BHCS maintains a Nurse Executive Fellowship program with the Southern Methodist University Cox School of Business. The program prepares BHCS nurse managers and directors for progressive leadership roles by developing advanced leadership and business skills. Each year, 25 nursing leaders complete the one-year fellowship, consisting of 12 intensive workshops and concluding with design and completion of a capstone project that must have significant impact for BHCS and show a return on investment, validated by a chief financial officer for one of the BHCS entities. This program provides BHCS with the dual benefits of more effective nurse leaders and the implementation of the capstone projects, which have demonstrated an aggregate return on investment to date of $2.4 million.[5]

MAGNET DESIGNATION

One of the most visible ways BHCS nurses are transforming leadership is through application of Magnet standards and attainment of Magnet status. The Magnet Recognition Program® recognizes health care organizations for quality patient care, nursing excellence, and innovations in professional nursing practice. Developed by the American Nurses Credentialing Center (ANCC), Magnet is the leading designation of successful nursing practices and strategies worldwide.[4] As of February 2011, five BHCS hospitals hold Magnet designation, and the goal is for every BHCS hospital to achieve this. Magnet standards are embedded in job descriptions and in the BHCS performance management system to clearly delineate and reward Magnet expectations.

The Magnet model is important because it emphasizes a hospital's ability to demonstrate specific outcomes that reflect advanced knowledge and national priorities. Examples of empirical outcomes include patient outcomes (e.g., risk-adjusted mortality, falls and associated injuries); nurse outcomes (e.g., level of nurse engagement, turnover and vacancy rates); organizational outcomes (e.g., efficiency and elimination of waste); and consumer outcomes (e.g., impact of community outreach programs). Magnet hospitals must demonstrate excellent clinical outcomes as well as a focus on patient-centered care. The Magnet model emphasizes both measurement and improvement in defined outcomes, consistent with an enhanced national focus on evidence-based medicine and value-based care.[3]

STANDARDIZATION OF CARE

In 2007, BHCS hired its first system chief nursing officer (CNO). To achieve greater standardization across BHCS facilities, each hospital CNO began reporting to the system CNO, an organizational structure that has driven BHCS toward more effective and efficient adoption, implementation, and dissemination of best nursing practices across the system.

Another important element for achieving standardization and promoting evidence-based practice across the system is that the BHCS Councils are organized primarily by service lines. Currently, these councils include the Staff Nurse Council, the Nurse Manager Council, the Emergency Department Council, the Women's Advisory Council, the Perinatal/Neonatal Council, the Perioperative Council, and the Critical Care Nursing Council. The councils, which include representatives from all facilities, develop and implement evidence-based initiatives to improve care and reduce waste across BHCS.

SYNERGY IN PRACTICE THROUGH IMPACT, RELATIONSHIPS, AND EVIDENCE

BHCS offers the ASPIRE program to promote growth in practice, education, research, and leadership by providing bonuses for completion of important projects that advance care. It encourages BHCS nurses to undertake quality improvement projects, research studies, and community outreach initiatives beyond the requirements of their job descriptions. The ASPIRE goals are to:

- Empower nurses to recognize and communicate the difference they make for patient outcomes;
- Differentiate professional nursing practice in terms of accountability, autonomy, and authority as it relates to outcomes;
- Promote collegiality, mentoring, and leadership in nursing;
- Foster the development of new knowledge, skills, and attitudes; and
- Embrace innovation and evidence-based decision making.

ASPIRE projects are diverse and innovative. Example titles of recent projects include "Implementation of a National Emergency Department Overcrowding Score Calculator," "Amputation Order Sets and Documentation Compliance for Input/Output and Weights on Specialty Care Unit," "An eJournal Club to Improve Use of Evidence-Based Practice in the Labor and Delivery Unit," and "Cue-Based Feeding."[5]

NURSING RESEARCH AND EVIDENCE-BASED PRACTICE

Knowledge, innovation, and evidence-based improvement are important areas of focus for BHCS nurse leaders. As part of its commitment to innovation (one of the five BHCS values, see Introduction, Figure I.1), BHCS hosts an annual Nursing Research and Evidence-Based Practice Summit for nurses to share presentations and nursing research studies.

The largest current evidence-based practice and nursing research project underway at BHCS is the work being done under a grant from the Deerbrook Charitable Trust (Chevy Chase, Maryland), pledging more than $12.4 million over three years to improve care for geriatric patients. Key initiatives within this work include:

1. Creating specialized geriatric nursing education programs, including a virtual center and computer simulation modeling.
2. Refining a comprehensive volunteer program for hospitalized older patients with the addition of Wii technology.
3. Creating education and best practice partnerships with skilled nursing homes.
4. Creating a consortium with regional geriatric experts in nursing universities and schools of anthropology throughout North Texas.
5. Assessing risks for chronically ill patients and refining a transitional care model to reduce their hospital readmissions and emergency room visits.

LESSONS LEARNED

One of the most important factors in BHCS's success in developing nurse leaders is its commitment to transparency. All patient care units in the organization have data posted to display staff turnover, staff satisfaction, and measures related to patient safety and health care quality. This transparency leads to open discussion of issues, exploration of solutions, and enhanced trust among employees. This, in turn, improves nurse retention and BHCS's ability to develop and train nurse leaders. Examples of nursing solutions to improve patient safety and quality of care or employee satisfaction that have been driven by the transparency created through shared governance and the open display of unit-level performance data include:

- Reductions in pressure ulcers and hospital-acquired infections
- Increased staff retention through peer interviewing
- Choice of equipment
- Introduction of self-scheduling procedures for staff on individual clinical units

Additional factors improving nurse retention and nurse leadership include:

- The Shared Governance Model, which empowers nurses to act as patient advocates
- BHCS's commitment to educating and developing nurses through programs such as the Advancing Nursing Excellence Scholarship and the Nurse Executive Fellowship Program
- The BHCS commitment to improving empirical outcomes such as patient outcomes, nurse-related outcomes, organizational outcomes, and consumer outcomes, consistent with ANCC Magnet status priority areas

Nurse managers at BHCS are also trained in behavioral interviewing techniques, and there is a Human Resources partner dedicated solely to nursing.

Furthermore, BHCS has learned the importance of finding "the right leaders" to drive change. These leaders need to share a vision, values, and goals that are consistent with the BHCS vision, values, and goals. Leaders set the tone related to how ambitious the goals of their staff will be. Nurse leaders must be aligned with the BHCS vision, values, and goals to encourage their frontline employees to adopt and achieve challenging goals within those "cascaded down" from the system goals related to People, Service, Quality, and Finance.

CONCLUSION

BHCS has a longstanding commitment to nurse leadership characterized by a focus on education and development, structural empowerment, standardization, evidence-based practice, research, empirical outcomes, and community outreach. Additional factors that drive BHCS's development of strong nurse leaders are transparency, the Shared Governance Model, and a dedication to finding "the right leaders" to drive change across the organization. BHCS's success in developing nurse leadership is demonstrated by the growing number of BHCS nurses who hold advanced degrees, the five BHCS hospitals that have attained ANCC Magnet status, the more than 90 nursing research projects that have enhanced quality and efficiency across the organization, and the attraction of large external private foundation grant funds to enable BHCS's implementation of best practices in geriatric care. The BHCS commitment to nurse leadership strongly aligns with national priorities that position the organization to anticipate and respond to the challenges facing the health care industry.

REFERENCES

1. Wilsey, H. L. 2004. *How we care: Centennial history of Baylor University Medical Center and Baylor Health Care System, 1903–2003.* Dallas: Baylor Health Care System.

2. Institute of Medicine of the National Academies. 2010. *The future of nursing: Leading change, advancing health*. Washington, D.C.: National Academies Press.

3. Luquire, R., and M. Strong. 2011. Empirical outcomes. In *Magnet: The next generation—nurses making the difference*, eds. K. Drenkard, G. Wall, and S. H. Morgan. Silver Spring, MD: American Nurses Credentialing Center.

4. American Nurses Credentialing Center. ANCC Magnet Recognition Program®. Online at: http://www.nursecredentialing.org/Magnet.aspx (accessed December 13, 2012).

5. *Baylor nursing annual report: July 2010 through June 2011*. Dallas: Baylor Health Care System.

6. Casanova, J. 2008. Medical staffs and nursing staffs: The need for joint leadership. *Physician Executive Journal* 34 (6): 24–27.

Infrastructure and Tools
for STEEEP Care

Chapter 8

STEEEP Academy

Bradley M. Leonard, Christopher Shutts, and Neil S. Fleming

CONTENTS

INTRODUCTION

BHCS is committed to providing physicians, nurses, and other health care leaders with the knowledge and the tools needed to deliver STEEEP care. This commitment requires teaching health care providers the appropriate methods and necessary skills to improve health care quality. In 2004, BHCS founded the "ABC Baylor" course (now called STEEEP Academy), based on the Intermountain Healthcare mini-Advanced Training Program led by Brent James,[1] to teach internal health care leaders theory and methods of rapid-cycle quality improvement. Course participants learn general principles of continuous quality improvement as well as health care-specific quality improvement tools and finish the course by designing and implementing a quality improvement project. STEEEP Academy training is an important part of BHCS's work establishing the culture and infrastructure to support quality improvement and has substantially contributed to its success in this area.[2] STEEEP Academy training fits within the seventh Institute for Healthcare Improvement Leadership Leverage Point—to build improvement capacity.[3]

In 2011, BHCS incorporated the ABC Baylor course into its newly founded STEEEP Academy, recognizing the course's emphasis on STEEEP care. The STEEEP Academy teaches physicians, nurses, and administrators, who are external to BHCS, the skills and techniques needed to lead quality improvement efforts in their own health care organizations. The curriculum emphasizes the elements of STEEEP care and the application of this framework to improving care, and teaches tools for cultural and process change to facilitate quality improvement in a variety of health care delivery settings.

RAPID-CYCLE QUALITY IMPROVEMENT EDUCATION

BHCS has been training its physician, nursing, and administrative leaders in the methods of rapid-cycle quality improvement since 2004.[4] The curriculum, co-taught by numerous BHCS leaders, instructs participants in the methods of designing, implementing, and evaluating quality improvement initiatives; helps them understand the relationship between quality and cost; and provides a general understanding of statistical variation and the practice of evidence-based medicine. It also introduces tools and techniques related to patient safety, leadership, teamwork, and change management strategies for quality improvement.[2]

Since 2004, 273 physicians, 617 nurses, and 733 administrative leaders at BHCS have completed this training, preparing them to lead improvement initiatives in their own departments. BHCS also has provided this training to leaders from other health care organizations, including small and rural hospitals that lack the resources to establish such programs independently.[5-7]

Quality Improvement Course Objectives

The STEEEP Academy teaches the following core principles of clinical quality improvement:

- Methods for rapid-cycle improvement based on PDCA (Plan-Do-Check-Act)
- Design of data collection tools
- Methods to analyze data to identify root causes
- Tools to define and understand problems leading to the prioritization, design, implementation, and evaluation of interventions
- Methods to streamline processes and eliminate errors, using Lean and Six Sigma methodologies to reduce variation

- Improvement of processes of care and patient-centered outcomes, based on the Institute of Medicine's six domains of health care quality (i.e., STEEEP)
- Standardization of care and other work processes
- Alignment of culture and leadership to promote, and implementation of the infrastructure to support, improvement and change management in the frontline of clinical care
- Lean 5S (sorting, straightening, sweeping, standardizing, sustaining): Leadership, teamwork, and change management based on multidisciplinary teamwork with the facilitation of a process improvement engineer

Plan-Do-Check-Act Model for Rapid-Cycle Improvement

The STEEEP Academy course trains participants in rapid-cycle improvement, which focuses on piloting and testing interventions through the PDCA model:

- **Plan** a change aimed at quality improvement
- **Do** the tasks required to implement the change, preferably on a small scale
- **Check** the results of the change
- **Act** to adopt, refine, or abandon the change

Each time this cycle is repeated as part of an iterative process, quality is further improved.

Multidisciplinary Quality Improvement Project

Each STEEEP Academy student is required to complete a 90-day rapid-cycle quality improvement project based on STEEEP principles, and pursuing a "SMART" goal:

S: Specific boundaries (scope), outcomes focused, specific target population
M: Measureable numerical goal with defined measures to quantify achievement
A: Agreed upon high-priority improvement area with an actionable change strategy
R: Realistic goal that is achievable within the time frame, but also will have a definite impact
T: Time bound with a clearly defined timeline for completion

Completing this project helps course participants internalize the tools and techniques taught during the didactic sessions by applying them to improve quality within the participant's specific realm within BHCS. This approach to improvement is consistent with fundamental process improvement principles that empower frontline workers because they know their work best. An important strength and point of the learning from these STEEEP Academy quality improvement activities is the multidisciplinary composition of the project team. A team typically includes 7 to 10 members (which may be more or less depending on the complexity of the project) who have different functional roles (e.g., physicians, nurses, clinical leaders, administrative leaders). Members include:

- Executive Sponsor (typically a department manager or higher) who must approve the project and who actively supports the project, removes barriers, and provides resources
- Team Leader (i.e., the STEEEP Academy participant)
- Facilitator/Coach (typically a process improvement engineer) who helps the team reach consensus on a topic and provides guidance on process improvement methods and tools during and after project completion
- Team Members who are frontline staff implementing the improvements (and, therefore, need an active voice in project development and execution)

To reinforce the cultural change, regular postcompletion follow-ups with participants and projects are required. Ongoing support is crucial for success and for improvement to become ingrained in students' actions.

Rapid-Cycle Quality Improvement Course Sample Agenda

Because people in different roles in health care organizations have different needs for quality improvement training, the STEEEP Academy offers courses ranging from a one-day course covering the basic process improvement principles (primarily designed for frontline staff) to advanced clinical and nonclinical focused courses that teach additional improvement tools, techniques, and concepts. The clinical STEEEP Academy course includes four day-long sessions and a graduation at which students present their quality improvement projects. A sample agenda from a clinical STEEEP Academy course is provided below.

Session 1

- Commitment to Quality
- Understanding the Problem in Health Care Quality
- Understanding Processes and Outcomes
- Clinical Transformation through Integration at Baylor Health Care System
- STEEEP Academy Methodologies
- Project Selection

- SMART Aim Statement
- Team Dynamics
- Mapping the Process
- Identifying Issues and Root Causes
- Wrap-Up and Project Learning Activities

Session 2

- Prioritizing Issues
- Selecting Measures
- Identifying and Prioritizing Solutions
- Designing Processes Utilizing Lean Principles
- Preparing for Implementation
- Change Management and Communication During Change
- Data Collection
- Analysis Tools
- Traditional View of Data Feedback
- Success Story—Quality Improvement Project
- Wrap-Up and Project Learning Activities

Session 3

- System Reliability in Health Care
- Determining Best Evidence
- Chronic Care
- The Patient-Centered Medical Home
- Recap of Methods & Tools (Jeopardy Game)
- Making Patient Care Safe
- Understanding Health Equity and Designing Improvement Processes
- Project Review
- Wrap-Up and Project Learning Activities

Session 4

- Growing Consumerism in Health Care
- Generational Diversity in the USA
- Social Media
- Financial Implications of Clinical Excellence
- Sustainment and Continuous Improvement
- Rapid Cycle Improvement Event
- Project Review
- Wrap-Up and Project Learning Activities

Graduation: Student Presents Rapid Cycle Improvement Project

TABLE 8.1 STEEEP Academy project alignment
with Baylor Health Care System's four areas of focus

Area	Issues/Goals/Initiatives
Service	Patient satisfaction (e.g., indicators HCAHPS, Press Ganey, and Point-of-Care patient satisfaction surveys); departmental service scores—how well the department/service line serves its customers
Quality	Projects that affect the outcomes of care given to the end-user (patient or population) (e.g., indicators including National Patient Safety Goal compliance, Quality Measures, Leapfrog, and National Quality Forum standards); in-service activities; efforts to eliminate unnecessary variance in processes that affect clinical outcomes
People	Mobilization of human resources (e.g., float pools, PRN programs, cross-training); recruitment, retention, training, and development; environmental work culture (e.g., Magnet designation)
Finance	Reducing waste/nonvalue-added activities; decreasing average length of stay; increasing revenue; increasing volume; improving coding.

QUALITY IMPROVEMENT COURSE ALIGNMENT WITH ORGANIZATIONAL OBJECTIVES

Table 8.1 provides examples of how STEEEP Academy projects align with the four BHCS areas of focus: Service, Quality, People, and Finance.

Example Quality Improvement Projects

STEEEP Academy projects focus on the elements of STEEEP care. Each project must have at least one major aim related to one of these six domains. An example project from each domain of care is presented below with the background, SMART aim statements, and results.

STEEEP Focus: Safe

Project Title: Increasing Hand Hygiene Compliance

Background: Hand washing is the most important way to prevent the spread of infections. Hand hygiene compliance at the facility was 84 percent over a seven-month period. This lack of compliance leads to preventable infections in hospitalized patients.

AIM Statement: By May 31, 2008, the facility will improve the hand hygiene compliance rate from 73 to 90 percent through the implementation of a strong educational and awareness program, providing foam dispensers and hand hygiene stations in proper locations, and providing staff with pocket hand sanitizers.

Results: The "You Bugged Me" program was established to hold staff accountable for proper hand hygiene practices. This program, along with the proper placement of foam dispensers and hand hygiene stations, increased hand hygiene compliance rates to 92 percent over an eight-month period, which helped prevent infections in hospitalized patients. The "You Bugged Me" program was adopted at a second facility, along with the visual management poster campaign "Got Foam." This second facility increased hand hygiene compliance from 70 to 98 percent. Additionally, through the adoption of these standards, BHCS has increased hand hygiene compliance rates across its hospitals from 85 percent in July 2008 to 97 percent in July 2011.

STEEEP Focus: Timely

Project Title: Push to Full: Improving Admission to Exam Time in the Emergency Department (ED)

Background: In April 2007, it took 63 minutes for a patient to get examined in the ED. The facility implemented methodology to get the patient from door to exam in 48 minutes. Subsequently, the ED Council has tracked this and other measures to improve timely ED care.

AIM Statement: Over the next 10 weeks, staff will reduce door-to-exam time in the ED by 20 percent by implementing the strategies of direct-to-bed triage, expedited bedside registration, and immediate notification of physicians when patients are placed in a treatment room.

Results: The target of 48 minutes was exceeded with 36 minutes being the average lowest monthly time from April 2007 to March 2008. From March 2010 to August 2011, the ED had only one month (February 2011) where the average time from door-to-exam exceeded 30 minutes.

STEEEP Focus: Effective

Project Title: Medication Reconciliation Improvement

Background: Medication reconciliation is a Joint Commission National Patient Safety Goal requirement. In fiscal year 2010, the facility medication reconciliation all-or-none bundle score was 69 percent.

AIM Statement: The facility will increase the medication reconciliation all-or-none bundle score from a rate of 69 to 86 percent by January 31, 2011.

Results: Through execution of a hospital-wide daily auditing process of all discharge/transfer patients standardized medication reconciliation forms and standardized training materials, the facility increased the medication reconciliation all-or-none bundle rate from 69.4 to 90 percent. For fiscal year 2011, this was the highest improvement across BHCS.

STEEEP Focus: Efficient

Project Title: "Let Me Catch My Breath"

Background: Patients at the facility were receiving therapeutic duplicates of medications (DuoNeb® and Spiriva®) that treat chronic obstructive pulmonary disease and asthma. This practice results in suboptimal outcomes for the patients, increased pharmacy and outpatient medication costs, and wasted effort by the respiratory therapy staff.

AIM Statement: By November 17, 2010, facility physicians, pharmacists, and respiratory therapists will reduce the incidence of patients receiving Spiriva and DuoNeb therapeutic duplications from 100 to 50 percent throughout the hospital by using physician education, therapeutic auto-interchange, and patient therapy monitoring.

Results: Through integration of best practices, collaborative efforts, and standardized education, the facility decreased the incidence of patients receiving Spiriva and DuoNeb therapeutic duplications by 55 percent, exceeding their goal. Through the elimination of wasteful rework, the project team saved $19,708.14.

STEEEP Focus: Equitable

Project Title: Collect Every Patient's Race, Ethnicity, and Primary Language Designation

Background: Identifying ethnic and minority groups for all patient visits helps identify gaps in the rates of preventive services received by disadvantaged groups. The facility identifies this information 39 percent of the time for all patients.

AIM Statement: By June 8, 2011, the facility will increase the percentage of electronic health records with patient designated race, ethnicity, and primary language identified from 39 to 50 percent for all patient visits.

Results: By providing easily accessible and standardized forms, the facility increased the percentage of identified patients from 39 to 55 percent (as of September 2011). The project team continues to improve the process to reach Kaiser Permanente's benchmark of 86 percent. These ongoing improvements will help identify additional areas for improvement to ensure we are providing the same quality care for all patients.

STEEEP Focus: Patient-Centered

Project Title: Family-Centered Care in the NICU: Open Access and Bedside Reporting

Background: There have been numerous complaints from families as a result of being asked to leave the neonatal intensive care unit (NICU) for various reasons. This directly influences the Press Ganey patient satisfaction score of "NICU was Family Friendly," which is currently at 82.5 percent (<10th percentile).

AIM Statement: The facility NICU will increase its "NICU was Family Friendly" Press Ganey survey mean score from 82.5 to 91.1 percent by June 30, 2011, by implementing policies for 24-hour access for parents and bedside change-of-shift report with family inclusion.

Results: Through the development of a standardized training program, display of visual management informational posters, and weekly rounding with families to obtain the voice of the customer, the facility increased the "NICU was Family Friendly" score from 83 to 100 percent. As a result of this project, the facility NICU was awarded a grant from the NICU Helping Hands Foundation for $300,000 to fund "Project NICU." The interventions from the project were adopted across BHCS as a best practice and were shared at the National NICU Leadership Forum in Las Vegas.

QUALITY IMPROVEMENT SUMMIT TO RECOGNIZE AND SPREAD SUCCESSFUL INITIATIVES

To recognize and celebrate the success of quality improvement projects, many of the projects or subsequent continuation of their efforts are submitted and recognized as part of the annual BHCS Bill Aston Quality Improvement Summit. At this event, quality improvement teams receive first-, second-, and third-place awards (including cash) for outstanding initiatives for each of the organization's four areas of focus (People, Service, Quality, and Finance) and first-place teams present their projects to an audience of hospital and system leaders.

LESSONS LEARNED

A rapidly evolving health care environment requires strategies for cultural change within health care delivery organizations. An organization cannot merely decide to be quality-based; it must also undergo a cultural shift to embrace continuous process improvement. STEEEP Academy courses teach change management theory and methods, along with tools of rapid-cycle health care quality improvement to promote cultural change.

The STEEEP Academy surveys participants to learn how the course has changed their thought processes, and uses the survey results to continue refining the courses' content and presentation. For example, one refinement currently being considered is to offer participants a refresher course to reinforce concepts learned and help identify new ways to apply quality improvement tools.

Courses have evolved to include attendees from a variety of functional roles. Most early participants of ABC Baylor were physicians; today, the STEEEP Academy courses target nurses, clinical leaders, and administrative leaders as well as physicians. The multidisciplinary perspectives and contributions of team members are an integral part of the success of the courses. Bringing together people with clinical and nonclinical backgrounds is beneficial because the definition of quality depends on one's perspective. While clinicians may be very focused on clinical indicators and patient outcomes, for patients, quality might mean a hot meal every day, and, for financial leaders, it might mean efficiency. Quality encompasses all of those things and more.

CONCLUSION

A culture of quality improvement is needed to link a vision for STEEEP care to practical execution and application. BHCS has been successful in forging this connection, and its rapid-cycle quality improvement training courses have been an integral part of this process. BHCS is committed to ensuring that its physicians, nurses, and health care leaders possess the knowledge and the tools needed to deliver STEEEP care and, through the STEEEP Academy, now offers the opportunity for other health care organizations seeking to bridge the health care "quality chasm" to benefit from the BHCS experience in this area.

REFERENCES

1. Intermountain Healthcare. 20-day course for executives & QI leaders—Advanced Training Program (ATP). Online at: http://intermountainhealthcare.org/qualityand-research/institute/courses/atp/Pages/home.aspx (accessed March 21, 2013).
2. Ballard, D. J., B. Spreadbury, and R. S. Hopkins, 3rd. 2004. Health care quality improvement across the Baylor Health Care System: The first century. *Proceedings (Baylor University Medical Center)* 17 (3): 277–288.
3. Reinertsen, J. L., M. Bisognano, and M. D. Pugh. 2008. *Seven leadership leverage points for organization-level improvement in health care*, 2nd ed. Cambridge, MA: Institute for Healthcare Improvement.
4. Haydar, Z., M. Cox, P. Stafford, V. Rodriguez, and D. J. Ballard, 2009. Accelerating best care at Baylor Dallas. *Proceedings (Baylor University Medical Center)* 22 (4): 311–315.
5. Haydar, Z., J. Gunderson, D. J. Ballard, A. Skoufalos, B. Berman, and D. B. Nash, 2008. Accelerating best care in Pennsylvania: Adapting a large academic system's quality improvement process to rural community hospitals. *American Journal of Medical Quality* 23 (4): 252–258.

6. Filardo, G., D. Nicewander, J. Herrin, J. Edwards, P. Galimbertti, M. Tietze, S. McBride, et al. 2009. A hospital-randomized controlled trial of a formal quality improvement educational program in rural and small community Texas hospitals: One year results. *International Journal for Quality in Health Care* 21 (4): 225–232.

7. Filardo, G., D. Nicewander, J. Herrin, P. Galimbertti, M. Tietze, S. McBride, J. Gunderson, et al. 2008. Challenges in conducting a hospital-randomized trial of an educational quality improvement intervention in rural and small community hospitals. *American Journal of Medical Quality* 23 (6): 440–447.

Chapter 9

Applications of Lean to STEEEP Care Improvement

J. Paul Dieckert and Margaret Henry

CONTENTS

INTRODUCTION

Scott & White Healthcare is a nonprofit collaborative health care system founded in 1897 in Temple, Texas, and is currently one of the nation's largest integrated health care systems. Scott & White's mission is to provide the most personalized, comprehensive, and highest quality health care, enhanced by medical education and research. The organization provides care to Central Texans in a 29,000-square-mile service area, and owns, partners, or manages 12 hospital sites and more than 65 primary care and specialty clinic locations in 46 medical specialties. It has more than 14,000 employees and 1,000 physicians and scientists, and is the primary clinical teaching facility to more than 400 medical residents and fellows in training at the Texas A&M Health Science Center College of Medicine.[1] Recently, Scott & White and Baylor Health Care System (BHCS) announced their intent to merge, creating the largest not-for-profit health system in the state of Texas, with combined revenues totaling approximately $7.7 billion in 2012.[1]

Since 2007, Scott & White has deployed Lean thinking with related projects and training across its organization. Lean seeks to maximize customer value while minimizing waste. Lean thinking changes the focus of management from optimizing separate technologies, assets, and vertical departments to optimizing the flow of products and services through entire value streams that flow horizontally across technologies, assets, and departments to customers.[2] This chapter describes the history, details, and results of Scott & White's implementation of Lean over the past six years and illuminates the potential of Lean thinking to improve quality across health care delivery organizations.

HISTORY OF LEAN THINKING AT SCOTT & WHITE

Scott & White Healthcare's engagement with Lean began in 2007. A timeline describing the organization's history with respect to Lean is presented in Table 9.1.

TABLE 9.1 Milestones in Scott & White's engagement with Lean

Date	Milestone
December 2007	• The Scott & White Healthcare chief executive officer and the executive vice president for quality and safety attend Lean Healthcare training at the University of Michigan through the College of Engineering
December 2007– April 2008	• Other key leaders attend Lean Healthcare training at the University of Michigan through the College of Engineering • Decision is made to move forward with embracing Lean methodology for process improvement and culture change
Late 2008	• Scott & White partners with Altarum Institute to provide Lean consulting services
2009	• Charter is developed for the Scott & White Continuous Learning and Improvement Program (CLIP) • An executive leader of the system-wide improvement effort is chosen, and a steering committee formed
2009–2010	• Lean training and project are deployed across Scott & White Healthcare
2012	• Strategic Alignment & Deployment (Hoshin Kanri) is used to cascade strategic goals and policy deployment through all 14,000 employees; Human Resources takes lead role and integrates with evaluation and pay systems • Lean Healthcare Strategies group is developed • Coaches are engaged to teach Scott & White leaders how to lead in a Lean organization
2012–2013	• Launch of Lean Management System training for Scott & White leaders; *Daily Lean* ensues, involving nearly all staff

DESIGN OF LEAN THINKING PROGRAMS AT SCOTT & WHITE HEALTHCARE

Lean programs at Scott & White have been designed from the beginning to meet the needs of the specific audience. The organization offers several courses, including:

- A four-day deep dive Continuous Learning and Improvement Program (CLIP)
- Two-hour Scott & White University courses designed to enable staff to attend training modules
- Continuing medical education course for physicians
- Continuing nurse education course
- Lean Management Systems training for leaders

Sample Agenda for CLIP Program

Day 1: Simulation

- Lean Philosophy and the Eight Wastes
- The Value of Gemba
- Visual Workplace
- Introduction to Huddles

Day 2: Simulation

- Introduction to Foundation Tools
- Concept of Andon
- Deeper Look at Standard Work
- 5S (sorting, straightening, sweeping, standardizing, sustaining) exercises

Day 3: Value Stream Mapping

- The Three Parts of a Value Stream
- Understanding Undesired Effects
- Teamwork on Real Problems
- Report Out

Day 4: A3 and Leadership

- Understanding Root Cause
- Fishbone, 5 Whys, Cause and Effect
- The Value of Metrics

- Teamwork on Real Problems (may use one from value stream mapping)
- Report Out
- Understanding Your Role in a Lean Culture

LEAN MANAGEMENT SYSTEM TRAINING

Lean Management System (LMS) training focuses on three major activities to enable leaders to improve quality and eliminate waste throughout the system:

- Leader Standard Work
  - Provides structure and routine for duties, and documents when the leader will be in the gemba (Japanese for "the real place") and available for continuous improvement matters
  - Enables leaders to shift from results only to focus on process *and* results
- Visual Controls
  - Visual displays make it easy for staff to evaluate expected versus actual performance on aligned metrics that matter to the team
  - Enables data to be recorded daily, and be visible and accessible
  - Allows leaders to identify areas where performance is lower than ·expected and quickly move the team toward action
- Daily Accountability (Huddles)
  - Enables leaders to meet daily with their teams and facilitate performance improvement
  - Helps leaders to prioritize efforts and control the pace of those efforts
  - Facilitates staff engagement

Sample Agenda for Lean Management System Training

Day 1: Overview of Lean Management and Introduction to Lean Management Principles

- Designed around observations of simulation teams working to improve daily work
- Leaders learn to build Lean Management Systems for the simulation and quickly translate those ideas to their own environments

Day 2: Introduction to Leader Standard Work and Lean Tiered Huddles

- Designed around observations of simulation teams working to improve daily work
- Leaders learn to see the absence and presence of LMS in the simulation and their own environment

Day 3: Gemba to Toyota and a Healthcare Facility to see the Artifacts of a LMS

- What do you see with your eyes; what is missing? Absence and presence of LMS

Day 4: Applying What You Learned to the Workplace

- Practice and modeling new behaviors

To date, 5,800 Scott & White employees have undergone CLIP training, including the four-day deep dive and the two-day continuing medical education/continuing nursing education training as well as the Scott & White University modules. There have been 392 leaders who have participated in LMS training. Over 100 major CLIP projects are implemented each year. Scott & White holds an annual CLIP Fair and celebration at which employees can showcase their Lean projects. A competition is judged by CEO Bob Pryor, who grants the President's Award to the team that best demonstrates "outstanding integration of the Lean healthcare philosophy through the effective use of CLIP tools producing superior outcomes."

CONTINUOUS LEARNING AND IMPROVEMENT PROGRAM STEERING COMMITTEE

The CLIP Steering Committee provides centralized oversight that facilitates learning through doing and fosters a culture in which every employee is a problem solver. The committee meets at least once per quarter, and is key to the recognition, encouragement, and celebration of success for the CLIP teams. It is committed to:

- Reduction of waste within the system;
- Identification of savings and efficiencies and commissioning efforts to capture those wins; and
- Encouraging employees at all levels to become problem solvers.

The committee's goals include:

- Creating a system-wide accountable culture, dedicated to improving process daily
- Reviewing, prioritizing, and approving as appropriate projects requiring central office support
- Communicating priorities, wins, and expectations across the system

- Providing coordination between projects and visibility of efforts within the organization
- Guiding organizational policies to support daily process improvement work
- Removing bureaucratic obstacles so improvement can occur

CONTINUOUS LEARNING AND IMPROVEMENT PROGRAM PROJECTS

Scott & White began its Lean journey with two main team-based project interventions: large value stream projects and A3s (so called because it uses a single A3-sized paper sheet to capture knowledge and progress for each problem-solving effort). Scott & White also employs specific tools within these interventions and as needed (e.g., visual management, 5S (sorting, straightening, sweeping, standardizing, sustaining), and other techniques). Scott & White believes that *learning by doing* is the best way to engage employees. The Plan, Do, Check, Act (PDCA) cycle (Figure 9.1) taught in training and reinforced in project work has been critical to the success of the CLIP program.

Many CLIP projects have focused on the design of new buildings or spaces. Scott & White has also utilized CLIP Lean Layout projects to leverage space and improve workflow. This has resulted in significant cost avoidance budget savings. An example of a CLIP project is displayed in Table 9.2.

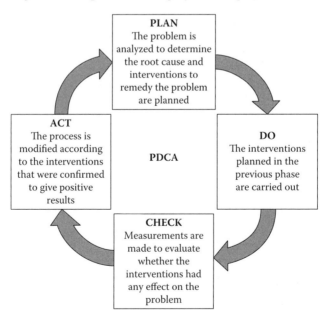

FIGURE 9.1 Plan-Do-Check-Act (PDCA) cycle of quality improvement.

TABLE 9.2 Example of Continuous Learning
Improvement Program (CLIP) project

Marble Falls Lean Layout	
Before	**What We Did**

Before

- Current & original blueprint layout is not efficient for either patients or staff
- Some clinics have more space than needed
- Some clinics lack appropriate spaces for their daily tasks
- Bottlenecks present in several areas

Goals

- Improve flow for patients and staff
- Determine actual amount and type of space needed for each clinic
- Minimize bottlenecks

What We Did

- Performed flow diagrams for patients and staff on original blueprints
- Identified bottle necks
- Determined relative location of each clinic
- Determined amount of space needed for each clinic
- Determined the type of space needed for each clinic
- Created work cells
- Centrally located workstations
- Moved physicians' offices closer to the patients
- Faster movers/high volume moved to front of clinic
- Shared procedure rooms and supply closets

Results

- Reduced walking distance (total average) = 19.1%
  - For patients: Reduced by 15%
  - For nursing staff: Reduced by 9%
  - For providers: Reduced by 40.8%
- Reduction in linear feet traveled = less time walking = more time providing patient care
- Additional 1,477 sq, ft. slated to be given back to shell repurposed as an Allergy clinic and audiologist clinic
- Additional revenue expected (based on Round Rock Clinic revenue) = $400,000 per year

Team

CEO Llano
CFO Llano
CMO Llano
CNO Llano
Director of Nurses
Clinic Manager Llano
ED Manager
Pediatric Nurse
OR/OB Manager
MD, Pediatrics, Marble Falls

"The Math"	
Space given to shell	2,720 sq. ft.
Approx. cost per sq. ft.	$85
Total cost savings	**$231,200**

CONTINUOUS LEARNING AND IMPROVEMENT PROGRAM RESULTS

From 2009 through 2012, Scott & White has tracked the following annualized improvement results from CLIP projects:

- Cost avoidance of $2,455,561
- Cost reduction of $200,000
- Collections increased by $2,533,480
- Revenue enhancements increased by $8,647,340
- Patient throughput increased by 709,020 patients
- Productivity increased by 944,580 minutes across all full-time employees
- Lead time decreased by 153,354 minutes
- Process time decreased by 504,212 minutes
- Staff walking distance decreased by 117,260 feet
- Patient wait time decreased by 83,510 minutes
- Staff wait time decreased by 788,060 minutes

LESSONS LEARNED

The success of Lean depends on many variables, including the organization's culture and size, and where it stands on its quality journey. One of the most important drivers of success is leadership support for and understanding of the Lean thinking and terminology. Leaders' commitment and understanding cascades to employees throughout the organization.

Scott & White has learned that patience is required to see the long-term changes brought about by Lean thinking. Long-term commitment cannot be sacrificed for short-term wins; organizations that want to promote a Lean culture must look to the future, set and pursue long-term goals, and adapt the goals when necessary. In addition, organizations must recognize that short-term losses may occur, but that this does not negate the long-term importance of having a Lean culture. Failed initiatives are as important from a learning perspective as those that work.

Scott & White also has learned that metrics are crucial. Improvement cannot be measured without data; however, early in the Lean journey, metrics need not be complicated. They may involve counting hand-offs, minutes spent waiting, or steps taken. Allowing people to measure simple things can provide important lessons.

Perhaps the most important lesson Scott & White has learned is the importance of communicating that the purpose of Lean initiatives is not just return on investment by eliminating waste and improving throughput—it is doing the right thing for patients. Success is measured by changes in how people are thinking; the appropriate returns on investment will follow if people learn how to solve problems.

CONCLUSION

Since 2007, Scott & White Healthcare has utilized Lean thinking throughout its organization, developing various courses to meet the needs of specific audiences. These courses include a four-day deep dive CLIP program as well as two-hour Scott & White University courses designed to enable staff to attend individual training modules. Projects emerging from these courses have resulted in a variety of improvements that influence all six domains of STEEEP care.[3] CLIP furthers Scott & White's mission to provide the most personalized, comprehensive, and highest quality health care, enhanced by medical education and research, and supports its philosophy of continuous learning and process improvement.

REFERENCES

1. Scott & White Health Care Fact Sheet. January 2013. Online at: www.sw.org (accessed April 9, 2013).
2. Lean Enterprise Institute. What Is Lean? Online at: http://www.lean.org/whatslean/ (accessed April 12, 2013).
3. Corrigan, J. M., M. S. Donaldson, L. T. Kohn, S. K. Maguire, and K. C. Pike. 2001. *Crossing the quality chasm: A new health system for the 21st century.* Washington, DC: National Academy Press.

Chapter 10

STEEEP Analytics

Donald Kennerly, Marisa Valdes, David Nicewander,

and Robert T. Green

CONTENTS

INTRODUCTION

For a health care delivery organization to achieve STEEEP care, it must commit to the development of robust infrastructure, an aspect of building capacity for improvement, the seventh Institute for Healthcare Improvement Leadership Leverage Point.[1] Such infrastructure includes effective systems for measuring and reporting the clinical and financial impacts associated with quality improvement. BHCS recognized the need for these systems early in its quality journey, and established resources related to database development and management through advanced programming, data integration from multiple sources, and reporting of performance measurement indicators. Collectively, these activities are provided by the BHCS STEEEP Analytics Department, a valuable organizational resource for measuring, analyzing, and reporting overall system performance as well as the effects of specific health care quality improvement initiatives.

ORGANIZATIONAL RESOURCE FOR ANALYTICS SERVICES

The STEEEP Analytics group within the Institute for Healthcare Research and Improvement (see Chapter 3) offers the following services to other departments and entities across BHCS:

- Data management, analysis, and reporting
- Implementation and reporting of performance measurement indicators
- Integration of data from multiple sources within BHCS, as well as state, regional, and national databases for benchmarking purposes
- Biomedical data management from electronic health records and other clinical systems
- System-wide support for standardized reporting and ad hoc data requests

PAY-FOR-PERFORMANCE THROUGH VALUE-BASED PURCHASING (VBP)

The Medicare VBP program is the first of several new pay-for-performance strategies developed by Centers for Medicare and Medicaid Services (CMS) under PPACA (Patient Protection and Affordable Care Act).[2] The VBP program is designed to promote the U.S. Department of Health and Human Services' triple aim to improve patient care, improve the health of individuals and communities, and lower health care costs.[3] Since October 1, 2012, 1 percent of a hospital's Medicare payment has been tied to its performance in the areas of clinical processes of care and patient experience (as measured by the HCAHPS (Hospital Consumer Assessment of Healthcare Providers and Systems) survey). Starting October 1, 2013, 30-day mortality measures also will be factored into each hospital's performance score. The total performance score will include clinical process measures (weighted 45%), patient experience measures (weighted 30%), and patient outcomes measures (weighted 25%) (Figure 10.1). VBP is intended to emphasize reimbursement for value rather than volume.[4]

Under VBP, health care systems could potentially gain or lose millions of dollars a year in Medicare reimbursement.[4] BHCS's ongoing commitment to STEEEP care has prepared it for this increased emphasis on performance on quality and patient satisfaction measures. The STEEEP Analytics Department and associated resources related to performance measurement and reporting

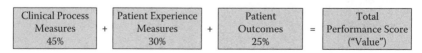

FIGURE 10.1 Hospital value-based purchasing program total performance score, starting October 1, 2013.

positioned BHCS to measure its performance on the measures included in the VBP total performance score before VBP became a reality. Having the STEEEP Analytics resource in place means BHCS is well positioned to respond to ongoing changes in the health care environment.

CENTERS FOR MEDICARE AND MEDICAID SERVICES CORE MEASURES

Core Measures, the publicly reported, recommended process of care measures developed by CMS and The Joint Commission, are one way to compare the quality of care that hospitals offer.[5] Core Measures reflect how often a hospital delivers recommended processes of care for high-priority conditions: acute myocardial infarction, heart failure, community-acquired pneumonia, and surgical infection prevention.[6] In 2003, the Hospital Inpatient Quality Reporting Program began requiring hospitals to submit their Core Measures performance data to CMS, which then publicized it on the Hospital Compare Web site.[7,8]

BHCS is committed to proactive analyses to "check" its processes, and began monitoring its Core Measures performance before the CMS reporting requirement took effect. To do this, BHCS implemented a system-wide software application (MIDAS+) in 2002 for the extensive data collection involved. BHCS's initial measurement of these performance measures required engagement of an external nurse abstractor group to conduct a retrospective review of patient charts for a random sample of up to 25 admissions per month with the relevant diagnoses for the period July 1, 2001 to June 30, 2002.[9] However, this work paid off; BHCS was well prepared when CMS began requiring hospitals to submit performance data for public reporting.

BHCS's data-driven mentality has enabled it to attain high reliability in Core Measures performance,[10] an aspect of its health care delivery that was instrumental in obtaining national recognition as a quality leader, winning the 2008 National Quality Healthcare Award from the National Quality Forum as well as the first Leapfrog Patient-Centeredness Award in 2007.

CLINICAL PREVENTIVE SERVICE DELIVERY

Another example of BHCS's commitment to data-driven performance improvement is seen in its work relating to the delivery of clinical preventive services in the primary care setting. Adults in the United States typically do not receive all recommended clinical preventive services for which they are eligible, resulting in missed opportunities for prevention and early detection. In 1999, HealthTexas Provider Network, the BHCS-affiliated ambulatory care physician network, implemented a multiyear quality improvement initiative targeting clinical preventive service delivery. Tools for improvement implemented included a flow sheet, a physician champion model, physician- and practice-level audit and feedback, and rapid-cycle quality improvement training. From 2000 to 2006, "recommended or done" clinical preventive service delivery increased from 68 to 92 percent, and from 2001 (when the distinction between "recommended" and "done" started being made) to 2006, "done" increased from 70 to 86 percent. Among the factors contributing to this sustained improvement were the resources for centralized data collection and analysis to support the improvement efforts.[11,12] STEEEP Analytics offers such a resource for collecting, analyzing, and reporting data.

MEASUREMENT OF HOSPITAL-STANDARDIZED MORTALITY RATES

Patient safety is another area in which BHCS has been proactive in mea- surement and reporting. There is currently no national agreed-upon metric for all-cause hospital mortality, but BHCS leaders believe that measuring in-hospital mortality is, nonetheless, important. BHCS has chosen to use hospital-standardized mortality ratios (HSMRs) for this purpose, where the HSMR is calculated as the observed deaths divided by expected deaths, with the latter being determined from the mean performance of acute care hospitals in Texas for the most recent year for which data are available. The mortality data for these calculations are extracted from the Texas Department of State Health Services Texas Health Care Information Collection.[13]

In 2005, BHCS leadership made reduction of inpatient mortality an orga- nizational objective, with the BHCS Board of Trustees passing a resolution to this effect (see Chapter 1). Annually, since 2005, BHCS has set mortality reduction goals for the system as a whole as well as for the individual hospitals, creating accountability for system and facility leaders through inclusion in the performance award program (see Chapter 4).

LESSONS LEARNED

A proactive approach to data collection, measurement, analysis, and reporting is essential to quality improvement. While the initial investment in resources and infrastructure to support such an approach may present challenges, it yields dividends by facilitating the identification, development, and implementation of appropriate quality improvement initiatives. Organizations cannot manage what they cannot measure.

A commitment to transparency is also essential and integral to quality improvement. Transparency of performance data must become part of the culture of the organization. People may resist this transparency by question- ing the credibility of the data, or whether the proper people and departments are getting credit for success, or whether everyone in the organization needs to see suboptimal performance data. But transparency creates accountability, and promotes the implementation of appropriate quality improvement initiatives when data indicate that performance needs to be improved.

An important lesson BHCS has learned through its data-driven initiatives relates to how to tell an employee or department that their performance data is suboptimal. These conversations can be challenging, and care needs to be taken to ensure the data are used to motivate improvement rather than to place blame. It is also important to enter the meeting with credible data and knowledge about how it was collected and analyzed, prepared for the possibility that the employee will believe the apparent deficit in performance is, in fact, a flaw in the data. Being ready to respond to such claims creates an opportunity to interest the employee in the organizational resources for data collection, measurement, analysis, and reporting, and their application to quality improvement.

CONCLUSION

Delivery of STEEEP care requires the resources and infrastructure for collecting, measuring, analyzing, and reporting relevant data. Health care organizations need systems for measuring and reporting the clinical and financial impacts of quality improvement. At BHCS, the STEEEP Analytics Department fulfills these roles, and has supported quality improvement successes as well as organizational preparedness for data-driven national initiatives, such as public reporting of Core Measures data and the Medicare VBP program. The current round of health reform emphasizes performance measurement and reporting, as reflected by the links created between Medicare reimbursement and performance on patient satisfaction, mortality, and readmissions measures.[2] These changes make the availability of a resource like STEEEP Analytics not merely valuable, but essential for a health care organization to remain competitive as well as to provide its patients with STEEEP care.

REFERENCES

1. Reinertsen, J. L., M. Bisognano, and M. D. Pugh. 2008. *Seven leadership leverage points for organization-level improvement in health care*, 2nd ed. Cambridge, MA: Institute for Healthcare Improvement.
2. Patient Protection and Affordable Care Act. Public Law 111–148—March 23, 2010. 124 Stat. 119. Online at: http://www.gpo.gov/fdsys/pkg/PLAW-111publ148/pdf/PLAW-111publ148.pdf
3. Berwick, D. M., T. W. Nolan, and J. Whittington, The triple aim: care, health, and cost. *Health Affairs* (Millwood) 27 (3): 759–769.

4. MX.com. 2013. Value-based purchasing: Improving the U.S. healthcare system by focusing on quality rather than quantity. White Paper. Online at: http://mx.com/resources/whitepapers/improving-us-healthcare-system-through-value-based-purchasing (accessed May 15, 2013).
5. The Joint Commission. Core measure sets. Online at: http://www.jointcommission.org/core_measure_sets.aspx (accessed January 30, 2013).
6. Masica, A. L., K. M. Richter, P. Convery, and Z. Haydar. 2009. Linking joint commission inpatient core measures and national patient safety goals with evidence. *Proceedings (Baylor University Medical Center)* 22 (2): 103–111.
7. QualityNet. Hospital inpatient quality reporting program overview. Online at: http://www.qualitynet.org/dcs/ContentServer?cid=1138115987129&pagename=Qnet-Public%2FPage%2FQnetTier2 (accessed January 30, 2013).
8. Medicare.gov. Hospital compare. Online at: http://www.medicare.gov/hospitalcompare/ (accessed January 30, 2013).
9. Ballard, D. J. 2003. Indicators to improve clinical quality across an integrated health care system. *International Journal for Quality in Health Care* 15 (Suppl 1): i13–23.
10. Hines, S., and M. S. Joshi. 2008. Variation in quality of care within health systems. *The Joint Commission Journal on Quality and Patient Safety* 34 (6): 326–332.
11. Ballard, D. J., D. A. Nicewander, H. Qin, C. Fullerton, F. D. Winter, Jr., and C. E. Couch. 2007. Improving delivery of clinical preventive services: a multi-year journey. *American Journal of Preventive Medicine* 33 (6): 492–497.
12. Silverstein, M. D., G. Ogola, Q. Mercer, J. Fong, E. Devol, C. E. Couch, and D. J. Ballard. 2008. Impact of clinical preventive services in the ambulatory setting. *Proceedings (Baylor University Medical Center)* 21 (3): 227–235.
13. Texas Department of State Health Services. Texas health care information collection. Online at: http://www.dshs.state.tx.us/THCIC/ (accessed March 7, 2013).

Chapter 11

STEEEP Care Operations

Donald Kennerly and Marsha C. Cox

CONTENTS

INTRODUCTION

Building improvement capacity, the seventh Institute for Healthcare Improvement (IHI) Leadership Leverage Point[1] requires health care systems to be technically capable of making, sustaining, and spreading improvements across facilities, and to take a proactive approach to doing so. For quality initiatives to change the culture of the organization, infrastructure and resources must be dedicated to their implementation and spread. Within BHCS, this is the role of the STEEEP Care Operations Department. This group connects departments, facilities, and service lines to implement and disseminate initiatives to achieve STEEEP care. It defines a proactive approach as "doing the right thing" rather than merely preventing the wrong thing from occurring.

ORGANIZATIONAL RESOURCE FOR HEALTH CARE IMPROVEMENT

The STEEEP Care Operations Department traces its roots to the first BHCS-wide clinical committee, the Quality Council, established in 1994, and the quality resolution passed by the BHCS Board in 2000 (see Chapter 1).[2] It incorporates both a health care improvement component and a Lean resource, and its mandate includes facilitating the alignment of process and clinical quality improvement with Lean. The STEEEP Care Operations group thus brings different components of STEEEP together, driving the integration of clinical quality improvement and efficiency.

The STEEEP Care Operations group is a system-level resource that engages health care improvement directors at the individual hospitals, providing coaching and guidance for improvement of processes, policies, procedures, and systems that impact the quality of patient care across BHCS. The hospital health care improvement directors are accountable for demonstrating improvements in their hospital's evidence-based care measures. They also serve as a resource regarding process improvement tools and methods within their hospital, identify health care processes that have the potential to advance STEEEP care and communicate these to other BHCS hospitals, champion the standardization of delivery of evidence-based care, and collaborate with the patient safety and risk management departments.

LESSONS LEARNED

BHCS has learned the importance of closely aligning the quality improvement goals and initiatives across the health care organization. The STEEEP Governance Council (see Chapter 1) manages STEEEP care at each hospital through the hospital-level STEEEP committees, and the STEEEP Care Operations group manages a health care improvement director at each hospital. These structures help ensure the alignment of goals and priorities across the system, and enable easy spread of improvement initiatives demonstrating success in one hospital to other entities in the system facing similar challenges.

Another important lesson relates to priority setting and the need to be disciplined about measurement. Measurement and improvement need to be "right sized;" organizations that try to improve everything simultaneously are unlikely to improve anything. One way BHCS decides which areas of care and quality measures to target is by focusing on national health care priorities. This approach has directed many of BHCS's efforts toward improving performance on the CMS Core Measures (see Chapter 10), the inpatient mortality rate (see Chapter 10), and goals related to the IHI 100,000 and 5 Million Lives Campaigns (see Chapter 1).

CONCLUSION

The BHCS STEEEP Care Operations group provides the resource BHCS needs to make, sustain, and spread quality initiatives across the system. This group brings together a Lean resource and a health care improvement component, and seeks to align clinical quality and efficiency within BHCS's improvement efforts. By interfacing with health care improvement directors at the individual hospitals, the STEEEP Care Operations group helps align and spread quality goals and initiatives across the system.

REFERENCES

1. Reinertsen, J. L., M. Bisognano, and M. D. Pugh. 2008. *Seven leadership leverage points for organization-level improvement in health care*, 2nd ed. Cambridge, MA: Institute for Healthcare Improvement.
2. Wilsey, H. L. 2004. *How we care: Centennial history of Baylor University Medical Center and Baylor Health Care System, 1903–2003.* Dallas: Baylor Health Care System.

Chapter 12

Evaluation of Clinical, Economic, and Financial Outcomes

Neil S. Fleming, Andrew Masica, and Ian McCarthy

CONTENTS

INTRODUCTION

Stewardship is one of the core BHCS values (see Introduction, Figure I.1), making the consumption of resources in relation to outcomes an important focal point of its quality improvement operations. A commitment to quality requires an investment of resources, which is critical to developing both the culture and the infrastructure to support improvement activities.[1] While cost and quality are often integrally related, quality can be improved without increasing costs—and can even result in reduced costs. The Institute of Medicine has identified unnecessary health care costs that quality improvement could reduce or eliminate: those stemming from duplication of services and treating avoidable complications, and the inefficiencies that arise when a more expensive treatment produces comparable clinical outcomes.[2] The goals of health care quality improvement should include obtaining better value for the resources expended; as such, the economic and other impacts associated with quality improvement initiatives need to be evaluated.[2]

ACHIEVING VALUE IN HEALTH CARE

Achieving value in health care requires costs of care to be weighed against outcomes, with the latter measured around the patient and over a patient's entire care cycle.[3]

Value assessments are often incorrectly perceived as equivalent to cost-effectiveness or cost-benefit analyses. While cost-effectiveness or cost-benefit analyses are important tools in assessing value, the concept of value is much broader. For example, cost-effectiveness analysis is fundamentally a comparative tool, intended to study the costs and outcomes of two competing treatments, and is of little use in the absence of a "head-to-head" comparison.[4]

Cost-benefit analysis typically compares the cost of implementing an intervention to the monetary benefit reaped from that intervention (e.g., money saved/costs avoided, or life years saved). Unlike cost-effectiveness, cost-benefit analyses, therefore, are not limited by reliance on a relative perspective, but rather by the difficulty of converting measures, such as life-years saved, into monetary units.[5] In contrast, a value analysis examines the total resources expended, a measure that can be meaningful either when comparing two options or when there is only one to consider, and requires no complicated conversion of measures.

Ideally, assessments of value, cost-effectiveness, or cost-benefit should include the perspectives of patients and families, employers, and payers, as well as of providers, and should consider medical and nonmedical costs and outcomes, to provide a more complete picture of health care value.[6] The scope of an ideal analysis in this area therefore extends beyond the patient/provider interaction and to the region or society as a whole. As such, the analysis would be considered more of an economic analysis than a pure financial analysis. The latter focuses predominantly on the observed costs and benefits of select entities, while the former considered (unobserved) opportunity costs as well as the impact on other entities not directly involved in the program.

FOUR STUDIES ON HEALTH CARE QUALITY AND COST FROM THE BAYLOR HEALTH CARE SYSTEM

BHCS prioritizes the accurate evaluation and quantification of its health care quality improvement efforts. Developing the capacity to conduct analyses is an important part of the BHCS commitment to quality, and experience has shown that BHCS providers are more willing to accept the locally generated evidence than findings from external studies because it is based on "real world" data derived from settings with which they are familiar. The presentation of scientifically developed evidence, particularly from a setting that resonates with clinicians' tangible frame of reference, creates a compelling case for adoption of system-wide initiatives.

TABLE 12.1 Summary of four studies on health care quality and cost from Baylor Health Care System

		Study	
Standardizing Care with a Pneumonia Order Set	Standardizing Care with a Heart Failure Order Set	Measuring the Financial and Nonfinancial Costs of Implementing Electronic Health Records	Effectiveness and Cost of a Transitional Care Program for Heart Failure
Pneumonia order set use resulted in: • Reduction in in-hospital mortality • Reduction in 30-day post-admission mortality • Increase in Core Measures compliance • Potential life years saved of 12 years per patient	Heart Failure order set use resulted in: • Increase in heart failure Core Measures compliance • Reduction in inpatient mortality • Reduction in 30-day mortality • Reduction in 30-day readmission • Reduction in direct cost	Implementing an electronic health record in an average five-physician practice resulted in: • Implementation cost of $162,000 • $85,500 in maintenance expenses during the first year • 611 hours to prepare for and implement the electronic health record system	An advanced practice nurse-led transitional care program resulted in: • Reduction in 30-day readmission rates • Little effect on length of stay or total 60-day direct costs • Reduction in hospital financial contribution margin of $227 per patient

The following four studies are examples of BHCS's evaluation of the impact of its quality improvement initiatives on both quality and costs. Table 12.1 provides a brief summary of all four studies' results. More detailed descriptions follow, and the full results have been published in the peer-reviewed literature.

1. Standardizing Care with a Pneumonia Order Set

The BHCS Adult Pneumonia Order Set was developed by a system-wide multidisciplinary team including pharmacists, nurses, respiratory therapists, care coordinators, health information management staff, and physicians specializing in infectious disease, pulmonology, internal medicine, and family practice. It was made available to physicians at all BHCS hospitals. Use of the standardized order set was encouraged, but not mandated.

From March 2006 to August 2008, compliance with Centers for Medicare and Medicaid Services (CMS) Core Measures for pneumonia, in-hospital

TABLE 12.2 The unadjusted and adjusted effect of Baylor Health Care System order set use on quality measures for adult pneumonia patients discharged from BHCS acute care hospitals, March 1, 2006–August 31, 2008

Outcome	Unadjusted	Adjusted[a]
In-hospital mortality, H.R. (95% C.I.)	0.62 (0.46; 0.85)	0.73 (0.51; 1.02)
30-day postadmission mortality, H.R. (95% C.I.)	0.76 (0.61; 0.96)	0.79 (0.62; 1.00)
Core measures compliance, R.R. (95% C.I.)	1.12 (1.08; 1.16)	1.08 (1.03; 1.12)

Note: H.R. = hazard ratio, R.R. = relative risk, C.I. = confidence interval.
[a] Adjusted for age, sex, race, hospital facility, payer type, discharge year, and All Patient Refined Diagnosis Related Group (APR DRG) risk of mortality.

mortality, and costs of care were compared between patients admitted to BHCS hospitals with pneumonia who were treated using the BHCS standardized order set, and patients who were admitted with pneumonia who were not. Patients in the latter group may have been treated using order sets developed by individual physicians or hospitals, or using line-by-line orders. Adjusted analyses showed reductions in both in-hospital mortality and 30-day postadmission mortality that bordered on statistical significance, and a significant increase in Core Measures compliance (Table 12.2). The mean differences (standard error) in in-hospital mortality and costs were estimated at 1.67 (0.62) percent and $383 (207), respectively, both showing a benefit with order set use. From the estimates of mortality and cost differences, the incremental cost-effectiveness ratio was estimated at $22,882 per additional life saved. Alternatively stated, using the BHCS order set to treat 2,000 patients with pneumonia would save an additional 33 lives and avoid $766,000 in direct patient care costs.[7]

2. Standardizing Care with a Heart Failure Order Set

A similar study evaluated the impact of implementing a standardized heart failure order set in BHCS hospitals on mortality, readmission, and costs of care.

As for pneumonia, BHCS developed and deployed a standardized heart failure order set, this time with content driven by the American College of Cardiology/American Heart Association clinical practice guidelines. Publicly reported process of care measures, in-patient mortality, 30-day mortality, 30-day readmission, length of stay, and direct costs of care (excluding overhead) were compared for heart failure patients treated with and without the order set, discharged between December 2007 and March 2009 who had not undergone a heart transplant and did not have a left ventricular assist device.

TABLE 12.3 Unadjusted and adjusted effect of Baylor Health Care System order set on quality measures for adult heart failure patients discharged from BHCS hospitals from December 2007 to March 2009

Safety and Effectiveness Indicators	Unadjusted	Propensity Score Adjusted[a]
In-hospital mortality, OR (95% CI)	**0.57 (0.34; 0.97)**	**0.49 (0.28; 0.88)**
30-day mortality, OR (95% CI)	0.78 (0.58; 1.05)	0.81 (0.58; 1.13)
30-day readmission, RR (95% CI)	0.93 (0.77; 1.14)	0.91 (0.73; 1.14)
Core Measures compliance, OR (95% CI)	**1.55 (1.15; 2.10)**	**1.51 (1.08; 2.12)**

Financial and Efficiency Indicators	Unadjusted	Propensity Score Adjusted[b]
Length of stay, difference (95% CI) (days)	–0.15 (–0.38; 0.08)	–0.07 (–0.34; 0.17)
Cost ($), difference (95% CI)[c]		
Initial admission direct cost	**–1408 (–2011; –806)**	**–685 (–1287; –87)**
30-day readmission direct cost	**–820 (–1500; –141)**	–665 (–1379; 49)
One-year readmission direct cost	**–1614 (–2676; –552)**	**–1224 (–2276; –171)**
Total direct cost (initial + 30-day readmission)	**–2229 (–3150; –1308)**	**–1350 (–2804;– 396)**
Total direct cost (initial + 1-year readmission)	**–3022 (–4240; –1806)**	**–1909 (–3143; –676)**

Note: OR = odds ratio, CI = confidence interval, RR = risk ratio. All significant results are in bold.
[a] Propensity score covariates: age, gender, race, type of physician (hospitalists vs. nonhospitalists), APR DRG risk of mortality, facility, payer type, and quarter of discharge.
[b] Propensity score covariates: age, gender, race, type of physician (hospitalists vs. nonhospitalists), APR DRG severity of illness, facility, payer type, and quarter of discharge.
[c] Cost difference obtained via bootstrap recycled prediction algorithm discussed in the statistical analysis section.

The study results are summarized in Table 12.3. Following propensity score adjustment to create comparability between the groups, order set use was associated with significantly increased compliance with the heart failure Core Measures and reduced inpatient mortality. Reductions in 30-day mortality and readmission approached significance. Direct costs for initial admissions alone and in combination with readmissions were significantly lower with order set use. The impact of the standardized order set on heart failure care translated into potential annual savings of 15,147 in-hospital deaths and $1.9 billion dollars nationally.[8]

As for pneumonia, these findings suggest that use of an evidence-based standardized order set may help improve outcomes and reduce costs of care.

The results of the pneumonia and heart failure order set analyses have driven adoption and widespread use of these order sets across BHCS, with use remaining above 95 percent, and support physician champions' use of the order sets as coaching tools. This underscores the impact local evaluation of health care quality improvement initiatives can have on buy-in and uptake.

3. Measuring the Financial and Nonfinancial Costs of Implementing Electronic Health Records

This study measured the cost of implementing an electronic health record system in 26 primary care practices in the BHCS-affiliated physician network, HealthTexas Provider Network (HTPN), taking into account hardware and software costs, as well as the time and effort invested in implementation. Results showed that, for an average five-physician practice, implementation cost an estimated $162,000, with $85,500 in maintenance expenses during the first year. The HTPN implementation team and the practice implementation team needed 611 hours on average to prepare for and implement the electronic health record system. "End users"—physicians, other clinical staff, and non-clinical staff—needed 134 hours per physician on average to prepare for use of the record system in clinical encounters.[9] This study underscores the nature of the investment required for quality improvement, especially the costs pertaining to time and effort, which are often "hidden" (i.e., not quantified) during such initiatives.

4. Effectiveness and Cost of a Transitional Care Program for Heart Failure

The BHCS evaluation of an advanced practice nurse–led transitional care program for patients with heart failure is described in Chapter 5. The program was associated with a statistically significant 48 percent reduction in 30-day readmission rates, had little effect on length of stay or total 60-day direct costs, and reduced the hospital financial contribution margin by an average of $227 per Medicare patient with heart failure under the CMS reimbursement scheme in place at the time.[10]

LESSONS LEARNED

A commitment to robust evaluation of any type of quality initiative is important both to determine its effectiveness and to provide feedback for decision makers at local and global levels. Data-driven evaluation facilitates the creation of a local evidence base that may be viewed as more relevant and compelling by both decision makers and frontline care providers.

Based on the studies described in this chapter, as well as the PDCA (Plan-Do-Check-Act) model (see Chapter 8), a "quality improvement" process could be outlined as:

- Propose the initiative
- Elicit physician and administrative opinions on the proposed initiative to ensure broad interest
- Deploy the initiative
- Evaluate the value of the intervention
- Continue, refine, or stop the initiative depending on the results of the evaluation

Building the capacity to perform these quality improvement evaluations requires a substantial resource commitment by the health care organization. BHCS employs health services researchers, biostatisticians, health economists, decision and computer scientists, and medical writers, among others, to assist in evaluating and disseminating the results of its quality improvement initiatives. Because of the power of local evidence, the ability to empirically test and evaluate initiatives at BHCS has been integral to the organization's success. This activity provides a "real-world" testing ground for initiatives and facilitates validation at all levels of the organization, which further lays the foundation for spread and sustainability of effective practices, leading to better clinical and financial outcomes.

CONCLUSION

Successful health care delivery organizations examine operational performance and financial implications in conjunction with clinical quality. Some clinical quality improvements bring simultaneous reductions in providers' costs; in other cases, the savings may play out only in the long-term or may occur in a different part of the health care system. When clinical quality improvement increases provider costs (either in the short term or permanently), the benefits to patients, nonetheless, may be so significant that it is worth identifying and addressing other areas of inefficiency to compensate for the increased costs.

Local evaluations of the effectiveness and cost implications of quality improvement initiatives provides relevant, "real world" data for decision makers and frontline providers, facilitating greater uptake and buy-in.

Health care organizations are being charged with providing more care and better outcomes while expending fewer resources, thus making rigorous evaluation of the cost and quality implications of improvement initiatives imperative. Such work can help health care organizations optimize their resource consumption without compromising clinical outcomes.

REFERENCES

1. Reinertsen, J. L., M. Bisognano, and M. D. Pugh. 2008. *Seven leadership leverage points for organization-level improvement in health care*, 2nd ed. Cambridge, MA: Institute for Healthcare Improvement.
2. Corrigan, J. M., M. S. Donaldson, L. T. Kohn, S. K. Maguire, and K. C. Pike. 2001. *Crossing the quality chasm: A new health system for the 21st century.* Washington, DC: National Academy Press.
3. Porter, M. E. 2010. What is value in health care? *New England Journal of Medicine* 363 (26): 2477–2481.
4. Glick, H. A. 2010. What's in a perspective? *Value Health* 13 (1): 2.
5. Gold, M. 1996. Panel on cost-effectiveness in health and medicine. *Medical Care* 34 (12 Suppl): DS197–199.
6. Ballard, D. J., B. Spreadbury, and R. S. Hopkins, 3rd. 2004. Health care quality improvement across the Baylor Health Care System: The first century. *Proceedings (Baylor University Medical Center)* 17 (3): 277–288.
7. Fleming, N. S., G. Ogola, and D. J. Ballard. 2009. Implementing a standardized order set for community-acquired pneumonia: Impact on mortality and cost. *The Joint Commission Journal on Quality and Patient Safety* 35 (8): 414–421.
8. Ballard, D. J., G. Ogola, N. S. Fleming, B. D. Stauffer, B. M. Leonard, R. Khetan, and C. W. Yancy. 2010. Impact of a standardized heart failure order set on mortality, readmission, and quality and costs of care. *International Journal for Quality in Health Care* 22 (6): 437–444.
9. Fleming, N. S., S. D. Culler, R. McCorkle, E. R. Becker, and D. J. Ballard. 2011. The financial and nonfinancial costs of implementing electronic health records in primary care practices. *Health Affairs* (Millwood) 30 (3): 481–489.
10. Stauffer, B. D., C. Fullerton, N. Fleming, G. Ogola, J. Herrin, P. M. Stafford, and D. J. Ballard. 2011. Effectiveness and cost of a transitional care program for heart failure: A prospective study with concurrent controls. *Archives of Internal Medicine* 171 (14): 1238–1243.

Chapter 13

Driving STEEEP Care across a Multihospital System

John B. McWhorter, III

CONTENTS

INTRODUCTION

STEEEP represents health care value of the highest order. The logic of continuous improvement of processes is self-evident; however, the pace at which health care improvements are adopted is slow to the point of embarrassment. Why did it take two decades to achieve the routine delivery of aspirin to patients arriving at the hospital with chest pain?[1] And, over a decade to "hardwire" hand washing between patient visits?[2] The answers are rooted in organizational culture and openness to the adoption of innovations.

Even within BHCS, some hospitals adopt innovations earlier and more rapidly than others. What causes a health care system to be an early adopter of innovation or a laggard? Generally, culture is influenced by leadership, but there are a multitude of tools and techniques available to motivate people to change. This chapter describes the BHCS journey to embrace change and adopt innovation.

BUILDING THE CHANGE PLATFORM

The crew chief of a NASCAR racing team has a multitude of tools to enhance the performance of the car. Similarly, there is an array of techniques to accelerate the pace of adoption of change available to health care organizations. Among those BHCS has found powerful in its STEEEP journey are transparency, visibility, competition, common metrics, goal setting, and reward and recognition.

BHCS took its first step toward accelerating quality improvement in the early 2000s when it committed to transparency within the organization. BHCS had long had a culture that emphasized delivery of "good news," but was reluctant to discuss failures in a meaningful way. Executive leadership made the decision to openly and transparently report its own performance metrics, and to compare performance between organizations.

The first time the Center for Medicare and Medicaid Services Core Measures performance was compared across BHCS hospitals, the chief medical officers, chief nursing officers, and presidents received quite a shock. However, it did not take long for the hospital at the "bottom" to communicate to its workforce that the hospital needed to accelerate the pace of change. The hospital medical staff governance committees had a different reaction, becoming defensive and questioning the credibility of the data. Nonetheless, it took less than six months for the "bottom scrapers" to move up in the rankings.

The combination of this transparency and the link established between Core Measures performance and leaders' compensation (see Chapter 4) in the system-wide focus on improving Core Measures performance has borne substantial fruit. In 2003, BHCS's system-wide performance on the 12-measure acute myocardial infarction (AMI) "bundle" was 81 percent, which was relatively good compared to hospitals across the nation. By 2007, performance had improved to 94 percent and, by December 2012, had topped 98 percent. Even more dramatic improvements were achieved in heart failure and pneumonia Core Measures performance, for which BHCS had substantially lower starting performance. In 2003, BHCS was only providing the full set of 10 evidence-based Core Measures for heart failure patients 55 percent of the time—about as often as a flip of the coin. By 2007, the system-wide focus on Core Measure performance had boosted performance to 86 percent and, by 2012, 97 percent of eligible heart failure patients were receiving all 10 recommended processes of care. Pneumonia care, for which BHCS faced the double challenge of starting at a performance level below 50 percent and having the number of measures included in the Core Measure set expand from 5 to 12 between 2003 and 2007, has similarly improved, with 98 percent of pneumonia patients admitted to BHCS hospitals receiving all the recommended processes of care in 2012. In the fourth area of care covered by the Core Measures, surgical care infection prevention, BHCS's performance on the 10-measure bundle has improved from 75 percent in 2006 to 95 percent in 2012.

BHCS's second step in building a platform for quality improvement was to make quality and quality improvement a high priority during governance and executive meetings. Quality routinely became a top agenda item at all medical staff meetings, executive meetings, and governance meetings, and was discussed and debated at every meeting.

Third, BHCS recognized the value of friendly competition as a driving force for improvement, and created a variety of competitive award and recognition programs for achievements in quality improvement, patient satisfaction scores, and utilization of newly implemented quality and safety tools.[3] Awards were available at both hospital and system levels, and friendly competition between departments was encouraged.

Competition encouraged innovation as hospitals and departments strove to gain or maintain their advantage with new methods of solving problems and improving quality. The problem with this approach was that it fostered the development of unique cultures and solutions within each hospital that could not be successfully replicated across BHCS, resulting in duplication of effort. A decision was reached to adopt common solutions using common language across the system and, before resources would be allocated or hospital projects approved, the hospital or team had to convince the decision makers that their program could be replicated across all hospitals if the pilot was successful. The resulting coordination led to a common understanding of solutions and accelerated system-wide adoption of successful programs.

FUELING THE RACE

BHCS's STEEEP journey can be thought of as a relay: After each stage, the baton is passed to a new runner. Transparency and competition served BHCS well as the first leg of the relay, but had we stopped at that point, progress would have slowed and eventually stopped. For the second leg of the relay, BHCS leaders recognized the need to provide "fuel" to keep the runners moving. This was achieved through performance measurement, incentive compensation, and goal setting (see Chapter 4). As this process matures, thoughts have turned to the third leg of the race, and the need to include incentives to motivate high-performing people and teams to help low-performing teams. BHCS is currently experimenting with different methods to reward high performers for assisting lower performers to improve outcomes.

SHARING BEST PRACTICES

In addition to the transparent sharing and comparing of performance data across BHCS facilities, BHCS benchmarks its performance against other high-performing health care systems across the nation. With so much performance data and academic literature readily accessible and searchable online, best practices can be rapidly identified and compared. BHCS holds an annual Quality Summit, maintains a searchable inventory of best practices that have been successful at BHCS, and provides an annual report to the Board of Trustees on best practices. BHCS also offers an annual President's Award at each hospital to recognize best practices and outstanding contributions to STEEEP, and monthly CEO Awards in which up to 24 individuals or teams are recognized for their contribution to best practices.

EVOLVING FROM EGOCENTRIC TO PATIENT-CENTRIC

The greatest transformation BHCS has had to facilitate in its STEEEP journey is one that occurs from the individual level up—moving from a perspective of doing things "my way" to doing them the system's way. This requires a complete change in attitude. BHCS has encouraged this transformation through bidirectional communication of goals and strategies; system-level goals in the areas of people, service, quality, and finance cascade down to individual employees, while individuals, departments, and facilities have to submit action plans and goals that are reviewed and adjusted to align them with the system's priorities. Overcoming resistance was a struggle, but was chipped away through individual meetings, performance appraisal sessions, team-building exercises, and benchmarking comparisons. Flexibility was also built into the system to encourage high performance and innovation. While individuals, departments, and hospitals are required to use system-mandated tools until their performance reaches a targeted benchmark, once they have passed that target, they are given license to experiment with other approaches.

LESSONS LEARNED

BHCS learned many lessons as it sought to drive improvement across its multiple and diverse hospital facilities. These are the most pertinent:

1. A sense of urgency must be created.

   The urgency may be driven by pain, fear, rewards, or people seeking recognition, but a motivation for change must be created. BHCS created this motivation using friendly competition, benchmarks, reward and recognition, and loss of reward through the performance award program. In extreme cases, people were asked to leave the organization when they could not meet goals.

2. A vision must be simple to explain and simple to understand.

   A vision that cannot be clearly communicated to the least sophisticated member of staff is not a shared vision. Every staff member should be able to develop a goal and associated strategic plan that fits under the vision.

3. Never underestimate the power of recognition.

As Quinton Studer (founder and chairman of the board at Studer Group) used to say, "No one has ever complained about receiving too much recognition." Recognition can be very inexpensive; a public appreciation at a board meeting, public event, or department director meeting. A written letter to someone's home or a donation to their favorite charity can go a long way to affirm good work. By recognizing the early adopters and the heroes of your own organization, linkage can be created between desired behavior and adoption of programs.

4. Harvest small wins and use them to drive friendly competition.

Early success provides motivation to continue and expand adoption of an initiative. Where the ultimate goal can only be achieved in the long term, intermediate milestones can provide early "wins." Achievements by early adopters can be broadcast through the organization and used to create healthy competition and motivation for others to change. For example, one BHCS hospital created and implemented a sepsis "bundle" that improved its performance on sepsis-related quality measures so dramatically that, when their results were trumpeted throughout the organization, the other BHCS hospitals wanted to implement it to achieve the same success.

5. Identify and address dissension.

Every change will have its resisters. Once it has been established that their resistance is not based on genuine grounds for concern about unintended consequences of the proposed change, dissenters must be made to understand that the change is nonnegotiable. One BHCS hospital has formalized this process, creating a list of nonnegotiables that every employee signed as part of his or her employment agreement.

REFERENCES

1. Stafford, R. S., V. Monti, and J. Ma. 2005. Underutilization of aspirin persists in U.S. ambulatory care for the secondary and primary prevention of cardiovascular disease. *PLoS Medicine* 2 (12): e353.
2. Haas, J. P., and E. L. Larson. 2008. Compliance with hand hygiene guidelines: Where are we in 2008? *American Journal of Nursing* 108 (8): 40–44; quiz 45.
3. Furman, C., and R. Caplan. 2007. Applying the Toyota Production System: Using a patient safety alert system to reduce error. *The Joint Commission Journal on Quality and Patient Safety* 33 (7): 376–386.

Chapter 14

Driving STEEEP Care across a Physician Provider Network

Carl E. Couch, F. David Winter, and William L. Roberts

CONTENTS

INTRODUCTION

Hospital-physician alignment is essential to improving health care quality and delivering STEEEP care. In 1994, BHCS established the HealthTexas Provider Network (HTPN), a physician network provider organization, as a step toward becoming an integrated health care delivery system. HTPN is a single-member 501(a) physician organization (with BHCS as the single member), formed under the Texas Medical Practice Act's exception to the state's prohibition on the corporate practice of medicine for certified organizations whose organizers, board, and executive leaders are physicians.[1] In the 19 years since its inception, HTPN has built its reputation as a high-quality, physician-led and patient-centered organization with extensive expertise in practice management and a strong code of conduct for its physicians and employees. In 2013, HTPN comprises 68 primary care centers and 129 specialty-care centers that include: 9 physiatric medicine centers, 7 hospitalist programs, 3 pulmonary critical care units, 13 liver disease outreach clinics, 3 advanced heart failure clinics, 3 senior health centers, 31 cardiovascular care sites, 4 computerized tomography centers, 1 magnetic resonance imaging center, and a family practice residency program.[2]

As a highly integrated unit, HTPN and BHCS share the same dedication to quality improvement, patient satisfaction, and the evidence-based practice of medicine. HTPN's commitment to patient centeredness—doing right by patients and doing it well—has led to substantial improvements in adult preventive medicine, disease management, as well as effective and efficient coordination of care at all stages of patients' lives. HTPN's continuing journey to provide STEEEP care is supported by a committee structure that fosters teamwork, collaboration, and a sense of partnership between leaders, physicians, patients, administrators, and staff.

In 2011 and 2012, HTPN was recognized as an American Medical Group Association Acclaim Award Honoree, an award that recognizes health care organizations that are embracing the Institute of Medicine's (IOM) aims for improvement and taking the steps necessary to bring their organizations closer to an ideal health care system: (1) measurably improving the quality and value of care, (2) improving patient experience and outcomes, (3) continuously learning and innovating, and (4) improving population health.[3]

ORGANIZATION AND INFRASTRUCTURE FOR QUALITY IMPROVEMENT

HTPN is a physician-led network and its organizational structures and governance encourage physicians to see themselves as a part of the whole and to be invested in continual improvement. With nearly 70 percent of HTPN physicians being involved in at least one organizational or governance committee either as a leader or a member, the committee structure provides an active forum through which physicians influence such health care system processes as clinical integration, business process redesign efforts, and strategic planning. This engagement in the broader health care system encourages a perspective that looks beyond the walls of the particular practice within which a physician provides care. HTPN's culture of collaboration and quality improvement is cultivated by a board and committee structure that demands the following: (1) physician involvement, (2) a strong commitment of senior leadership to improving the quality of care delivered to patients, (3) the willingness of leaders from both the medical group and hospital system to invest in each other's infrastructure, and (4) a physician recruitment process that emphasizes teamwork to address the needs of every patient.

Board and Committee Structure

The HTPN Board of Directors makes routine business decisions and oversees the medical aspects of practice. HTPN's bylaws require primary care physicians (family practitioners, internists, and pediatricians) to make up 60 percent of Board membership. Board activities include approving budgets, appointing executives, monitoring network implementation, credentialing physicians, establishing medical management and quality assurance policies, and implementing risk sharing and incentive plans.

Board decisions are supported by a committee structure that promotes teamwork and empowers physicians to take an active role in management, and sustains two-way communication between the board and care-site levels (Figure 14.1). More than 25 physician-led committees and subcommittees have been created to address all aspects of practice management and health care delivery, from finance and ethics to research, patient safety, and ambulatory electronic health records. In addition to the high rate of physician involvement in these committees, HTPN recruits patient representatives to gain their perspective on quality improvement efforts.

Senior leaders from HTPN and BHCS actively participate in each other's governance structures. For example, both the president and chief clinical officer of HTPN serve on BHCS's STEEEP Governance Council. The president of

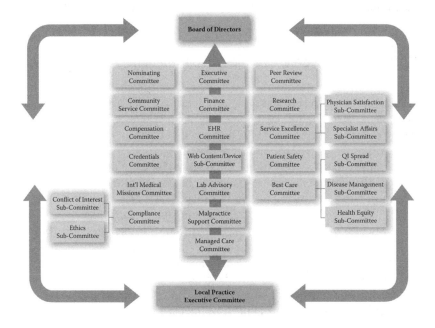

FIGURE 14.1 HealthTexas Provider Network committee structure.

HTPN also serves on the BHCS Board of Trustees and Executive Council. In return, the BHCS chief executive, financial, and operating officers, and several BHCS hospital presidents regularly attend HTPN Board meetings. Investing in each other's infrastructure advances accountability and collaboration across all care settings, a key strategy for building a high-performance medical group.

Best Care Committee

In 1999, HTPN established a Quality Committee (now known as the Best Care Committee) to set goals for improving clinical care, collecting data, and implementing goals related to preventive and early diagnostic measures, and the delivery of excellence in the management of chronic illnesses. Driven by the IOM's call to provide STEEEP care,[4] the Best Care Committee strives to improve the quality of patient care at every level of the organization. The committee is chaired by a physician leader and consists of patients, executive stakeholders, and physicians from various care sites within HTPN. Its specific goals are to (1) provide physicians with reliable data that enable them to identify best practices and opportunities for improvement, (2) implement evidence-based, system-wide standards of care, (3) advance clinical care through the development of standards and protocols, and (4) recruit patients to serve as members of the committee to provide input and feedback regarding quality projects.

Clinical Performance Excellence Department

HTPN's Clinical Performance Excellence Department establishes clinical skills guidelines to ensure and promote clinical excellence within HTPN. The department offers the following programs on a regular basis to improve the quality of care delivered by HTPN physicians:

- *Clinical Skills Orientation*: An all-day clinical skills class involving didactic instruction and selected demonstration of the 20 clinical skills most often performed in HTPN clinics.
- *"Focus Four"*: Tutorials delivered during lunch hours that cover the four critical skills areas of (1) performing EKGs, (2) blood pressure measurement, (3) medication injections, and (4) hand washing.
- *"Train the Trainer"*: A program designed to place within HTPN a clinical employee who assists with the required annual check-off of skills for each clinic. This program gives each trainer hands-on opportunities to teach critical skills during the training class.
- *Onsite Visits*: A trained clinical registered nurse is made available for clinic visits to evaluate clinical staff and operations with the aim of improving clinical outcomes within HTPN.

- *The Nursing Task Force*: Represents a cross section of HTPN clinics and meets monthly to discuss clinical nursing issues and review and update nursing policy.

Physician Recruitment

Physician recruitment plays an important role in maintaining HTPN's culture of patient-centeredness and quality improvement. Its recruitment efforts focus on finding physicians who are willing to commit to common values, work as a team to care for patients, and share best practices for running their care sites. Physicians are required to sign a Code of Conduct[5] (Figure 14.2) that characterizes a unified culture of shared accountability among all HTPN physicians. By agreeing to this Code of Conduct, HTPN physicians confirm their commitment to competence, trustworthiness, timeliness of care, collegiality, courtesy, and patient-centricity. Once on board, new physicians are mentored by experienced physicians to build relationships across care practice sites.

MAJOR INITIATIVES TO IMPROVE CARE QUALITY

HTPN's quality improvement efforts are driven by a vision it shares with BHCS of clinical integration, standardization, efficiency, care coordination, and accountability across all settings. Applying the STEEEP framework as a guide, HTPN has developed and implemented a variety of quality initiatives (Table 14.1). Efforts to ensure delivery of adult preventive health services, alignment with a new model of patient-centered primary care, and improvements in ambulatory care coordination are just a few examples along HTPN's continuing journey to create an ideal health care delivery model. Setting benchmarks, collecting data, and measuring progress against internal and industry standards drive all of HTPN's efforts toward streamlining and improving the patient experience.

Adult Preventive Health Services

The HTPN multiyear, multifaceted initiative to improve delivery of adult preventive services is described in Chapter 10. A retrospective study conducted in 2005 estimated that, with the improvements in preventive service delivery, HTPN had prevented 36 deaths and 97 incidents of cancer, 420 coronary disease events (including 66 sudden deaths) and 118 strokes, and 87 osteoporosis-related fractures.[6]

PHYSICIAN CODE OF CONDUCT

RELATIONSHIP TO STAFF:

- Treat staff with dignity and respect.
- Work to lead a team where our philosophy, integrity, commitment, compassion, and caring is observed by those around us.
- Strive to make others better by expecting more of ourselves.
- Influence and communicate with those around us in a positive and cooperative way.
- Thank and recognize those who allow us to do what we do.
- Look for opportunities to do things better.
- Listen to the input of others and take an active ownership role to implement change.
- Educate rather than criticize.
- Work to be leaders who are respected because of our actions.

RELATIONSHIP TO PHYSICIANS:

- Treat our colleagues with respect.
- Communicate effectively with each other to enhance continuity and quality of care.
- Look for the good in others and share these views with patients to improve perception and experience with HealthTexas primary and specialty care physicians.
- Foster the spirit of teaching and learning from each other.
- Look for opportunities to make each other better.
- Never criticize another physician's treatment or actions amongst staff or patients, but view differences as opportunities to improve.
- Encourage fun and interaction amongst colleagues both in and out of the workplace.
- Honor the uniqueness of others.
- Treat our colleagues in the way in which we want to be treated.
- Give a helping hand should someone need it.

RELATIONSHIP TO PATIENTS:

- Treat patients with respect and dignity.
- Learn about the person as well as the condition.
- Work together with our patients as a team.
- Strive to make each patient feel as though he or she is our only patient.
- Make patients feel that we are always on their side because effective care can never be delivered in opposition.
- Engage, listen, and clearly explain issues to our patients so that time spent with us exceeds their expectations.
- Aim to return phone calls promptly.
- Thank patients for waiting if we are running late.
- Earn patients' loyalty through our behavior.

FIGURE 14.2 HealthTexas Provider Network (HTPN) Physician Code of Conduct.

TABLE 14.1 HealthTexas Provider Network initiatives aligned
with the domains of STEEEP care

STEEEP Domain	Example Initiatives
Safe	Clinical skill training and verification, patient event reporting
Timely	Urgent/after hours care offered by majority of primary care sites, same-day appointments
Effective	Adult preventive health services, disease management program, elder house calls, use of standardized care practices
Efficient	Electronic health records, automated audits and quality improvement reporting, standardization of medical supplies
Equitable	Outreach clinics for liver, kidney, and heart failure
Patient-centered	Patient-centered medical home, ambulatory care coordination, advanced medical planning for elder populations

Patient-Centered Medical Home

The patient-centered medical home (PCMH) is a model of twenty-first-century primary care that combines teamwork, access, and technology to deliver quality care and improve health. It is rapidly gaining support across the health care industry as an approach to making health care more personalized, coordinated, effective, and efficient. The foundation of the PCMH model is that each patient has a relationship with a primary care clinician who leads a team that takes collective responsibility for patient care, providing for the patient's health care needs, and arranging for appropriate care with other qualified clinicians. Specialists also work in a PCMH if they agree to cover all aspects of the patient's care, including immunizations and preventive services. The model also emphasizes coordination of care facilitated by health information technologies, quality and safety including use of evidence-based medicine, increased access to care, and reimbursement structured to recognize the value added by the medical home.[7]

HTPN's strong foundation in primary care and prevention has led to the successful redesign of its care sites to support the PCMH model. Sixty HTPN primary care clinics, representing more than 300 providers, have received PCMH designation from the National Committee for Quality Assurance (NCQA).[8] The NCQA standards constitute one of the most widely used formal PCMH evaluation programs. The 2011 NCQA standards (which took effect after the HTPN PMCHs were recognized, but with which they will have to comply for renewal) align closely with elements of the federal Centers for Medicare and Medicaid Services "meaningful use" requirements for electronic health records (EHRs) and emphasize use of systematic, patient-centered, coordinated care practices. Meeting the NCQA standards for PCMH recognition prompted redesign efforts within HTPN practices to improve the patient experience and incorporate key elements of managing patient populations, including previsit planning, expanded patient access, and ambulatory care coordination. Implementation of the PCMH model has also led to increased adoption of standardized guidelines across HTPN practices.

Ambulatory Care Coordination

Care coordination is one of several IOM-identified national priorities for action to achieve STEEEP care.[4,9] HTPN established a care coordination department in 2010 with the explicit goal of closing gaps in care in the ambulatory setting. In this setting, patient transitions between providers (retail clinic, primary care practice, specialty care practice, hospital, rehab, or even home health) can be inefficient and may compromise quality of care.

HTPN's ambulatory care coordination department employs a staff of more than 20 ambulatory care coordinators (ACCs). Some ACCs are registered nurses, while others are experienced medical assistants. These coordinators capitalize on their relationships with HTPN care providers, including physicians, nurse practitioners, medical assistants, and physician assistants, to foster coordinated, efficient care. ACCs' focus is on four specific areas of work: patient care advocacy, hospital discharge transition and follow-up, preventative services, and disease management. They follow the patient throughout the course of care, using both outpatient EHRs and hospital inpatient portal systems to facilitate optimal patient services across the care continuum. In the areas of preventive services and disease management, each care coordinator performs outreach and follow-up activities according to standardized protocols established by the Disease Management Committee.

The ACC Department supports more than 45 HTPN care sites and 245 providers, averaging 65 patient contacts per day, and has led to many positive outcomes. In one example, an ACC made contact with a 65-year old male who had not had a colonoscopy in 20 years. The ACC scheduled the colonoscopy for the patient and followed up with him to make sure he made his appointment. Results of the examination revealed four premalignant polyps that were successfully removed. HTPN aims to provide all patients with a seamless, well-coordinated, system of effective and efficient care that begins in their personal lives and extends without variation in quality to every corner of the health system.

Quality Metrics and Dashboards

HTPN physicians are held to high standards of care and are consistently monitored and held accountable for quality and service. The implementation of EHRs facilitates close monitoring of key quality indicators. Data extracted from EHRs are used to create quality improvement reports, audits of disease management, and adult preventative health services metrics. These quality metrics are one component of the "physician dashboard" that shows each physician his/her performance in the areas of finance, service, quality, and compensation. Physicians are audited every three months to create summary reports for practices and physicians with the capability to drill down to patient detail. Improvement reports are created and updated weekly to give physicians timely feedback on their progress toward meeting their goals for adult preventative health services, chronic disease management, and congestive heart failure measures. All of these reports are formatted as "clinical dashboards" that are highly intuitive and easy to interpret. Good performance and opportunities for improvement are highlighted in the reports with green and red dashboard icons. Icons link to a report showing the specific metric and which patients are not in compliance with evidence-based recommendations. This enables physicians to better manage chronic disease and preventative health services and take action in a timely manner.

Specialty metrics in the areas of cardiovascular disease, endocrinology, otolaryngology, gerontology, hepatology, pediatrics, pulmonology, rheumatology, thoracic surgery, neurosurgery, and general surgery have been recently established as well. HTPN has begun the process of gathering data from the EHR to form baseline results for these metrics so that performance goals can be determined for its specialists. Once HTPN begins tracking results for these metrics, performance reports (dashboards) will be created to present summary results and track performance.

Because transparency is an essential component of accountability, all reports and results are posted on HTPN's intranet and in poster form at all care sites, accessible by all physicians and employees to create friendly competition to motivate improvement. Transparency also increases acceptance and eases implementation of quality initiatives. Experience with numerous improvement initiatives across BHCS has found that physicians are more likely to implement a process when they are presented with data that show it works.

LESSONS LEARNED

The greatest lesson learned along the HTPN quality improvement journey is that, while changing health care delivery is challenging, the results of these efforts can better the lives of patients. Physicians respond to data that they trust. The Best Care Committee spent many years verifying data and demonstrating to HTPN physicians where they had opportunities for improvement. Physician champions were engaged to educate others about the data and about ways to improve individual scores. HTPN was also proactive about aligning its goals with those of BHCS and integrating the domains of STEEEP into its culture. The network has remained focused on developing, implementing, and expanding improvement initiatives. Some of the lessons learned on HTPN's journey toward an ideal health care delivery system include:

- *Put patients first*: The concepts of doing right by patients and doing it well guide all quality improvement initiatives.
- *Encourage and empower employees at all levels*:. Helping employees identify and implement techniques to improve health care quality, providing the training and tools they need to be successful, and rewarding them accordingly, are vital to success.
- *Make collective, incremental changes*: Small changes throughout an organization can add up to real results in improving care. Steps to improvement do not always have to be monumental to make a difference.
- *Teamwork and communication are crucial*: Create an organizational infrastructure that allows leaders, physicians, patients, administrators, and support staff to come together as a team, work collaboratively on initiatives, share information, and develop a true sense of partnership and trust.
- *Cascade organizational goals and objectives*: Cascading goals from top to bottom allows employees to set goals for themselves that they know will support the accomplishment of entity goals and, therefore, that they are motivated to achieve.
- *Measure results*: Tracking progress and performance through evidence-based research/tools, and making results transparent throughout the organization and sharing information facilitate learning and the refinement of best practices.

CONCLUSION

The integral partnership created by HTPN and BHCS has produced multiple benefits for patients, as well as for physicians and the hospital system. Active participation in each others' governance structures has created accountability and facilitated collaboration and coordination between BHCS and HTPN as they seek to provide STEEEP care across the full continuum of care. From its earliest initiatives aimed at improving the delivery of adult preventive services to implementation of the PCMH model, HTPN remains committed to improving best care practices, outcomes, patient satisfaction, and coordinated care across the health care continuum. As health reform initiatives direct the focus of health care toward population-based management and value-based purchasing focusing on patient outcomes, the close alignment between BHCS and HTPN will be an important factor in optimizing resource use to improve patient outcomes and access to care, while reducing costs.

REFERENCES

1. Chapter 162.001(b) of the Texas Occupations Code (formerly 5.01(a) in the Medical Practice Act). Online at: http://www.statutes.legis.state.tx.us/Docs/OC/htm/OC.162.htm

2. HealthTexas Provider Network. Online at: https://www.dfwdoctorjobs.com/Pages/Index.aspx (accessed January 8, 2013).

3. American Medical Group Association. Acclaim Award. Online at: http://www.amga.org/AboutAMGA/Awards/Acclaim/index_acclaim.asp (accessed May 15, 2013).

4 Corrigan, J. M., M. S. Donaldson, L. T. Kohn, S. K. Maguire, and K. C. Pike. 2001. *Crossing the quality chasm: A new health system for the 21st century.* Washington, DC: National Academy Press.

5. HealthTexas Provider Network. Code of Conduct. Online at: https://www.dfwdoctorjobs.com/Pages/Codeofconduct.aspx (accessed May 15, 2013).

6. Silverstein, M. D., G. Ogola, Q. Mercer, J. Fong, E. Devol, C. E. Couch, and D. J. Ballard. 2008. Impact of clinical preventive services in the ambulatory setting. *Proceedings (Baylor University Medical Center)* 21 (3): 227–235.

7. Patient-Centered Primary Care Collaborative. Joint Principles of the Patient-Centered Medical Home. Online at: http://www.pcpcc.net/content/joint-principles-patient-centered-medical-home (accessed May 15, 2013).

8. National Committee for Quality Assurance. Patient-Centered Medical Home Program. Online at: http://www.ncqa.org/Programs/Recognition/PatientCenteredMedicalHome-PCMH.aspx (accessed May 15, 2013).

9. Adams, K., and J. M. Corrigan, eds. 2003. *Priority areas for national action: Transforming health care quality.* Washington, D.C.: National Academies Press.

Achieving STEEEP Care

Chapter 15

Safe Care*

Jan Compton and Donald Kennerly

CONTENTS

INTRODUCTION

Patient safety is an integral component of STEEEP care. As defined by the Institute of Medicine (IOM), safe care should avoid injuries to patients from care that is intended to help them.[1] Consistent with this definition, the BHCS patient safety vision has three components: (1) achieving no preventable deaths, (2) ensuring no preventable injuries, and (3) seeking no preventable risk.[2,3] These goals require strategic efforts in the categories of culture, processes, and technology.

BHCS established a system-level Office of Patient Safety (OPS), which has achieved significant standardization of safety processes and implementation of evidence-based patient safety practices. Associated with these improvements, BHCS has made significant progress toward reducing hospital-standardized

---

* An earlier version of this chapter appeared in the American Journal of Medical Quality (Kennerly D., Richter K.M., Good V., Compton J., Ballard D.J. 2011. Journey to no preventable risk: the Baylor Health Care System patient safety experience. *American Journal of Medical Quality* 26(1): 43–52).

mortality rates and rates of hospital-acquired adverse events. This chapter will describe these improvements, as well as specific techniques BHCS has used to achieve them.

ORGANIZATIONAL RESOURCE FOR PATIENT SAFETY

BHCS established the OPS in 2005. Consistent with the IOM's recommendation for "all health care settings to establish comprehensive patient safety programs operated by trained personnel within a culture of safety,"[4] the OPS seeks to intensify existing patient safety programs, promote an organizational culture conducive to recognizing and resolving situations that pose a risk of patient injury, develop patient safety innovations, and guide employees in the adoption of the values of a safety culture. Its system-wide activities include the BHCS hospitals, HealthTexas Provider Network ambulatory care sites, and the Baylor Quality Alliance (BHCS's accountable care organization). This global approach facilitates the widespread standardization of processes and outcomes.[5]

BHCS also established a system-level Patient Safety Committee in 2005, with broad professional and institutional representation, to advise and guide the OPS. The OPS also relies heavily on data analytic support from the STEEEP Analytics Department (see Chapter 10) in its work to support patient safety improvement across BHCS facilities by: (1) assisting them to set goals that are challenging but attainable, (2) using measurement systems to show current performance, and (3) providing resources, such as coaching and training.

BIENNIAL PATIENT SAFETY SITE VISITS

As part of its efforts to measure and improve patient safety across the system, the OPS introduced biennial site visits to explore facility effectiveness with regard to patient safety. Site visits are akin to a health "checkup." Their purpose is to identify facility-specific patient safety concerns that require follow up, good/best practices for dissemination across the system, and areas of improvement, identified at multiple hospitals, that can be spread across BHCS to improve patient safety. Site visits are preceded by a detailed data review by the site visit team. This review and the site visit findings are summarized in a formal document describing opportunities for shared learning. The biennial site visits facilitate the dissemination of evidence-based best practices and help the OPS formulate future areas of focus to improve patient safety throughout BHCS.

Patient safety site visits utilize a focus group format and are intended to be a "well checkup" rather than a regulatory visit (i.e., they do not have punitive intentions). Frontline staff from all areas—evening as well as day staff—are included. Representatives attend from various areas of the organization, including the Office of Patient Centeredness, senior leadership, Risk Management, Human Resources, Health Care Improvement, and Baylor Information Services, to collectively learn about concerns specific to their functional departments and provide immediate feedback when issues are raised.

STANDARDIZATION OF CARE TO IMPROVE PATIENT SAFETY

In addition to the changes driven by the OPS, the BHCS Best Care Committee (the STEEEP Governance Council's precursor) championed greater standardization of evidence-based care across the system, which contributes to all domains of STEEEP. Standardization was achieved with the use of order sets, particularly those for common conditions, such as heart failure and community-acquired pneumonia.

BHCS has also driven patient safety and quality improvement using a Physician Champion model. System- and hospital-level physician champions are compensated for providing intellectual capital and leadership related to order set design, order set deployment, and clinical process improvement. Using academic detailing principles, these physicians motivate, encourage, and offer medical expertise to collaboratively design solutions to address challenges to quality improvement and to support standardization of evidence-based processes of care.[6] Patient Safety Physician Champions work at the hospital level to facilitate the alignment of system and hospital patient safety goals, assist with adverse event (AE) review and patient safety rounds, and to represent patient safety at major medical and executive committee meetings.

PATIENT SAFETY STRATEGIES AND GOALS

BHCS's strategies and tactics to decrease mortality, AEs, and patient risk can be divided into the three categories of culture, processes, and technology.[7]

Culture

Reliable industries have long recognized the importance of cultural change to improve safe practices and improve quality.[7] To identify and address cultural "potholes" and work toward a culture of safety, BHCS uses a Survey of the Attitudes and Practices of Patient Safety. Answers to survey questions are based on one of two forms: frequency (e.g., always, sometimes, most of the time, rarely, never) or agreement (strongly agree, agree, neutral, disagree, and strongly disagree). This instrument measures four domains: leadership, teamwork, reporting and feedback, and resources. This biennial survey, which began in 2005, facilitates data-driven conversations that are needed to improve patient safety across the system.

Gaps identified through the cultural self-assessment are addressed via multidisciplinary project-based initiatives, such as:

- Stop the Line[8]
  Stop the Line encourages employees to speak up anytime they have a patient safety concern by using the words: "I need some clarity." This helps to clarify expectations, provides employees with a script, and promotes unambiguous support of those who speak up in good faith.
- Teamwork Improves Patient Safety[9]
  One route for improving safety is to ensure that individuals, organizations, and teams learn from their errors; cultures must exist to make this process safe and, therefore, successful. The Teamwork Improves Patient Safety program provides teams with the tools they need to adopt a culture of patient safety.
- Standardized Communication or SBAR (Situation-Background-Assessment-Recommendation) Training[10]
  With SBAR, employees standardize communication by presenting the Situation, Background, Assessment, and Recommendation in an ordered statement. For example, a nurse calling a physician with a question about a patient's care would present the situation in a 5- to 10-second statement; give the background (objective data, such as vitals and labs); provide an assessment (a possible diagnosis of the problem); and offer a recommendation (a statement of what the nurse thinks needs to be done for the patient).

Patient Safety Processes

BHCS's second major strategic category for patient safety improvement is the area of clinical processes. Goals are set based on patient benefit, alignment with regulators and payers, alignment with other existing and planned programs, and the amount of "leadership capital" needed to effect meaningful change. Processes, which are measured using the percentage adoption of the target practice, include these goals:

- Increase evidence-based order set use[11]
- Increase use of World Health Organization Safe Surgery Saves Lives (WHO SSSL) processes[12]
- Reduce adverse drug events[13]
- Increase adherence to National Patient Safety Goals[14]
- Increase use of National Quality Forum Safe Practices[15]

- Reduce use of urinary catheters[16]
- Reduce hospital-acquired pressure ulcers[17]
- Increase obstetrical excellence
- Reduce falls[18]
- Increase employee influenza vaccination[19]

Technology

The third strategic category for patient safety improvement within BHCS is technology: preventing AEs, and improving patient safety and patient centeredness through electronic medical records and clinical decision support, computerized physician order entry, and bar code medication administration. Although health information technology has considerable promise to improve patient safety, its complexity can lead to unintended and unforeseen consequences. It is imperative for health information technology efforts to be aligned with the maxim to "first do no harm." This requires multidisciplinary coordination between relevant departments to create an integrated, system-wide approach to identifying errors, evaluating causes, and taking appropriate actions to improve performance.[20]

OUTCOMES RELATED TO PATIENT SAFETY

Hospital-Standardized Mortality Ratio

The first goal of the BHCS patient safety vision is to achieve no preventable deaths. Defining a "preventable death," however, is typically not straightforward.[21] To examine mortality, BHCS calculates hospital standardized mortality ratios (HSMRs) (see Chapter 1).

Hospital-Acquired Adverse Events

The second goal of the BHCS patient safety vision is to achieve "no preventable injuries." Like preventable deaths, preventable injuries can be challenging to define and measure.[13] Voluntary AE reporting systems underreport adverse outcomes, primarily capturing "near misses."[22,23] To obtain a more objective measure of the AE rates in its hospitals, BHCS adapted and implemented the Institute for Healthcare Improvement (IHI) Global Trigger tool as the Baylor Adverse Event Measurement Tool (BAEMT).[24,25]

The BAEMT uses a trigger tool methodology to retrospectively identify AEs through standardized review of randomly selected patient records from which the AE rate is estimated. Like the IHI Global Trigger Tool, the BAEMT looks for AEs in six broad areas: medical care, surgical, medication, intensive care, perinatal, and emergency department,[26] but asks nurse reviewers to provide more detailed characterization of identified AEs, including the type, NCC MERP (National Coordinating Council for Medication Error Reporting and Prevention) harm score, a judgment of preventability, whether the AE was present on admission, and whether it stemmed from care provided or omission of indicated care. Nurse reviewers are also asked to write a brief structured summary of the AE. These additional details enable BHCS to use the BAEMT data for system-wide learning and improvement, focusing primarily on hospital-acquired AEs.[24,25]

FUTURE WORK IN PATIENT SAFETY

The third aim of the BHCS patient safety vision is to seek no preventable risk. Although specific metrics for preventable risk are still under development, BHCS has identified several initiatives to help achieve this aim. In addition to embracing the tenets of high-reliability organizations and reliability in health care,[27] a specific initiative is consistent use of the WHO SSSL checklist to improve the reliability of surgical care.[12] On September 29, 2009, the Operating Policy and Procedure Board of Directors unanimously adopted a resolution to fully implement the WHO SSSL checklist, affirming its commitment to surgeons, anesthesia personnel, and staff to facilitate team success in doing all the right things, on all patients, all of the time.

BHCS also plans further improvements in its patient safety culture, including measurement of the implementation effectiveness of "Stop the Line," reduced tolerance for disruptive behavior, and growing transparency regarding AEs. In addition, BHCS plans to further improve patient safety processes by intensifying reductions in procedure- and surgery-related AEs (identified as the most common type by the BAEMT) and exploring management of fatigue. In the area of technology, BHCS plans to increase electronic order set deployment (more than 300 have been deployed as of 2012), bar coded prescription administration, electronic alerts for prescription and diagnosis interactions, and use of electronic reminders.

CONCLUSION

Although changes in culture, processes, and technology are recognized as having the potential to improve patient safety and health care quality, there is little evidence that connects such changes to measurable patient outcomes, such as inpatient mortality and AE rates. The journey to safe patient care requires a long-term vision, system-wide alignment of strategies and processes, and an understanding from organizational leadership that improved quality and safety are fundamental business objectives. Goals to improve specific aspects of patient safety, such as preventable deaths and injuries, must be carefully and specifically defined, and metrics must be chosen to reliably determine progress (or a lack thereof) toward the outcomes related to these aims. BHCS has demonstrated that a balanced focus is required among patient safety culture, processes, and technology to achieve sustainable patient safety improvements.

REFERENCES

1. Corrigan, J. M., M. S. Donaldson, L. T. Kohn, S. K. Maguire, and K. C. Pike. 2001. *Crossing the quality chasm: A new health system for the 21st century.* Washington, DC: National Academy Press.
2. Champy, J., and H. Greenspun. 2010. *Reengineering health care* 2010. Upper Saddle River, NJ: FT Press.
3. Harrington, L., D. Kennerly, and C. Johnson. 2011. Safety issues related to the electronic medical record (EMR): Synthesis of the literature from the last decade, 2000–2009. *Journal of Healthcare Management* 56 (1): 31–43; discussion 43–44.
4. Institute of Medicine. 2004. *Patient safety: Achieving a new standard for care.* Washington, D.C.: National Academies Press.
5. Ballard, D. J., B. Spreadbury, and R. S. Hopkins, 3rd. 2004. Health care quality improvement across the Baylor Health Care System: The first century. *Proceedings (Baylor University Medical Center)* 17 (3): 277–288.
6. Ballard, D. J., G. Ogola, N. S. Fleming, D. Heck, J. Gunderson, R. Mehta, R. Khetan, and J. D. Kerr. 2008. The impact of standardized order sets on quality and financial outcomes. In *Advances in patient safety: New directions and alternative approaches,* eds. K. Henriksen, et al. Rockville, MD: AHRQ Publications, nos. 08-0034 (1–4).
7. Leonard, M., S. Graham, and D. Bonacum. 2004. The human factor: The critical importance of effective teamwork and communication in providing safe care. *Quality and Safety in Health Care* 13 (Suppl 1): i85–90.
8. Furman, C., and R. Caplan. 2007. Applying the Toyota Production System: Using a patient safety alert system to reduce error. *The Joint Commission Journal on Quality and Patient Safety* 33 (7): 376–386.
9. Firth-Cozens, J., Cultures for improving patient safety through learning: The role of teamwork. *Quality in Health Care* 10 (Suppl 2): ii26–31.
10. Compton, J., K. Copeland, S. Flanders, C. Cassity, M. Spetman, Y. Xiao, and D. Kennerly. 2012. Implementing SBAR across a large multihospital health system. *The Joint Commission Journal on Quality and Patient Safety* 38 (6): 261–268.
11. Fleming, N. S., G. Ogola, and D. J. Ballard. 2009. Implementing a standardized order set for community-acquired pneumonia: Impact on mortality and cost. *The Joint Commission Journal on Quality and Patient Safety* 35 (8): 414–421.
12. Haynes, A. B., T. G. Weiser, W. R. Berry, S. R. Lipsitz, A. H. Breizat, E. P. Dellinger, T. Herbosa, et al. 2009. A surgical safety checklist to reduce morbidity and mortality in a global population. *New England Journal of Medicine* 360 (5): 491–499.
13. Kohn, L. T., J. M. Corrigan, and M. S. Donaldson. 1999. *To err is human: Building a safer health system.* Washington, DC: National Academy Press.

14. Joint Commission. National patient safety goals. Online at: http://www.jointcommission. org/standards_information/npsgs.aspx (accessed October 30, 2012).

15. Agency for Healthcare Research and Quality. 30 safe practices for better health care. Online at: http://www.ahrq.gov/qual/30safe.htm (accessed October 30. 2012).

16. Berenholtz, S. M., P. J. Pronovost, P. A. Lipsett, D. Hobson, K. Earsing, J. E. Farley, S. Milanovich, et al. 2004. Eliminating catheter-related bloodstream infections in the intensive care unit. *Critical Care Medicine* 32 (10): 2014–2020.

17. Duncan, K. D. 2007. Preventing pressure ulcers: The goal is zero. *The Joint Commission Journal for Quality and Patient Safety* 33 (10): 605–610.

18. Sutton, J. C., P. J. Standen, and W. A. Wallace. 1994. Patient accidents in hospital: Incidence, documentation and significance. *British Journal of Clinical Practitioners*, 1994. 48(2): p. 63–66.

19. Zimmerman, R. K., M. P. Nowalk, C. J. Lin, M. Raymund, D. E. Fox, J. D. Harper, M. D. Tanis, and B. C. Willis. 2009. Factorial design for improving influenza vaccination among employees of a large health system. *Infection Control and Hospital Epidemiology* 30 (7): 691–697.

20. Kohn, L. T., J. M. Corrigan, and M. S. Donaldson. 1999. *To err is human: Building a safer health system.* Washington, DC: National Academy Press.

21. Wilson, D. S., J. McElligott, and L. P. Fielding. 1992. Identification of preventable trauma deaths: Confounded inquiries? *Journal of Trauma* 32 (1): 45–51.

22. Cullen, D. J., D. W. Bates, S. D. Small, J. B. Cooper, A. R. Nemeskal, and L. L. Leape. 1995. The incident reporting system does not detect adverse drug events: a problem for quality improvement. *The Joint Commission Journal on Quality Improvement* 21 (10): 541–548.

23. Rozich, J. D., C. R. Haraden, and R. K. Resar. 2003. Adverse drug event trigger tool: A practical methodology for measuring medication related harm. *Quality and Safety in Health Care* 12 (3): 194–200.

24. Kennerly, D. A., M. Saldaña, R. Kudyakov, B. da Graca, D. Nicewander, and J. Compton. 2013. Description and evaluation of adaptations to the Global Trigger Tool to enhance value to adverse event reduction efforts. *Journal of Patient Safety* 9 (2): 87–95.

25. Good, V. S., M. Saldana, R. Gilder, D. Nicewander, and D. A. Kennerly, 2011. Large-scale deployment of the Global Trigger Tool across a large hospital system: Refinements for the characterisation of adverse events to support patient safety learning opportunities. *BMJ Quality and Safety* 20 (1): 25–30.

26. Griffin, F. A., and R. K. Resar. 2007. *IHI Global Trigger Tool for measuring adverse events.* Cambridge, MA: Institute for Healthcare Improvement.

27. Ballard, D. J., G. Ogola, N. S. Fleming, B. D. Stauffer, B. M. Leonard, R. Khetan, and C. W. Yancy. 2010. Impact of a standardized heart failure order set on mortality, readmission, and quality and costs of care. *International Journal for Quality in Health Care* 22 (6): 437–444.

Chapter 16

Timely and Effective Care

Andrew Masica

CONTENTS

INTRODUCTION

High-quality health systems consistently deliver care that is evidence-based and clinically indicated for individual patients at appropriate time points in their care episodes (collectively representing the concepts of effectiveness and timeliness). Timeliness refers to the provision of health care services with continually reduced waiting times and without delays—for both the patient and the provider.[1] Delays in diagnosis and treatment can lead to physical and emotional harm; therefore, prompt service is essential in improving the health care experience. Effectiveness within the context of the clinical setting refers to using evidence-based interventions demonstrated to have better outcomes than alternative approaches,[1] particularly those shown to be beneficial in real-world health care delivery environments. Interventions may include therapy, diagnostic tests, and preventive care. Effective evidence-based care must not be underused or overused, and ineffective potentially harmful care must be avoided altogether.

TIMELINESS AND EFFECTIVENESS (CLINICAL EXCELLENCE) SUBCOMMITTEE

In addition to its performance award program (see Chapter 4), BHCS utilizes its STEEEP Governance Council (SGC) to connect its efforts and investments to achieve synergy across the domains of STEEEP (see Chapter 1). As one of five SGC subcommittees, the Timeliness and Effectiveness Subcommittee provides clinical leadership for BHCS quality improvement efforts that are primarily related to direct patient care, e.g., use of a new clinical care pathway for a specific condition. Given this focus, the committee is composed of a higher percentage of physicians than the other SGC subgroups, and has added the term "Clinical Excellence" to its nomenclature to emphasize its prerogative in this area.

The committee's scope of work centers on identifying and supporting implementation of health care delivery practices that:

- are evidence-based;
- work in "real world" clinical settings;
- provide value (in terms of a favorable incremental quality improvement-to-cost ratio); and
- are consistent with established guidelines and best practices while representing an appropriate use of resources.

The committee oversees high-impact clinical initiatives, and is co-chaired by a system-level vice president (a physician with experience in evidence-based medicine, quality improvement tactics, and health services research), and a system-level director from the department of the chief nursing officer (who is well versed in practice adoption strategies). Other committee members are system leaders representing a range of clinical disciplines and nonclinical BHCS departments. Guiding principles for the committee (many of which are aligned with or adapted from the Institute of Medicine's prior descriptions of timeliness and effectiveness)[1] include:

- Delivery of the "right care at the right time" should have the highest priority.
- Initiatives receiving committee support should have a smooth clinical workflow and be both feasible and sustainable in direct patient care environments.
- Unnecessary delays in care should be minimized.
- Clinical care processes should be centered on patient welfare.
- Care improvement initiatives should be based on systematically acquired evidence to determine whether a proposed intervention produces better outcomes than alternatives.
- Underuse of effective care and overuse of ineffective care should be avoided.
- Evidence-based practice is supported by integrating evidence with clinical expertise and patient values.
- Continued expansion of the knowledge base about effective care and its use in health care settings should be promoted.
- Initiatives that fall under the committee's scope undergo a systematic review process before any implementation decisions.

- Clinical practitioners (and BHCS at an organizational level) are encouraged to be reflective and systematic in studying their own patterns of care and outcomes.
- Clinical improvement initiatives must be consistent with other STEEEP council activities.

IMPLEMENTATION AND PROGRAM EVALUATION SUCCESS STORIES

As an example of the type of work supported by the SGC and its Timeliness and Effectiveness Subcommittee, BHCS has demonstrated success using a multifaceted implementation approach in the inpatient setting for adoption of a standardized clinical care pathway for patients with pneumonia.[2,3] In addition to deploying an evidence-based pneumonia order set, there was a concurrent pneumonia education program for nursing staff, activation of physician pneumonia champions at the system and hospital levels, and a tracking program (including a feedback loop to physicians) for order set use. This approach was highly effective in improving adoption of the order set, with a 50 percent increase in use over a 30-month period; adherence has consistently remained above 80 percent across all BHCS acute care hospitals since 2008. A similar implementation program helped drive adoption of a congestive heart failure care pathway to >70 percent usage across BHCS during the first full year following rollout.[4]

Moving beyond the process measure of practice adherence, BHCS has formally assessed the impacts of these implementation programs for its pneumonia and heart failure care pathways on clinical and cost outcomes (see Chapter 12).

Importantly, having locally generated evidence regarding the pneumonia and heart failure care pathways' beneficial impacts was a major factor in achieving physician acceptance and changing behavior at the facility level. This influence is attributed to the belief that data from one's own practice environment often seem less remote and more reliable than results from a highly controlled clinical trial.[5,6]

These evaluations of the effect of standardized order set implementation are only two examples of the numerous instances where a stepwise cycle of quality improvement (Figure 16.1) was applied to clinical care initiatives with good results at BHCS. Sustained success is best achieved if this systematic approach is embedded into organizational operations.

LESSONS LEARNED

Like many innovative concepts in health care, hardwiring timeliness and effectiveness into daily operations is associated with many challenges. One

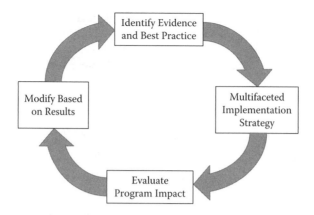

FIGURE 16.1 Stepwise cycle of quality improvement used at Baylor Health Care System.

key issue is determining what should be done first when competing priorities exist and resources are limited. Within BHCS, the SGC sets these priorities and coordinates the implementation of quality projects based on evidence gathered from robust evaluation.

A second challenge lies in duplication of efforts across different hospitals (or even within hospitals). Although BHCS has a corporate-level quality improvement structure, local hospital teams are encouraged to develop, implement, and track results of improvement projects at their own facilities. With multidisciplinary representation from all BHCS facilities, the SGC serves to bring local evidence to the system as a whole, and make recommendations based on the implications of these local programs.

Finally, BHCS physicians largely operate under a fee-for-service, independent practitioner model. Thus, some of the financial incentives afforded in other scenarios (e.g., a scenario including employed physicians) to promote adoption of specific clinical practices have not been feasible historically. As BHCS and other delivery systems shift toward a population health management, accountable care model, additional leverage should be available to encourage evidence-based and clinically appropriate care.

CONCLUSION

Similar to the other core aims of STEEEP health care, timeliness and effectiveness need clear governance. BHCS has established this by appointing a clinically oriented subcommittee operating under its SGC in these areas. Ultimately, the BHCS Timeliness and Effectiveness Subcommittee is charged with supporting delivery of "the right care for a specific patient at the right time," through a systematic approach of (1) best practice identification;

(2) multifaceted, strategic implementation; and (3) impact evaluation. The presence of this type of clinical oversight group is a central component of a health system quality improvement enterprise.

REFERENCES

1. Corrigan, J. M., M. S. Donaldson, L. T. Kohn, S. K. Maguire, and K. C. Pike. 2001. *Crossing the quality chasm: A new health system for the 21st century.* Washington, DC: National Academy Press.
2. Fleming, N. S., G. Ogola, and D. J. Ballard. 2009. Implementing a standardized order set for community-acquired pneumonia: Impact on mortality and cost. *The Joint Commission Journal on Quality and Patient Safety* 35 (8): 414–421.
3. Ballard, D. J., G. Ogola, N. S. Fleming, D. Heck, J. Gunderson, R. Mehta, R. Khetan, and J. D. Kerr. 2008. The impact of standardized order sets on quality and financial outcomes. In *Advances in patient safety: New directions and alternative approaches,* eds. K. Henriksen, et al. Rockville, MD: AHRQ Publications, nos. 08-0034 (1–4).
4. Ballard, D. J., G. Ogola, N. S. Fleming, B. D. Stauffer, B. M. Leonard, R. Khetan, and C. W. Yancy. 2010. Impact of a standardized heart failure order set on mortality, readmission, and quality and costs of care. *International Journal for Quality in Health Care* 22 (6): 437–444.
5. Horn, S. D., and J. Gassaway. 2010. Practice based evidence: Incorporating clinical heterogeneity and patient-reported outcomes for comparative effectiveness research. *Medical Care* 48 (6 Suppl): S17–22.
6. Tunis, S. R., D. B. Stryer, and C. M. Clancy. 2003. Practical clinical trials: Increasing the value of clinical research for decision making in clinical and health policy. *JAMA* 290 (12): 1624–1632.

Chapter 17

Efficient Care

Robert T. Green and Donald Kennerly

CONTENTS

INTRODUCTION

In an efficient health care system, resources are used to achieve the best value for the money spent.[1] When care is delivered inefficiently, resources are used without direct benefit to the patient, which results in waste. At least two ways to improve efficiency exist: (1) reduce waste and (2) reduce administrative or production costs.[2] Making care more efficient while maintaining or improving health care quality is an important focus for BHCS. Achieving this goal requires strong collaboration between finance and quality leaders, consistent with the fifth of the Institute for Healthcare Improvement Seven Leadership Leverage Points: make the chief financial officer a quality champion.[3] BHCS has demonstrated such collaboration between finance and quality leaders for years as part of its longstanding commitment to STEEEP care.

APPROACHES TO ORGANIZING AND MANAGING SYSTEM-WIDE QUALITY INITIATIVES

BHCS's longstanding commitment to collaboration between leaders in the area of quality and finance (see Chapter 5) and the structure of the STEEEP Governance Council (SGC), which brings together clinical, financial, and administrative leaders (see Chapter 1), mean the organization is prepared to respond rapidly to changes in the health care environment. Current challenges include payment reforms and reimbursement changes, such as those introduced by the Medicare Value-Base Purchasing (VBP) program, which focuses incentives on value, quality, and performance. Poor-performing hospitals stand to lose millions of dollars in Medicare reimbursements with the introduction of VBP.[4] BHCS, because of its ongoing commitment to STEEEP care, has little to fear. It is positioned well for this increased emphasis on reimbursing value rather than volume. Specifically, BHCS's commitment to measuring and reporting its performance (see Chapter 10) meant that it was collecting and analyzing the measures included in the VBP total performance score before the program came into existence, and, therefore, was able to predict and anticipate the likely effects on its reimbursement.

MEDICARE BREAK-EVEN

Another specific challenge BHCS faces in the area of efficiency is the drive toward Medicare Break-Even, calculated by BHCS as cost reductions required to break even on Medicare business and commercial and managed care business assuming Medicare payment rates. From a business perspective, BHCS needs to cover both its direct and indirect costs, where direct costs are those for direct patient care and indirect costs are more general costs that are not identifiable to only one area, and are typically allocated across different areas. This means that BHCS must reduce costs so that total costs (direct plus indirect) are equivalent to reimbursement in order to break even. Currently, BHCS and other health care delivery organizations face Medicare reimbursement reductions related to the Patient Protection and Affordable Care Act. Commercial and managed care payment reductions are expected to follow these decreases. An increase in the number of Americans qualifying for Medicare, along with relatively high unemployment rates, are causing a decline in the proportion of payments from commercial payers. For these reasons, many markets are moving to new payment models, such as tiered networks, bundled/episode-based payments, risk sharing/accountable care organizations, and prospective capitation.[3] Health care delivery organizations need to have the requisite structure and competencies to support a rapid transition from volume-based payment to value-based payment.

The evolution of new payment models will require that metrics adapt alongside them. Table 17.1 compares selected current metrics under a fee-for-service payment model to selected future metrics under a fee-for-value payment model.

Creating a highly efficient cost structure to address these new payment models will require sustained effort across multiple fronts of BHCS. These include operational excellence, business restructuring, and clinical restructuring (Figure 17.1). Driving out waste and rework will be an important focus in each of these areas.

TABLE 17.1 Selected fee-for-service and fee-for-value payment metrics

Selected Current Metrics (Fee-for-Service)	Selected Future Metrics (Fee-for-Value)
Volume (daily census, admissions, emergency department visits, observations, surgeries)	Covered Lives (premium revenue per member per month, cost of care per member per month, incurred but not reported claims)
Payer Mix (commercial, government, or self-pay)	Patient Experience (communication, staff responsiveness, pain management, cleanliness/quietness, discharge information, overall hospital rating)
Price Increases	Utilization (MRI utilization rates)
Days Cash on Hand	Days Cash on Hand
Debt-to-Capital Ratio	Debt-to-Capital Ratio
Risk	Process Measures (acute myocardial infarction, heart failure, pneumonia, sepsis, smoking cessation, diabetes management)
Throughput (average length of stay, Medicare length of stay, emergency room length of stay)	Health Outcomes (mortality index, complication index, potentially avoidable admission, readmission)
Staffing (full-time employees, agency/contracted workers)	
Acuity (case mix index, Medicare case mix index)	

Creating a highly efficient cost structure requires:

Operational Excellence	Business Restructuring	Clinical Restructuring
Budgets and Controls	Mergers and Acquisitions	Care Processes
Revenue Cycle	Enhanced Capital Allocation	Physician Integration
Supply Chain	Operating Model Redesign	Narrow Networks
Measurement and Reporting	Portfolio Optimization	Service Distribution Optimization
Productivity	Payment Transition (fee-for-service to fee-for-value)	Care Continuum Coordination
Expense Management		Information Technology Operable Information Optimization
Progress Toward Comprehensive Cost Reduction		
Effective Transition/Change Management and Execution		
Hard	Harder	Hardest
Many Providers		Selected Leading Providers

FIGURE 17.1 Creating a highly efficient cost structure.

Improving efficiency of care related to processes will require Lean methodology to be deployed across sites of care and support functions. Some of the value streams currently being addressed across BHCS include:

- Emergency department registration
- Operating room throughput
- Strategic sourcing
- Emergency department throughput
- Operating room charge capture
- Diagnostic imaging
- Preadmission testing
- Inpatient length of stay

Some BHCS hospitals have also established Strategies and Tactics Operations Committees and are working at the local level to identify and reduce variation in cost drivers among physicians.

To ensure accountability for efficient care, tactical plans related to operational excellence, business restructuring, and clinical restructuring are embedded into the system-wide budget and strategic financial plan.

LESSONS LEARNED

The first lesson BHCS has learned in its journey toward providing more efficient care is that efficiency needs to be prioritized at the structural level. Organizations cannot become efficient overnight; they must intentionally develop structures to facilitate greater efficiency. BHCS formed the SGC to ensure that financial concerns were incorporated into system-wide quality improvement objectives and initiatives.

The second lesson is that finance and quality leaders must form a partnership to drive STEEEP care. A holistic approach to process improvement is required. BHCS is committed to strengthening the connection between quality and financial objectives.

The third lesson is that the organization must strengthen its commitment to delivering high-value health care (quality of care for the cost of care). Payment reform and reimbursement changes focus incentives on value, quality, and performance, and health care delivery organizations must rapidly respond to these changes while retaining a patient-centered focus.

CONCLUSION

Making care more efficient while maintaining or improving health care quality is an important goal for BHCS, consistent with the provision of STEEEP care.

Achieving this goal requires strong collaboration between finance and quality leaders. This partnership and the organization's commitment to patient value and its infrastructure supporting the delivery of STEEEP care have positioned it for success in a rapidly changing health care environment.

REFERENCES

1. Palmer, S., and D.J. Torgerson. 1999. Economic notes: Definitions of efficiency. *British Medical Journal* 318 (7191): 1136.
2. Corrigan, J. M., M. S. Donaldson, L. T. Kohn, S. K. Maguire, and K. C. Pike. 2001. *Crossing the quality chasm: A new health system for the 21st century.* Washington, DC: National Academy Press.
3. Reinertsen, J. L., M. Bisognano, and M. D. Pugh. 2008. *Seven leadership leverage points for organization-level improvement in health care*, 2nd ed. Cambridge, MA: Institute for Healthcare Improvement.
4. MX.com. 2013. Value-based purchasing: Improving the U.S. healthcare system by focusing on quality rather than quantity. White Paper. Online at: http://mx.com/resources/whitepapers/improving-us-healthcare-system-through-value-based-purchasing (accessed May 15, 2013).

Chapter 18

Equitable Care

Clifford T. Fullerton

CONTENTS

INTRODUCTION

According to the Institute of Medicine, the goal of a health care system is to improve health status and to do so in a manner that reduces health disparities among particular subgroups.[1] When health care is delivered equitably, access to care and quality of services are based on individuals' specific needs rather than personal characteristics unrelated to the reason for seeking care. Quality of care should not vary based on characteristics, such as gender, race, age, ethnicity, income, education, disability, sexual orientation, or location of residence.[1] BHCS has a longstanding commitment to equitable care dating back to 1903, when the first hospital in the system was founded by George W. Truett, pastor of the First Baptist Church of Dallas, envisioned as "a great humanitarian hospital, one to which people of all creeds and those of none may come with equal confidence."[2] This chapter describes some of the specific strategies and initiatives BHCS has implemented in its efforts to drive health care equity across the organization.

STRUCTURES TO SUPPORT HEALTH EQUITY

The BHCS STEEEP Governance Council (SGC) connects efforts and investments to achieve integration across the domains of STEEEP (see Chapter 1). Equity initiatives are primarily driven by the Equity Subcommittee.

Other structures supporting equitable care within BHCS include the BHCS Institute of Chronic Disease and Care Redesign, which works to improve access for patients through its Chronic Disease Council and Transitional Care Governance Council (which includes an Equity Subcommittee). The Chronic Disease Council helps ensure that patients with chronic disease, regardless of race, ethnicity, insurance status, or other personal characteristics, have access to care to help manage their condition. It works closely with seven HealthTexas Provider Network (HTPN) community care clinics located at four BHCS hospitals to provide this care.

In the ambulatory care setting, HTPN's Best Care Committee (see Chapter 14) includes a subcommittee on equity, responsible primarily for addressing diabetes disparities and increasing the collection of data related to race, ethnicity, and primary language. These data enable HTPN to better understand the gaps in care that may arise through racial, ethnic, and language differences, and to redesign care to meet the specific needs of different populations.

VOLUNTEERS-IN-MEDICINE
FOR COMMUNITY HEALTH IMPROVEMENT

The Volunteers-in-Medicine program is HTPN's community health improvement and service campaign. Since 1998, the Volunteers-in-Medicine program has provided HTPN physicians and staff with opportunities to improve health equity throughout the Dallas–Fort Worth community. Through a number of innovative programs coordinated by the Office of Community Care, physicians and staff can donate time, services, and money to achieve these goals:

1. Expand access to care for the medically underserved
2. Improve the health status of the medically underserved
3. Provide physician leadership throughout the community
4. Support HTPN's nonprofit status
5. Create a culture of service throughout the organization

Originally built around the idea of having a defined strategy for physician-based community service work, the Volunteers-in-Medicine program has grown to provide opportunities for employed physicians to participate in a coordinated approach to community service as well as supporting several medical missions to developing countries. It thereby furthers HTPN's commitment to providing patient care, medical education, research, and community service.[3]

COMMUNITY-BASED PARTNERSHIP
TO REDUCE EMERGENCY DEPARTMENT UTILIZATION
AMONG THE UNINSURED

National data indicate that nearly 19 percent of nonelderly individuals are without health insurance.[4] Being uninsured is more common among individuals with lower incomes and education levels, and among ethnic minorities.[4] Minority and low-income Americans without insurance generally lack a regular source of medical care and suffer from medical conditions that are either preventable or easily treated in the outpatient setting.[5]

Project Access Dallas (PAD) is a community-wide, faith-health partnership that was developed to provide access to care and preventive services for low-income working individuals without health insurance residing in Dallas, Texas. PAD's geographical focus is Central Dallas, an area characterized by high proportions of groups who are likely to use the emergency department (ED) as a usual source of care.[6]

PAD was the result of a long-term partnership between faith-based organizations, government agencies, social service organizations, hospitals, the local medical society, several universities, and a medical school. BHCS is one of the key community partners of PAD. By creating an organizational and administrative infrastructure, PAD provides coordinated access for the uninsured to existing faith-based community health clinics, volunteer primary and specialty care physicians, and local hospitals and pharmacies.[6]

Physicians, hospitals, and ancillary partners who volunteer in the program determine their level of participation by agreeing to donate their services to see a set number of patients per year. Patients are referred for enrollment in the program from volunteer physicians, partnering charity health clinics, and partnering hospitals. When a patient is enrolled in PAD, he or she is assigned a primary care physician, receives $750 per year in pharmacy benefits, and has access to free specialty care, labs, ancillary procedures, care coordination, and inpatient hospital care.[7]

Since PAD began seeing patients in April 2002, the program has steadily grown to include more than 2,200 physicians, 17 hospitals, 14 community and charity health clinics, 10 ancillary service support organizations, 2 national laboratory service organizations, and more than 40,000 nationwide pharmacies.[7] A 2012 study found that PAD program enrollees had significantly fewer ED visits and fewer inpatient hospital days than comparable nonenrollees. Direct hospital costs were 60 percent and indirect costs 50 percent lower for enrollees.[6]

IMPROVING CARE THROUGH A DIABETES EQUITY PROGRAM

In 2009, BHCS was awarded a $1.7 million grant from The Merck Company Foundation to improve and expand diabetes care by developing community collaborations throughout Dallas County as part of the Diabetes Equity Program (DEP). BHCS and its community partners created the DEP because Type 2 diabetes is one of the most prevalent and fastest growing chronic diseases in the United States, with the burden of illness falling disproportionately on minorities.[8] African American and Hispanic patients experience higher rates of diabetes-related mortality and complications than Caucasian patients, and are less likely to receive recommended processes of care.[9,10] BHCS recognized that improved community health can be achieved through medical, public health–oriented community interventions, and various forms of partnerships.[11,12]

BHCS formed a community partnership including HTPN, PAD, and Dallas Charity Clinics to implement the DEP. The goal was to reduce health care disparities by improving access to and quality of diabetes care, and health outcomes for low-income, minority, uninsured, and underserved individuals residing in Dallas County. The DEP was implemented at multiple sites in underserved communities located throughout Dallas County.

The program uses the patient education component of CoDE© (Community Diabetes Education), which has been successfully implemented in one PAD enrollment and medical home site, CitySquare (formerly Central Dallas Ministries Community Health Services), and has demonstrated a significant improvement in glycemic control (as measured by HbA1c levels) for patients who participated in the program for 12 months.[13] CoDE utilizes a certified community health worker to deliver an educational diabetes curriculum that was initiated through a grassroots, community-based effort to improve access to diabetes educational services, and reduce health disparities in the large population of uninsured, underserved Mexican Americans living in East Dallas.

The CoDE model was implemented in five community clinics, providing patients with a structured, systematic approach to managing diabetes. DEP patients achieved significant improvements in the primary outcome measure, glycemic control (HbA1c), with the mean decreasing from 8.7 percent at baseline to 7.4 percent. These findings suggest that this community health worker–led model of care is an effective model for diabetes management that can be successfully replicated in clinics serving low-income, Hispanic populations.[14]

BHCS's successful implementation of the DEP in Dallas communities provides a roadmap for reducing health disparities. New delivery of care models that use community health workers to provide patient education and care coordination have the ability to transform health care and improve outcomes for patients with chronic conditions.[14]

LESSONS LEARNED

BHCS has learned that for equity to be prioritized across the organization, it must be incorporated into the organization vision, mission, and values.

At BHCS, the commitment to equity is most clearly invoked by the mission statement: "... to serve all people through exemplary health care, education, research, and community service." The BHCS value of servanthood also drives the provision of equitable care throughout the system.

The second lesson BHCS has learned is that providing opportunities for employees to become involved in community outreach can be a powerful vehicle in achieving equitable care. BHCS and HTPN have long encouraged physicians to donate their time and talents to the community. The Volunteers-in-Medicine program and the various community partnerships between BHCS and organizations, such as PAD and community health clinics, enable physicians and others to prioritize community service. This work facilitates improved health care access, care delivery, and care outcomes throughout the community.

As it has enhanced its focus on equity as part of its commitment to STEEEP care, BHCS also has learned that system-wide standardization in implementing and measuring the results of quality initiatives is integral to improvement. BHCS achieves standardization through several councils dedicated to equitable care, including the SGC and its Equity Subcommittee, the Chronic Disease Council, and the HTPN Best Care Committee and its equity subcommittee. System-wide, culturally sensitive standardization of chronic care across the care continuum helps to ensure equitable care and outcomes for all patients.

CONCLUSION

BHCS is committed to providing equitable patient care—defined as care that provides consistent quality and is unrelated to patient characteristics, such as gender, ethnicity, geographic location, and socioeconomic status—as part of STEEEP care. Structures supporting equitable care within BHCS include the SGC, the Chronic Disease and Transitional Care Governance Council, and the HTPN Best Care Committee. BHCS and HTPN are central players as well in several specific initiatives to improve health equity throughout the Dallas–Fort Worth community, contributing resources and providing mechanisms through which employees can volunteer their time and talents. BHCS also conducts research to identify effective means of achieving equitable care. Results of one such project suggest the community health worker model may be a powerful tool in this area, particularly for chronic disease management.

REFERENCES

1. Corrigan, J. M., M. S. Donaldson, L. T. Kohn, S. K. Maguire, and K. C. Pike. 2001. *Crossing the quality chasm: A new health system for the 21st century.* Washington, DC: National Academy Press.

2. Mayberry, R. M., D. A. Nicewander, H. Qin, and D. J. Ballard. 2006. Improving quality and reducing inequities: A challenge in achieving best care. *Proceedings* (Baylor University Medical Center) 19 (2): 103–118.

3. Intermountain Healthcare. 20-day course for executives & QI leaders—Advanced Training Program (ATP). Online at: http://intermountainhealthcare.org/qualityandresearch/institute/courses/atp/Pages/home.aspx (accessed March 21, 2013).

4. The Kaiser Commission on Medicaid and the Uninsured. 2011. *The uninsured: A primer.* Menlo Park, CA: The Henry J. Kaiser Family Foundation.

5. Lurie, N., and T. Dubowitz. 2007. Health disparities and access to health. *JAMA* 297 (10): 1118–1121.

6. DeHaven, M., H. Kitzman-Ulrich, N. Gimpel, D. Culica, L. O'Neil, A. Marcee, B. Foster, M. Biggs, and J. Walton. 2012. The effects of a community-based partnership, Project Access Dallas (PAD), on emergency department utilization and costs among the uninsured. *Journal of Public Health* (Oxford) 34 (4): 577–583.

7. Project Access Dallas. Online at: http://www.projectaccess.info/ (accessed February 26, 2013).

8. Centers for Disease Control and Prevention. 2005. *National diabetes fact sheet: General information and national estimates on diabetes in the United States.* Atlanta: CDC.

9. Heisler, M., D. M. Smith, R. A. Hayward, S. L. Krein, and E. A. Kerr. 2003. Racial disparities in diabetes care processes, outcomes, and treatment intensity. *Medical Care* 41 (11): 1221–1232.

10. Sequist, T. D., G. M. Fitzmaurice, R. Marshall, S. Shaykevich, D. G. Safran, and J. Z. Ayanian. 2008. Physician performance and racial disparities in diabetes mellitus care. *Archives of Internal Medicine* 168 (11): 1145–1151.

11. Anderson, N L., E. R. Calvillo, and M. N. Fongwa. 2007. Community-based approaches to strengthen cultural competency in nursing education and practice. *Journal of Transcultural Nursing* 18 (1 Suppl): 49S–59S; discussion 60S–67S.

12. Srinivasan, S., and G.W. Collman. 2005. Evolving partnerships in community. *Environmental Health Perspectives* 113 (12): 1814–1816.

13. Culica, D., J. W. Walton, and E. A. Prezio. 2007. CoDE: Community diabetes education for uninsured Mexican Americans. *Proceedings* (*Baylor University Medical Center*) 20 (2): 111–117.

14. Walton, J. W., C. A. Snead, A. W. Collinsworth, and K. L. Schmidt. 2012. Reducing diabetes disparities through the implementation of a community health worker-led diabetes self-management education program. *Family & Community Health* 35 (2): 161–171.

Chapter 19

Patient-Centered Care

Terri Dyksterhouse Nuss

CONTENTS

INTRODUCTION

Servanthood (being of service to others) is one of the key BHCS values. Patient centeredness is the fundamental method of facilitating service and achieving trust. Patients need to be actively invited at every encounter, by every care-giver, to (1) participate in their own care; (2) offer their needs, values, prefer-ences; and (3) understand all of their options and the related consequences and commitments before making informed decisions. Important questions that health care systems must address include: How can health care delivery organizations accomplish this alongside highly directive, fast-moving pro-cesses that create time urgencies? And, how can they ensure that care is indi-vidualized while reaping the patient outcome benefits that can be achieved by applying standardized evidence-based care? BHCS has been addressing these challenges through its longstanding commitment to improving care through patient-centered concepts.

STRUCTURES TO SUPPORT PATIENT-CENTERED CARE

BHCS established the Ideal Patient Experience Charter in 2005 under which an Ideal Patient Experience Team was created. The team's goals were to create system-wide requirements to govern the Ideal Patient Experience, improve patient satisfaction scores across BHCS, systematize methods to obtain patient input, and use patient-centered measures in the BHCS overall marketing strategy.

In 2006, BHCS established the system-wide Office of Patient Centeredness. BHCS was innovative in understanding the need for infrastructure to define and support patient-centered effort. As recently as 2011, industry survey results suggest that as few as 6 percent of health care delivery systems in the United States have an executive leader devoted to patient-centered care.[1]

GOVERNANCE COMMITMENT TO PATIENT-CENTERED CARE

The ongoing BHCS Board commitment to patient centeredness is evident in the organization's goals and leadership incentive program. Patient centeredness is captured through patient satisfaction goals under the BHCS's "Service" area of focus. These goals are cascaded down to all employees, and are incorporated into the performance award program for leaders, placing a portion of their compensation at risk.

The Board's commitment to patient centeredness was recognized nationally in 2007 when BHCS won the first annual Leapfrog Patient-Centered Care Award. The BHCS Board's and executive leader's focus on improving patient centeredness have been instrumental in BHCS's improved performance on the "likelihood to recommend" and overall patients satisfaction scores over the past five years (Figure 19.1).

In 2009, the BHCS Board further demonstrated its commitment to improving patient centeredness by bringing the Patient- and Family-Centered Institute Training Seminar to Dallas. BHCS co-hosted this nonprofit national event with Children's Hospital, and sent 64 leaders, physicians, and staff to the three and a half-day seminar to gain better understanding of what patient centeredness means.

PROMOTING AND ESTABLISHING
A PATIENT-CENTERED CULTURE

Improving patient-centered care requires a major cultural shift throughout the organization. One of the early challenges associated with establishing a patient-centered culture at BHCS was alignment of the measurement and goal processes across the system. In 2006, four different vendors managed patient-centered metrics across the system, and patient surveys were often biased and administered only at the point of care. The first step in improving patient centeredness was to standardize the measurement and reporting of patient satisfaction. Around this same time, organizations across the United States were shifting toward use of the HCAHPS (Hospital Consumer Assessment of Healthcare Providers and Systems) survey to measure patient satisfaction and to ensure alignment with national priorities related to patient-centered care.

BHCS implemented central reporting for patient satisfaction metrics in its monthly Best Care Reports (now, STEEEP Care reports) and began educating leaders about the metrics through the BHCS Leadership Development Institute, communication plans, intranet Web sites, and multidisciplinary council meetings. For frontline staff, BHCS focused its communications regarding patient centeredness on bedside behaviors (including scripting of communication with patients and families), family/friend access, inviting patients to participate, following up with patients after discharge with care calls, and developing Codes of Conduct in the medical practices. The message was kept steadily in front of employees through publication of staff and patient stories in newsletters sent to employees' homes. BHCS also added an introduction to the tenets of patient-centered care to its two-day orientation program for new employees.

A new strategy employed by BHCS is inclusion of patients and families in operational councils and committees as "advisors" to give voice to the patient's perspective, as recommended in the Institute for Healthcare Improvement Seven Leadership Leverage Points: "Put[ting] patients and families on the improvement team is not only an important force in driving the achievement of measured results, but it is also the leverage point with the greatest potential to drive the long-term transformation of the entire care system."[2] Patients' recommendations have helped BHCS to redesign discharge lobbies, new facilities for women's and cancer services, and medication reconciliation forms. Patients attend the national Institute for Patient- and Family-Centered Care and bring back recommendations and discoveries. They participate in strategy sessions, attend steering team meetings, and help BHCS employees better understand what it means to deliver patient-centered care.

EXAMPLES OF PATIENT-CENTERED CARE INITIATIVES: 'EVIDENCE-BASED CARING' TACTICS

BHCS trains its staff in the use of several techniques to support and facilitate patient-centered care. Implemented with the help of StuderGroup® and continued with Studer's permission, several of these techniques are described below.

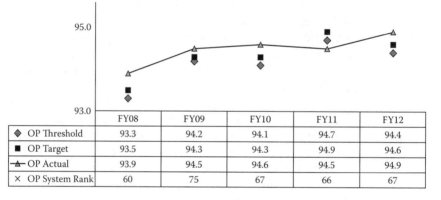

BHCS Inpatient Likelihood to Recommend Mean Score

	FY08	FY09	FY10	FY11	FY12
◆ IP Threshold	90.1	91.5	90.5	91.5	91.7
■ IP Target	90.8	91.8	90.7	91.8	91.9
▲ IP Actual	90.5	90.9	91.7	91.8	92.0
× IP System Rank	91	90	93	94	93

A

BHCS Outpatient Likelihood to Recommend Mean Score

	FY08	FY09	FY10	FY11	FY12
◆ OP Threshold	93.3	94.2	94.1	94.7	94.4
■ OP Target	93.5	94.3	94.3	94.9	94.6
▲ OP Actual	93.9	94.5	94.6	94.5	94.9
× OP System Rank	60	75	67	66	67

B

FIGURE 19.1 Patient satisfaction "likelihood to recommend" scores in the inpatient, outpatient, emergency department, and ambulatory services (FY 2008–FY 2012).

AIDET

AIDET stands for Acknowledge, Introduce, Duration, Explanation, Thank You. AIDET is intended to help employees communicate more effectively with patients, families, and each other through use of an expected communication structure that creates order, respect, and consistency. Managers and staff are trained to use AIDET techniques when rounding on patients and families, while physicians learn in orientation, through physician-specific communications from the chief medical officer, and in classes designed for physicians *by* physicians, how important their behaviors and words are. BHCS provides AIDET training materials in paper form, in MP3 format, and on video.

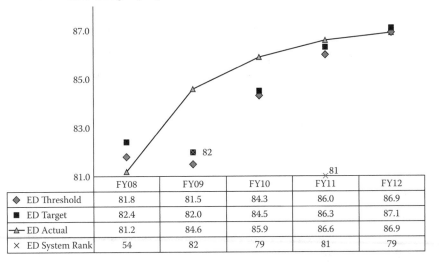

BHCS Emergency Department Likelihood to Recommend Mean Score

	FY08	FY09	FY10	FY11	FY12
◆ ED Threshold	81.8	81.5	84.3	86.0	86.9
■ ED Target	82.4	82.0	84.5	86.3	87.1
–▲– ED Actual	81.2	84.6	85.9	86.6	86.9
✕ ED System Rank	54	82	79	81	79

C

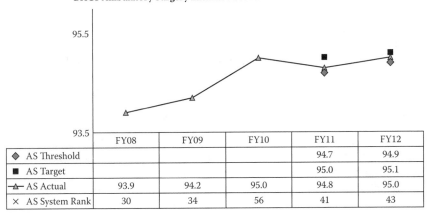

BHCS Ambulatory Surgery Likelihood to Recommend Mean Score

	FY08	FY09	FY10	FY11	FY12
◆ AS Threshold				94.7	94.9
■ AS Target				95.0	95.1
–▲– AS Actual	93.9	94.2	95.0	94.8	95.0
✕ AS System Rank	30	34	56	41	43

D

FIGURE 19.1 (*Continued*)

Rounding for Outcomes

"Rounding for Outcomes" is the consistent practice of setting aside regular, predictable times to work with each patient or family to share the plan of care, identify gaps in care, assess whether reasonable progress has occurred in relation to expected care outcomes, and ensure that the patient's needs, values, and preferences are invited at each decision point. BHCS uses four types of rounding:

- Leaders and physicians rounding on staff to build relationships and ensure tools and time are in place.
- Leaders rounding on patients and sometimes families to ensure care is progressing and concerns are met.
- Nursing and other clinicians rounding on patients.
- Internal department leaders rounding on each other as internal customers all seeking to support the patient and family.

Standardized documentation templates have been developed and are used for rounding meetings.

Bedside Shift Report

One of the most challenging practices to implement has been the bedside shift report. The incoming and departing caregivers meet at the patient's bedside at shift change, or during any departmental transition, to discuss the patient's recent activities, plan of care, symptoms, tests, and concerns. Physical examination may also be performed at this time. Patients (and families when requested) participate, which enables critical information sharing in a brief amount of time. The bedside shift report can lead to feelings of vulnerability among employees when they have to say, "I don't know," in front of patients; nevertheless, drawing the patient into the conversation allows information to be shared among all parties and helps to build trust and confidence of patients and families.

Care Calls

Care calls are calls that are made pre- or posthospital visit to prepare a patient for a visit, gather information about a visit, or aid in the transition to home or to another facility. These calls focus on transition readiness, quality outcomes, patient safety, and care continuity, and they improve patient satisfaction when they are performed well.[3] BHCS implemented a robust and standardized process for placing HIPAA-compliant discharge calls to and leaving HIPAA-compliant messages for patients discharged from inpatient, emergency, and surgical environments. The purpose is to ascertain whether they have questions about their discharge instructions, medications, symptoms, or the initiation of follow-up appointments with their physician.[3] Nearly 30,000 calls are made monthly across BHCS to ensure that patients leave with the resources and information needed for a solid, expected recovery. The evidence is clear from the BHCS results for the HCAHPS domain for discharge readiness—connecting with the patient to assess readiness with direct conversation can improve results for this domain by 40 to 70 percentile points in comparison to other facilities.

BHCS has developed a robust electronic health record module to manage general discharge calls as well as chronic disease calls that require more comprehensive resources. Data from this module, which are being used to develop a predictive model for readmission, reveal that the greatest challenge for discharging patients is ensuring they understand medications and side effects and can recall their discharge instructions. Answering patients' questions about these issues has improved transitions in care at BHCS.

Opening Access to Family and Friends

More than any other tactic, ensuring that loved ones have access to the patient is critical to achieving patient-centered care. These are the people who will not only see the patient through the crisis, but will take the patient home to continue care and recovery as well.

In 2010–2011, BHCS "opened access" to the patient. The greatest challenge to open access was fear of violating HIPAA. The nursing, patient centeredness, and compliance departments worked together to identify areas and processes of concerns, and to educate employees about the difference between "incidental disclosure" and a true violation.[4] Without the direct engagement of the compliance leaders, this work would have been unable to advance.

In the course of this work, BHCS learned several important lessons: patients define who family is, the organization needs to invite the family to help us with the patient, and together BHCS and the patient's family can help the patient achieve desired outcomes through increased trust and transparency.

Shared Decision Making: The Ultimate Partnership

Shared decision making recognizes that in every discussion between a patient and a provider about a medical treatment, there are two experts involved: the physician is the expert on what risks and benefits the treatment carries, while the patient is the expert on himself, his health care goals, and his priorities. Shared decision making tools seek to facilitate a meaningful discussion between these experts, so that the risks and benefits of treatment are appropriately weighed against the patient's goals. For example, such a tool may present a patient with an easy-to-read explanation of his individual risk for certain complications (in place of a generic informed consent form) in preparation for the discussion with his physician. This information should enable more meaningful discussion about the patient's expectations and concerns.

Randomized controlled trials testing the effects of the decision aids used to facilitate shared decision making have found that they appear to have a positive impact on patient-provider communication, to improve patients' knowledge and the accuracy of their risk perception, and increase satisfaction with the decision made.[5] In both randomized controlled trials and observational studies, use of such decision aids also reduce the choice of major elective surgery (for example, hip and knee replacements) in favor of conservative options, and reduce use of tests or treatments of ambiguous benefit (for example, prostate-specific antigen screening, and hormone replacement therapy).[5,6]

BHCS is still at the very early stages of implementing shared decision making, but has established a steering committee on shared decision making to start educating providers on this concept, and its tools and application.

CHALLENGES

BHCS has encountered several cultural challenges in its journey toward patient-centered care. Building good patient relationships requires the investment of time, consistency, and effort. Employees need to trust that changing their behavior and making the investment will be worthwhile. Strong leadership actively and visibly supporting this work is required to create this trust.

A second challenge is related to evidence-based care. Many interventions to improve the safety and effectiveness of care are supported by randomized controlled trial evidence and many providers have come to expect or even require such evidence before they are willing to accept a new practice. However, robust studies of patient-centered behaviors are for the most part nonexistent. Even when clear evidence for patient-centered behaviors exists, the demand is often made for the evidence to be recreated in the local context and the business case established. This cautious approach slows adoption and leaves improvement a step behind in a dynamic, ever-changing patient care environment.

Furthermore, health care providers and organizations tend to be very risk-averse—a culture that hampers data access and transparency. It particularly hampers attempts to determine how patient-centered behaviors drive better outcomes.

Another challenge lies in explicitly distinguishing the differences between system-centered, leadership-centered, physician-centered, and patient-centered behaviors. These are not always readily apparent, and many times are driven by resource constraints in one area or another. Paradoxically, these behaviors must all be integrated to create the positive patient-centered experience.

The greatest challenge in improving patient-centered care, however, lies simply in discipline. If a change is important, it must be implemented, measured, and monitored under the PDCA (Plan-Do-Check-Act) approach. Leadership must be diligent in monitoring, reporting, providing feedback, and coaching. These activities must happen every day, and the behaviors needed from leaders cannot be delegated until they are consistently and firmly embedded in the culture with steady evidence to validate their impact. This can be challenging to maintain once the initial excitement of implementing a new practice and seeing its effects wear off, as the work is often tedious. But, perseverance is essential to making the change "stick."

LESSONS LEARNED

Patient centeredness is central to STEEEP care at BHCS. Ultimately, quality outcomes in health care cannot be achieved without robust, patient-centered methods and behaviors by everyone who "touches" the patients and their families, either directly through the delivery of clinical care or indirectly through their interactions with the organization's systems.

Necessary changes to improve and sustain patient-centered behaviors include Board and leadership commitment, alignment of patient satisfaction goals for all employees, standardization of processes that inform behaviors, and the ongoing discipline of practicing the behaviors and monitoring the results. These changes require a cultural shift in which employees recognize that everyone in the organization "owns" patient centeredness because everyone contributes to that experience. Everyone at all levels of the health care organization (especially at the frontline) needs to understand that he or she is accountable for the right words, actions, follow through, and transparency. And, then each needs the courage to advocate for it with every patient, and during every encounter.

CONCLUSION

No simple recipe exists for improving patient-centered care; it is a cultural, industry, regional, community, and consumer change movement. In recognizing and addressing these complexities, BHCS has been developing and implementing methods for improving patient centeredness as it strives to provide STEEEP care. As health care organizations prepare for an era in which outcomes-based, efficient care will be more important than ever, BHCS continues to seek, develop, and apply innovative ways to improve patient-centered care for the 2.5 million patients who pass through its doors each year.

Patient Story: Open Access

Karen Campbell, a nurse at Baylor Regional Medical Center Grapevine, used to believe open access was not in the best interest of patients, families, or caregivers. When her facility introduced open access in 2010, she was concerned that negative things might happen—that children might become sick or injured while visiting the intensive care unit, for example. However, a recent experience transformed her skepticism into an "open attitude" about open access.

Campbell was caring for an elderly man with leukemia who chose to begin hospice care. His family came to visit him for what would be the last time. His daughter arrived at the hospital with her nine-month-old baby girl. She told Campbell, "I know you don't allow babies in the ICU." She was pleasantly surprised to learn that because of Baylor Grapevine's open access policy, babies were allowed in the ICU.

Campbell asked if the baby had recently been sick, and her mother said no. This meant that the baby was able to visit her grandfather, who had not met her since her birth. "The baby made him smile from ear to ear," Campbell recalls. "It was a special time for him. It was wonderful to see the look on the patient's face when he got to see his nine-month-old granddaughter. He passed two days later."

After the patient died, his family thanked Campbell for allowing his granddaughter to visit him and for giving them that happy memory.

Naturally, Baylor's ICUs have guidelines to protect everyone's safety. Visiting children need to be supervised by their parents, for example. But, as Campbell points out, "You have to ask what you would want if you were in that place." In this case, a 10-minute visit to the ICU created a wonderful experience for the patient and a lasting memory for his family.

REFERENCES

1. Shaw, G. 2011. The new patient experience imperative. *HealthLeaders Media Intelligence* August.
2. Reinertsen, J. L., M. Bisognano, and M. D. Pugh. 2008. *Seven leadership leverage points for organization-level improvement in health care*, 2nd ed. Cambridge, MA: Institute for Healthcare Improvement.
3. Cochran, V. Y., B. Blair, L. Wissinger, and T. D. Nuss. 2012. Lessons learned from implementation of postdischarge telephone calls at Baylor Health Care System. *Journal of Nursing Administration* 42 (1): 40–46.
4. Nuss, T. D. 2013. Patient privacy in an open access environment. *Compliance Today* April, 66–73.
5. Stacey D., Bennett, C. L., Barry, M. J., Col, N. F., Eden, K. B., Holmes-Rovner, M., Llewellyn-Thomas, H., Lyddiatt, A., Légaré, F., Thomson, R. 2011. Decision aids for people facing health treatment or screening decisions. *The Cochrane Database of Systematic Reviews.* Oct 5; (10): CD001431.
6. Arterburn, D., Wellman, R., Westbrook, E., Rutter, C., Ross, T., McCulloch, D., Handley, M., Jung, C. 2012. Introducing decision aids at Group Health was linked to sharply lower hip and knee surgery rates and costs. *Health Affairs (Millwood)* 31 (9): 2094–2104.

STEEEP Care in Practice: Service Lines and Other Lines of Business

SAFE • TIMELY • EFFECTIVE

STEEEP®

EFFICIENT • EQUITABLE

PATIENT-CENTERED

S

SAFE

Avoiding injuries to
patients from care that is intended
to help them.

T

TIMELY

Reducing waits and sometimes
harmful delays for both those who receive
care and those who give care.

E

EFFECTIVE

Providing services based on scientific knowledge to all who could benefit and refraining from providing services to those not likely to benefit (avoiding under use and overuse, respectively).

EFFICIENT

Avoiding waste, including waste of equipment, supplies, ideas and energy.

EQUITABLE

Providing care that does not vary in quality because of
personal characteristics such as gender, ethnicity, geographic
location and socioeconomic status.

PATIENT-CENTERED

Providing care that is respectful of and responsive to
individual patient preferences, needs and values, and ensuring
that patient values guide all clinical decisions.

Chapter 20

Cardiovascular Services

Bradley M. Leonard, William B. Cooksey,

Michael D. Sanborn, Mark Valentine, Michael J. Mack,

David L. Brown, Kevin R. Wheelan, and Nancy Vish

CONTENTS

INTRODUCTION

Cardiovascular disease is a common cause of mortality and morbidity and is associated with high rates of hospital utilization; for example, one in every four heart failure patients must be readmitted to the hospital within 30 days of discharge.[1] The Cardiovascular Service Line, one of nine major clinical service lines at BHCS, seeks to improve care for patients with cardiovascular illnesses. Since its beginnings as a small group of internists and surgeons in the mid-twentieth century, the service line has grown to include eight regional heart and vascular treatment centers and two specialty hospitals dedicated to providing STEEEP cardiovascular care. The service line's core goals of clinical excellence, patient satisfaction, health care team satisfaction, and fiscal responsibility form the foundation of daily operations and metrics by which success is measured. Standardization of data collection, reporting methods, and common care practices have been instrumental to continued quality improvement. The ongoing commitment, support, and engagement of physician and administrative leaders throughout BHCS have been an integral part of these successes.

BRIEF HISTORY AND FACILITIES

For more than half a century, BHCS has delivered quality heart and vascular care alongside innovative clinical research programs that both contribute to the advancement of science and benefit the community by delivering new drug treatments and therapies. BHCS currently includes eight regional heart and vascular treatment centers and two specialty hospitals committed to delivering safe, quality, and compassionate care to heart and vascular patients.

Cardiovascular care at BHCS expanded rapidly in the 1990s, and a vision evolved of redefining the relationship between physicians and the hospital to create a sustainable integrated heart and vascular delivery system focused on high-quality, cost-effective care. Plans were formulated for the development of a specialty hospital (Baylor Heart and Vascular Hospital (BHVH)) that would be jointly owned by the BHCS, hospital-based cardiologists, and vascular surgeons as well as external physicians groups.

BHVH opened in 2002 and provides inpatient and outpatient services focused on preventive health care and comprehensive cardiovascular disease management. Designed as a patient-centered facility, BHVH has cardiac catheterization and electrophysiology laboratories, surgical suites, a cardiac rehabilitation area, and an imaging department. It is also home to the Baylor Heart and Vascular Institute and the Community Resource Center, where educational resources are available to patients, families, and community members interested in learning more about heart and vascular health.

The next major expansion of BHCS's heart and vascular treatment services came in 2007, when a group of practicing cardiovascular physicians and surgeons created The Heart Hospital Baylor Plano (THHBP), a 68-bed hospital, in partnership with Baylor Regional Medical Center at Plano. Recognized as the first and only freestanding, full-service hospital in the region dedicated solely to heart and vascular health care, the THHBP today is a 116-bed facility led by 123 physician partners. The hospital provides inpatient and outpatient care, including diagnostic, interventional, surgical and rehabilitation services; wellness and prevention support; and comprehensive cardiovascular research. In five short years, it has become the ninth largest cardiac surgery program in the United States and one of the foremost valve surgery centers in the world. In 2012 there were 24 hospitals across the United States that performed statistically more favorably than the rest of the hospitals in the United States in risk-adjusted overall quality performance, in both heart bypass and aortic valve replacement surgery. Two of those were BHCS hospitals, Baylor University Medical Center in Dallas and THHBP.*

The expansion of cardiovascular services at BHCS has occurred beyond its two specialty hospitals. During the same period, BHCS extended high-technology cardiac care to cardiovascular treatment centers within its regional hospitals across the Dallas–Fort Worth metroplex, giving patients access to high-quality, comprehensive care at convenient locations.[2]

STANDARDIZATION OF CARE

Following the example of the BHCS Best Care Committee (now the STEEEP Governance Council) established to coordinate health care improvement initiatives across BHCS, a Cardiovascular Best Care Committee was formed in 2007 and tasked with driving quality improvement across the Cardiovascular Service Line. A core leadership group consisting of selected physician leaders at each care facility, as well as administrative and clinical representatives, was established. It was charged with developing system-wide reporting structures, implementing evidence-based best practices, coordinating regular meetings of cardiovascular clinicians throughout BHCS, and collaborating with clinical and administrative stakeholders to aid the adoption of improvement measures. Subcommittees were also organized and tasked with identifying, prioritizing, and operationalizing quality improvement projects for specialty areas, such as heart failure, cardiovascular surgery, coronary intervention, and cardiac electrophysiology. This focused commitment to quality prompted several initiatives that have led to improved health outcomes, reduced costs of care, and increased adherence to standard performance and quality measures across the Cardiovascular Service Line. These initiatives have occurred most notably in the areas of heart failure and cardiovascular surgery.

Quality Outcomes Performance

The collection and use of standardized clinical data are critical to the assessment of patient outcomes and in research efforts focused on improving the

---

* The Society of Thoracic Surgeons developed a comprehensive rating system for the quality of cardiac surgery among hospitals across the country. Approximately 6% of hospitals received the "3 star" rating for aortic valve surgery and 15% of hospitals received the "3 star" rating for coronary bypass surgery, which denotes the highest category of quality in these areas. Only 2.5% of hospitals received the "3 star" rating in both areas. In the current analysis of national data covering the period from January 2010 through December 2012 (valve) and January 2012 through December 2012 (bypass), the cardiac surgery performance of the hospitals are established in the highest quality tiers, thereby receiving STS three-star ratings. The STS National Cardiac Database measures outcomes on over 90% of the 1,100 cardiac surgery programs in the U.S.

quality of patient treatments. The American College of Cardiology (ACC) and the Society of Thoracic Surgeons (STS) are nationally recognized leaders in cardiovascular care quality improvement. They have established clinical practice guidelines and quality standards that are widely followed by cardiovascular physicians and surgeons. One of the first recommendations of the Cardiovascular Best Care Committee was to make data collection, as outlined by these organizations, mandatory for all clinicians across the Cardiovascular Service Line. This mandate has been widely accepted and followed by cardiovascular clinicians, in large part because they were already accustomed to the requirements and guidelines established for their disciplines. At BHCS, it has facilitated sharing of data across individual treatment centers, provided a means to measure individual facility and physician performance against national benchmarks, and informed all decisions about changes in processes of care across the service line.

Improving Heart Failure Outcomes

BHCS identified inpatient heart failure (HF) care as an important target for quality improvement, and a Heart Failure Mortality Task Force was convened in 2008 to identify specific strategies to reduce HF mortality across the system. The task force evolved into a multidisciplinary Heart Failure Strategy Group (Figure 20.1) in late 2010, whose specific aim was to develop and implement a BHCS-wide plan to reduce mortality and 30-day readmissions by using standardized methods to optimize in-hospital and out-of-hospital processes of care. An inventory of HF initiatives across the Cardiovascular Service Line

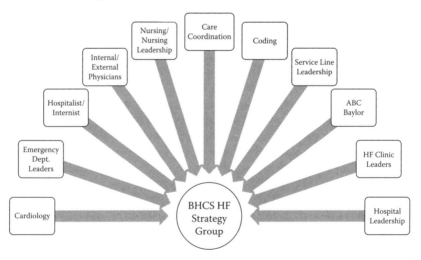

FIGURE 20.1 Multidisciplinary composition of the BHCS Heart Failure (HF) Strategy Group.

at that time revealed more than 60 projects, many of which duplicated efforts and were implemented by different teams with different processes at individual facilities within the health care system. The strategy group employed the BHCS standardized processes for rapid-cycle quality improvement (STEEEP Academy) to map their processes, identify failures and successes, and set priorities and action plans for improvement (Figure 20.2). Deployment of a standardized heart failure order set and establishing accreditation goals are among the initiatives that have led to significant improvements in cardiovascular care across BHCS.

Standardizing Care with a Heart Failure Order Set

BHCS researchers conducted a study in 2010 that examined the impact of its standardized heart failure order set on mortality, readmission, and quality and costs of care across 10 of its hospitals including 8 acute care hospitals and 2 specialty heart hospitals.[3] Order set use was associated with significantly increased heart failure core measures compliance and reduced inpatient mortality, and direct costs for initial admissions alone and in combination with readmissions were significantly lower with order set use (see Chapter 12).

These findings suggest that implementing an evidence-based standardized order set can contribute to improving outcomes, reducing costs of care, and increasing adherence to evidence-based processes of care.

Transitional Care Program for Heart Failure

In another effort to reduce readmission rates for patients with heart failure, BHCS performed a prospective study to test the effectiveness and cost of a transitional care program for patients with heart failure led by an advanced practice nurse.[4] The study found that the intervention significantly reduced risk-adjusted 30-day readmission rates by 48 percent during the postintervention period and, under the payment system in place at the time reduced the hospital's financial contribution margin (profit) on average $227 for each Medicare patient with heart failure (see Chapter 5). These findings underscore the potential of transitional care programs to be effective in a real-world setting. However, payment reform may be required for these types of intervention to be financially sustainable by hospitals when they incur program costs.

SCPC Accreditation

Accreditation is one means by which BHCS ensures that it is meeting the highest standards of patient care. Based on the recommendations of a multidisciplinary BHCS committee created to examine heart failure readmission processes and challenges, all cardiovascular service units across BHCS have received Heart Failure Accreditation from the Society of Cardiovascular

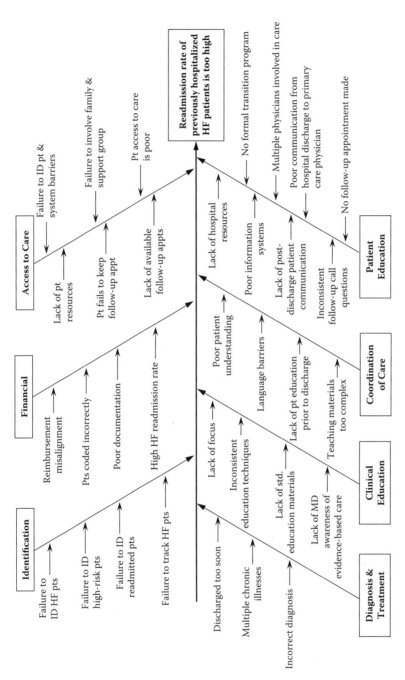

FIGURE 20.2 Cause and effect (fishbone) diagram modeling processes related to heart failure care. The diagram was created to identify targets for improvement as part of a Baylor Health Care System-wide effort to reduce patient readmissions for heart failure.

Patient Care.[5] Accreditation requires that each service unit undergo a rigorous evaluation and improvement process, including an onsite survey, validating that it is in compliance with the highest national standards of care for patients suffering from heart failure. The result of this care is typically better clinical outcomes, lower hospital readmission rates, and cost reductions. Key areas in which each facility must demonstrate expertise include emergency department integration with emergency medical services, emergency assessment of patients with symptoms of acute heart failure, heart failure patient education, process improvement and staff training, organizational structure, commitment to providing the best care, and heart failure community outreach.

Alignment with National Standards

As part of its continuing commitment to providing the highest quality patient care across the Cardiovascular Service Line, BHCS clinicians have aligned their best practices and standards of quality with measures and guidelines set forth by the Joint Commission as well as national societies specializing in cardiovascular care. The benchmarks of these organizations provide a framework for collecting and analyzing health outcome data, evaluating the effectiveness of clinical practices, and, ultimately, implementing quality improvement processes to ensure delivery of the safest, most timely and effective care possible:

- *STS Risk Assessment*: STS risk assessment[6] is a method developed by the STS to predict the risk of mortality and morbidity after adult cardiac surgery on the basis of patient demographic and clinical variables that exist prior to surgery. In 2010, BHCS mandated its use for all cardiac surgery patients, and started requiring second surgical opinions for patients with a predicted risk of mortality of >5 percent. In addition to serving as a useful tool for physicians and patients for understanding the possible risks of surgery, STS risk scoring enables clinicians to compare predictions with actual outcomes (risk adjusted mortality), and can help inform quality improvement processes within individual service units and across the BHCS Cardiovascular Service Line.
- *Phase of Care Mortality Analysis*: Phase of Care Mortality Analysis (POCMA) is a systematic method of mortality review based on the following concepts: (1) all cardiac surgical deaths undergo a root cause of death analysis and (2) the clinical course of cardiac surgery patient is a series of events, therapeutic decisions, interventions, and responses to treatment that are independent.[7] For each death, the analysis requires categorizing the mortality trigger into one of five time frames: preoperative, intraoperative, ICU, postoperative floor, and after discharge. POCMA motivates surgeons and hospital leadership to develop and refine their processes of care and provides a structured platform for

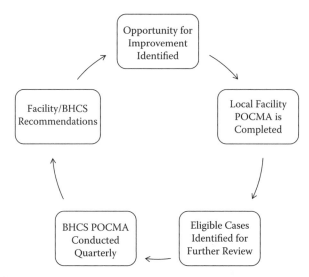

FIGURE 20.3 BHCS System-Wide Phase of Care Mortality Analysis (POCMA). Following POCMA at each local facility, eligible cases (including "low risk" mortalities) are presented at system-wide, surgeon-led POCMA meetings held quarterly. Specific recommendations are referred back to each facility including its medical executive committee. System-wide opportunities for improvement and plans of actions are then identified and acted upon.

discussion, education, quality improvement, and enhanced outcomes. A system-wide POCMA strategy has been developed at BHCS that includes both individual facility-level review processes as well as system-wide procedures for reviewing cases of "low risk" mortality or stroke, or other suboptimal outcomes (Figure 20.3). These are multidisciplinary review processes that include surgeons, anesthesiologists, cardiologists, nurses, and other relevant care providers.

• *Appropriate Use Criteria (AUC) for Coronary Revascularization:* Coronary revascularization is the process of restoring the flow of blood to the heart by opening or bypassing blockages in coronary arteries. Inappropriate use of revascularization can be potentially harmful to patients and generate unwarranted costs, whereas appropriate procedures can improve clinical outcomes.[8] BHCS cardiologists and cardiovascular surgeons have adopted system-wide use of AUC for coronary revascularization outlined by the American College of Cardiology Foundation, Society for Cardiovascular Angiography and Interventions, Society for Thoracic Surgeons, and the American Association for Thoracic Surgery, along with other key specialty and subspecialty societies.[9] The underlying philosophy, endorsed by clinicians and leadership at BHCS, is that ongoing review of clinical practices using these criteria will help guide a more effective, efficient, and equitable allocation of health care resources that will result in better patient outcomes.

RESEARCH AND EDUCATION

Research to discover new ways to diagnose and treat heart and vascular conditions is an important part of BHCS's commitment to ensuring STEEEP cardiovascular care. Cardiovascular physician specialists at three major research centers within BHCS—The Soltero Cardiovascular Research Center, the Baylor Heart and Vascular Institute (BHVI) at BHVH, and the Cardiovascular Research Institute at The Heart Hospital Baylor Plano—are involved in national and international clinical research trials that afford patients access to breakthrough technologies and emerging drug treatments and therapies while contributing to the advancement of medical science. Cardiovascular research efforts across BHCS are ultimately focused on breakthroughs that translate into meaningful outcomes for patients, including more accurate diagnosis, faster recovery, or more effective treatment. BHVI further serves as an important referral center for both physicians and patients seeking information about and access to treatment for cardiovascular disease. Information and education are core components of patient-centered care and help lead to improved cardiovascular health outcomes for patients. The institute houses a community resource center that is open to the public and provides information on recognizing the signs of heart disease, understanding treatment options, and connecting with support groups.

To further promote and support research aimed at improving cardiovascular health, a Cardiovascular Research Review Committee was established in 2007 with the mission of assessing the scientific merit of BHCS cardiovascular research proposals and recommending funding from the BHCS Foundation. The committee meets at least once a year to evaluate the progress of ongoing research projects and to review new project proposals.

CARDIOVASCULAR SERVICE LINE STRUCTURE: FUTURE DIRECTIONS

Cardiovascular services at BHCS have previously been grouped into five traditional specialties: noninterventional cardiology, interventional cardiology, cardiac surgery, radiology, and electrophysiology. As the service line evolves to meet the growing demand for services and the system's heightened emphasis on patient centeredness, it is moving away from this traditional procedure-based organization and toward a new structure that emphasizes multidisciplinary care teams and clinical collaboration focused around specific cardiovascular problems or conditions.

The treatment of cardiovascular disease has become increasingly complex owing to the development of new devices and approaches to care, an increasing amount of scientific evidence-based data, and the expansion of appropriate use criteria. The goal of the multidisciplinary "heart team" is to optimize the management of multifaceted patient care issues through joint and shared decision making among different medical care stakeholders, as well as patients and their families.[10] Within the Cardiovascular Service Line at BHCS, a coronary team will include a primary cardiologist, an interventional cardiologist, a cardiovascular surgeon, and emergency care providers if needed. An arrhythmia team will include a primary cardiologist, a cardiac electrophysiologist, and a cardiovascular surgeon. Similar teams with the necessary care providers will be organized to treat patients with problems associated with the mitral valve, aortic valves, aorta(s), and heart failure.

The BHCS Cardiovascular Council will oversee the various heart team efforts as well as other system-wide quality improvement initiatives. This council consists of a leadership team that includes a chair and the active presidents of BHCS's two specialty heart hospitals. The council includes representatives in the areas of cardiovascular surgery, noninvasive cardiology, heart and ventricular assist devices, vascular care, cardiac electrophysiology, thoracic care, and anesthesia. A representative from BHVI also sits on the council. Together, these council members will be responsible for improving patient outcomes through continued measurement and reporting, enhancing the heart team structure to accommodate clinical developments and evolving patient needs, developing and disseminating evidence-based best practices, and identifying new opportunities for cardiovascular research and innovation.

LESSONS LEARNED

Several key themes have emerged from quality improvement endeavors in BHCS's Cardiovascular Service Line.

First, standardized collection and reporting of clinically accurate and relevant data are essential not only for identifying priorities for improvement, but for motivating physician commitment to adopting improvement measures. Producing transparent patient outcome data, for example, capitalizes on the desire of physicians to do the best for their patients. These peer-by-peer comparisons make it more likely that physicians will work together to discuss ideas to improve patient outcomes.

Second, quality improvement takes a substantial investment of time and resources. Strong administrative leaders and an established quality- and patient-centered culture have been crucial elements of the service line's successes. Finally, best practices need not be reinvented. Many of the quality improvement initiatives embraced by the Cardiovascular Service Line come from adherence to best practices codified by standard-setting organizations in the fields of cardiology and cardiothoracic surgery and are key aspects of the culture of safety advanced by clinicians and administrative leaders.

CONCLUSION

Consistent with BHCS's goal of delivering best care, the Cardiovascular Service Line is committed to ensuring that patients receive the most comprehensive, advanced, and highest quality heart and vascular care possible. This service line has been guided by the principles of delivering STEEEP care and has embraced evidence-based standards of excellence defined by federal governmental and national quality organizations. This commitment to quality extends to all facets of the service line, from administrative and clinical leaders to physicians, nurses, and care coordinators. It is also aided by a quality-focused infrastructure that supports data collection, analysis, and evaluation as a means to drive improvements in the delivery of the best possible cardiovascular care.

REFERENCES

1. Ross, J. S., J. Chen, Z. Lin, H. Bueno, J. P. Curtis, P. S. Keenan, S. L. Normand, et al. 2010. Recent national trends in readmission rates after heart failure hospitalization. *Circulation: Heart Failure* 3 (1): 97–103.
2. Wilsey, H. L. 2004. *How we care: Centennial history of Baylor University Medical Center and Baylor Health Care System, 1903–2003*. Dallas: Baylor Health Care System.
3. Ballard, D. J., G. Ogola, N. S. Fleming, B. D. Stauffer, B. M. Leonard, R. Khetan, and C. W. Yancy. 2010. Impact of a standardized heart failure order set on mortality, readmission, and quality and costs of care. *International Journal for Quality in Health Care* 22 (6): 437–444.
4. Stauffer, B. D., C. Fullerton, N. Fleming, G. Ogola, J. Herrin, P. M. Stafford, and D. J. Ballard. 2011. Effectiveness and cost of a transitional care program for heart failure: A prospective study with concurrent controls. *Archives of Internal Medicine* 171 (14): 1238–1243.
5. Society for Cardiovascular Patient Care. Online at: http://scpcp.org/ (accessed May 15, 2013).
6. Society of Thoracic Surgeons. STS Web risk calculator. Online at: http://riskcalc.sts. org/STSWebRiskCalc261/STS%20Web%20Risk%20Calculator%20Descriptor.pdf (accessed May 15, 2013).
7. Shannon, F. L., F. L. Fazzalari, P. F. Theurer, G. F. Bell, K. M. Sutcliffe, and R. L. Prager. 2012. A method to evaluate cardiac surgery mortality: Phase of care mortality analysis. *The Annals of Thoracic Surgery* 93 (1): 36–43; discussion 43.
8. Ballard, D. J., and B. M. Leonard. 2011. National priorities partnership focus on eliminating overuse: Applications to cardiac revascularization. *American Journal of Medical Quality* 26 (6): 485–490.
9. Patel, M. R., G. J. Dehmer, J. W. Hirshfeld, P. K. Smith, and J. A. Spertus. 2009. ACCF/SCAI/STS/AATS/AHA/ASNC 2009 Appropriateness criteria for coronary revascularization: A report by the American College of Cardiology Foundation Appropriateness Criteria Task Force, Society for Cardiovascular Angiography and Interventions, Society of Thoracic Surgeons, American Association for Thoracic

Surgery, American Heart Association, and the American Society of Nuclear Cardiology endorsed by the American Society of Echocardiography, the Heart Failure Society of America, and the Society of Cardiovascular Computed Tomography. *Journal of the American College of Cardiology* 53 (6): 530–553.

10. Holmes, D. R., Jr., J. B. Rich, W. A. Zoghbi, and M. J. Mack. 2013. The heart team of cardiovascular care. *Journal of the American College of Cardiology* 61 (9): 903–907.

Chapter 21

Emergency Services

Nestor R. Zenarosa, Rosemary Luquire, and Kristine K. Powell

CONTENTS

INTRODUCTION

The hospital emergency department (ED) is the place that Americans turn to first when they have an illness or injury that demands immediate attention.[1] EDs are seeing a growing number of patients without medical insurance and insured patients whose physicians are unavailable during off-peak hours.[1] As the "front door" to the hospital, the ED also has the first and, perhaps, most critical opportunity to influence both patient perception of care and clinical quality. The challenge of meeting these demands is compounded by the rapidly growing number of patients visiting EDs each year.[2] The decision by emergency department leaders at BHCS to outsource ED staffing and management to a single entity in the 1970s was a pivotal step in the evolution of the ED Service Line. This partnership has enabled rapid deployment of best practices, established care guidelines, and quality improvement processes in keeping with BHCS's mission of providing STEEEP care.

BACKGROUND AND FACILITIES

BHCS currently provides emergency medical care in 10 regional hospitals serving more than 470,000 ED patients annually, with plans to expand service to eight free-standing emergency hospitals in North Texas.

Emergency Health Care Services was formed in 1972 as the contracting entity to help serve Baylor University Medical Center's (BUMC) physician staffing needs. The pattern of care and care management established at BUMC was extended to community medical centers that became part of BHCS.[3] In the 1990s, Emergency Health Care Services evolved into EmCare, Inc., a national shareholder-owned company that now services more than 500 hospitals nationwide.[4]

In 2012, BHCS joined forces with Emerus—a Texas-based emergency hospital system designed by board-certified ER (emergency room) specialists—to extend delivery of emergency care to eight free-standing emergency hospitals by 2014. The facilities will be open 24 hours a day. Trauma patients will be stabilized and transferred to a trauma center and there will be beds available for patients who need to stay overnight. The goal is to make emergency services more convenient to the growing population while relieving some of the congestion, thereby improving quality of care in BHCS's existing EDs.[5]

INFRASTRUCTURE FOR QUALITY IMPROVEMENT

The ED Service Line is dedicated to providing patients and families with the best emergency care services in an expeditious, high-quality, and cost-effective manner. Both internal and external structures have been instrumental to the quality improvement process across the service line. First, BHCS's partnership with EmCare, Inc. as its single source for ED staffing and management has enabled the development and implementation of system-wide processes and procedures since the 1980s. It also has engendered improved organizational performance by providing strong strategic leadership.[6] The commitment of BHCS leaders and all ED clinicians to providing STEEEP care, including the application of best practices, risk mitigation, and process improvement strategies, has helped elevate the quality and consistency of emergency medical care provided throughout the entire health care system.

Internally to BHCS, the ED Council provides the multidisciplinary leadership and teamwork necessary to implement and promote improvements in the delivery of STEEEP emergency care. The Council is led jointly by a physician, nursing director, and executive sponsor, and includes medical directors and nursing managers from each BHCS emergency department, as well as representatives from the Offices of Patient Centeredness and Patient Safety, Quality Improvement, and Ancillary Support Services. The Council meets monthly to share best practices, review metrics, and set goals for improvement.

Subcommittees meet quarterly to discuss specific improvement goals in the areas of data management, patient centeredness, operational efficiency, and national accreditations.

MAJOR IMPROVEMENT INITIATIVES

Overcrowding, inefficient patient flow processes, and fragmented care following discharge from the hospital are among the biggest challenges facing the ED. As part of its continuing commitment to providing timely, effective emergency care, BHCS has implemented several important quality improvement initiatives.

Rapid Medical Assessment to Improve Patient Throughput

Lack of critical-care beds and general overcrowding are foremost among the challenges facing EDs nationwide. At BUMC, overcrowding was addressed by implementing a Rapid Medical Assessment (RMA) and a five-level emergency severity index triage system to accelerate patient flow.[6] The five levels were:

1. Emergent with life/limb threatening condition
2. Emergent with potential life/limb threatening condition
3. Urgent
4. Semiurgent
5. Nonurgent

Level 3 patients, who comprised more than 40 percent of the total, were identified as a large problem in the flow of care, causing ~10 percent of patients to leave without being seen. The RMA intervention consisted of an RMA team (made up of a physician, registered nurse, and ED technician), and designated subwaiting rooms equipped with recliners to which the nurse directed patients who could be treated without lying down and whose condition could be dealt with in little more than a routine 15-minute office visit. RMA can be used in a variety of ways based on how the ED is staffed and how the department is laid out, but the concept remains the same: RMA is used when there are more people than beds. Finding and treating patients who do not require lying down enables the ED to use each bed more efficiently.

BUMC's implementation of RMA led to several measurable improvements in both patient care and staff and patient satisfaction: (1) the percentage of patients who were likely to recommend BHCS facilities rose from 77 to 99 percent and has remained high, (2) the percentage of Level 3 patients who left without being seen dropped from 14 to 2 percent, (3) employee turnover dropped from 28 percent at the beginning of the year to less than 4 percent for the remainder of the year, and (4) RMA and other efforts decreased patient ED length of stay by 40 percent. More broadly, the RMA led to the development of "vertical flow models" to improve patient throughput in EDs across BHCS. These process flow models vary depending on the staff, resources, and demands unique to each ED, but are designed around the concepts of keeping ambulatory patients upright (and maximizing the use of ED beds for the patients who most need them). Use of Lean thinking and BHCS's internal rapid-cycle quality improvement training (see Chapter 8) were instrumental in the development of these models.

Improving Sepsis Care and Mortality

Sepsis is a serious medical condition caused by an overwhelming immune response to infection. It afflicts an estimated 750,000 patients in the United States each year, and has a mortality rate of approximately 30 percent.[7,8] Because many septic patients first present to the ED, emergency clinicians are uniquely positioned to identify patients early and begin treatment with evidence-based therapies, such as timely antibiotic and fluid administration, to decrease mortality.[9] Sepsis care was consequently identified as a key area for quality improvement across the ED Service Line.

BHCS implemented the recommendations set forth by the Surviving Sepsis Campaign (SSC).[9] ED leadership introduced a Sepsis Screening Tool in 2009 to help clinicians evaluate patients' risk for sepsis using four screening criteria for systemic inflammatory response syndrome: elevated heart rate, elevated respiratory rate or low partial pressure of carbon dioxide, elevated or low temperature, and high or low white blood cell count. If two or more criteria are met and infection is suspected, the screen is deemed positive, prompting immediate physician evaluation, additional laboratory tests, rapid intravenous fluid infusion, and antibiotics administration. These steps are designed to decrease the time to diagnosis and facilitate rapid treatment.

BHCS also adopted a severe sepsis protocol, specifying use of a six-hour care bundle, a set of evidence-based measures that must be completed within six hours of diagnosis, developed by the SSC in collaboration with the Institute for Healthcare Improvement.[10,11] Use of the six-hour bundle ensures consistent application of best practices in sepsis care and provides a foundation for measuring and improving sepsis outcomes. Implementation of both the Sepsis Screening Tool and the six-hour care bundle contributed to a 25 percent reduction in sepsis mortality across BHSC between 2008 and 2011, saving 413 lives. In 2013, BHCS adopted use of a severe sepsis and septic shock management bundle endorsed by the National Quality Forum. This bundle includes three-hour and six-hour bundles intended for adult patients who present with symptoms of severe sepsis and septic shock.

ED Staff Rounding on Patients

The ED is the first point of entry into the hospital for many patients. Their experience not only affects them personally, but also leaves a lasting positive or negative impression about the care they received and the health care system as a whole.

In 2006, three BHCS ED units participated in a research study that examined the effects of 3 staff rounding protocols on patient safety and satisfaction in 28 EDs across the country.[12] The three protocols combined produced positive results across five measures:

- 23 percent reduction in patients who left the ED without being seen
- 23 percent reduction in patients who left against medical advice
- 59 percent reduction in falls
- 35 percent reduction in patients' use of the call light
- 40 percent reduction in the number of family members and patients approaching the nursing station to inquire about the patient's care.

Patient satisfaction ratings for overall care and pain management also increased significantly. The protocol that incorporated an individual patient care tactic asking patients to name their most important expectation for the ED visit, produced the greatest improvements.

These findings sparked a renewed interest in patient satisfaction at one of the BHCS EDs that participated in the study, including greater emphasis on patient throughput and engagement of frontline staff with individual patients. This ED has implemented mandatory staff training on basic communication and patient satisfaction skills and, to maintain accountability, hourly rounding performance is tracked weekly, reported to administration monthly, and posted for the ED staff. ED physicians also receive individual patient throughput reports from the ED medical director, and a dedicated ED patient satisfaction team holds monthly meetings to review and discuss processes and results and to make recommendations. Events to recognize and reward staff accomplishments help sustain staff morale and their commitment to delivering the highest quality ED care.

Improving Arrival to Exam Time

ED crowding compromises quality of care and patient satisfaction and, when patients leave without treatment, it causes significant lost revenue for hospitals. Crowding can be mitigated by improving patient flow and, beginning in 2013 and 2014, hospitals will be required to report on several ED crowding-related measures to the Centers for Medicare and Medicaid Services to help drive efficiency improvements.[13]

ED leaders at one BHCS ED identified patient throughput as a key area for quality improvement in 2007. They began a rapid-cycle improvement project to improve throughput by reducing door-to-exam time by 20 percent. In April 2007, the average wait time for an ED patient to receive a medical screening exam was 63 minutes. A team of frontline clinical staff developed and implemented a three-phase strategy aimed at reducing door-to-exam time to 48 minutes through direct-to-bed triage, expedited bedside registration, and immediate notification of physicians when patients are placed in a treatment room. In only eight weeks, the ED demonstrated a 40 percent reduction in door-to-exam time, as the mean decreased to 36.5 minutes. In addition to dramatically improving patient satisfaction scores, the ED's "left without treatment" rate plummeted from an average of 5.4 percent to a low of 0.5 percent, well below the suggested national target of 2 percent. These initiatives earned the hospital a 2008 National Press Ganey Success Story Award for demonstrating innovation and leadership to measurably improve patient care and clinical quality.[14] All EDs across BHCS have since devoted attention to improving arrival to exam time through implementation of different patient flow initiatives.

Postdischarge Telephone Calls

Hospital discharge often involves communication of complex information, including diagnostic test results or instructions about medications or follow-up care. These generally occur at a time when patients and families are stressed. Failure to communicate this information accurately and effectively can cause harm to the patient ranging from confusion to an adverse event resulting in a return visit to the ED or even death. Based on evidence that postdischarge telephone calls can improve patient satisfaction and increase compliance with medication instructions and other physician recommendations,[15] the ED Council at BHCS developed and implemented a standardized process for placing postdischarge telephone calls.[16]

In August 2010, BHCS staff made 26,803 postdischarge calls with an average contact rate of 34.5 percent (9,240 direct contacts with the patient or the patient's caregiver). The phone call was introduced to the patient at the time of discharge with the provider explaining that he/she would like to reach the patient within the next 24 to 48 hours. Staff standardized the call using a HIPAA-compliant directed conversation. They also used a script to ask whether patients had any questions about their discharge instructions, medications, and symptoms, and to initiate a follow-up appointment with their physician.

Of the 9,240 direct contacts, 1,041 interventions were provided including clarification of medication and/or home instructions (n = 346, 34%) and reminders for follow-up appointments or assistance with referrals (n = 314, 30%).

Patients who reported new or unresolved symptoms were instructed to return to the ED or their primary care physician (n = 346, 33%).[16]

These data showed that many patients require information after returning home. Based on the success of post-ED discharge calls, BHCS is expanding the standardized follow-up calls to other care settings.

LESSONS LEARNED

Data collection and transparent reporting are cornerstones and drivers of quality improvement across the ED Service Line. Measures include length of stay, door-to-provider time, left without being seen percentage, sepsis mortality, heart failure and pneumonia care, and patient satisfaction. ED performance data are reported monthly both at the system and hospital levels. These measurement and reporting efforts have helped (1) identify areas for improvement, (2) evaluate the impact of improvement initiatives and (3) promote sharing of best practices between individual ED departments across BHCS. High levels of alignment and engagement across clinical disciplines and staffing areas, accountability of key stakeholders, and an unwavering focus on delivering patient-centered care have been essential to the development and implementation of improvement initiatives. Quality improvement tools used included customer service tactics and standardized protocols and order sets.

CONCLUSION

Quality improvement in the BHCS ED Service Line has been guided by a focus on patient satisfaction, clinical best practices, and improving patient throughput. The decision by BHCS leaders to partner with a single source for ED staffing and management has facilitated rapid improvements in the quality and consistency of emergency care provided across BHCS, creating an environment that is positioned to meet the growing demand for ED care. The standards and metrics by which ED leaders and clinicians are held accountable constitute an integral part of the quality improvement process, as is application of the tools of rapid-cycle improvement.[17]

REFERENCES

1. Institute of Medicine Committee on the Future of Emergency Care in the United States Health System. 2007. *Hospital-based emergency care: At the breaking point.* Washington, DC: National Academies Press.
2. Centers for Disease Control and Prevention. Ambulatory health care data: Survey results and products. Online at http://www.cdc.gov/nchs/ahcd/ahcd_products.htm: (accessed June 25, 2013).

3. Wilsey, H. L. 2004. *How we care: Centennial history of Baylor University Medical Center and Baylor Health Care System, 1903–2003.* Dallas: Baylor Health Care System.

4. EmCare, Inc. About EmCare. Online at: http://www.emcare.com/About-EmCare.aspx (accessed May 15, 2013).

5. Jacobsen, G. 2012. Baylor Health Care System plunges into free-standing ER business. Online at: http://www.dallasnews.com/business/health-care/20120529-baylor-health-care-system-plunges-into-free-standing-er-business.ece (accessed May 15, 2013).

6. EmCare, Inc. A system-wide approach to creating high performance emergency departments. Online at: https://www.emcare.com/Solutions-for-Hospitals/White-Papers/A-System-Wide-Approach-to-Creating-High-Performanc.aspx (accessed May 15, 2013).

7. Angus, D. C., W. T. Linde-Zwirble, J. Lidicker, G. Clermont, J. Carcillo, and M. R. Pinsky. 2001. Epidemiology of severe sepsis in the United States: Analysis of incidence, outcome, and associated costs of care. *Critical Care Medicine* 29 (7): 1303–1310.

8. National Center for Health Statistics, Health, United States 2007 with chartbook on trends in the health of Americans. Hyattsville, MD: U.S. Government Printing Office.

9. Levy, M. M., R. P. Dellinger, S. R. Townsend, W. T. Linde-Zwirble, J. C. Marshall, J. Bion, C. Schorr, et al. 2010. The Surviving Sepsis Campaign: Results of an international guideline-based performance improvement program targeting severe sepsis. *Critical Care Medicine* 38 (2): 367–374.

10. Levy, M. M., P. J. Pronovost, R. P. Dellinger, S. Townsend, R. K. Resar, T. P. Clemmer, and G. Ramsay. 2004. Sepsis change bundles: Converting guidelines into meaningful change in behavior and clinical outcome. *Critical Care Medicine* 32 (11 Suppl): S595–597.

11. Institute for Healthcare Improvement. IHI severe sepsis bundle. Online at: http://www.ihi.org/knowledge/Pages/SevereSepsisBundles.aspx (accessed May 15, 2013).

12. Meade, C. M., J. Kennedy, and J. Kaplan. 2010. The effects of emergency department staff rounding on patient safety and satisfaction. *Journal of Emergency Medicine* 38 (5): 666–674.

13. McHugh, M., K. Van Dyke, M. McClelland, and D. Moss. 2011. *Improving patient flow and reducing emergency department crowding: A guide for hospitals.* Rockville, MD: AHRQ Publication No. 11(12)-0094.

14. Baylor Health Care System Online Newsroom. 2008. Frontline Emergency Team earns two national awards. Online at: http://media.baylorhealth.com/channels/Grapevine/releases/Frontline-Emergency-Team-Earns-Two-National-Awards (accessed May 15, 2013).

15. Braun, E., A. Baidusi, G. Alroy, and Z. S. Azzam. 2009. Telephone follow-up improves patients satisfaction following hospital discharge. *European Journal of Internal Medicine* 20 (2): 221–225.

16. Cochran, V. Y., B. Blair, L. Wissinger, and T. D. Nuss. 2012. Lessons learned from implementation of postdischarge telephone calls at Baylor Health Care System. *Journal of Nursing Administration* 42 (1): 40–46.

17. Ballard, D. J., B. Spreadbury, and R. S. Hopkins, 3rd. 2004. Health care quality improvement across the Baylor Health Care System: The first century. *Proceedings (Baylor University Medical Center)* 17 (3): 277–288.

Chapter 22

Critical Care Services

Rosemary Luquire and Robert W. Baird

CONTENTS

INTRODUCTION

Nearly 80 percent of all Americans experience a critical illness or injury in their lifetime, either as the patient, family member, or friend of a patient.[1] The intensive care unit (ICU), where critical care is often delivered, saves lives, but also faces challenges to providing patients with the best possible care including a high risk of infection and other medical complications. In these "high stakes" environments, even a seemingly small quality improvement measure can mean the difference between life and death. The BHCS Critical Care Service Line is committed to the continued advancement of critical care practice, implementing standardized, evidence-based practices supported by continuous cycles of research and quality improvement initiatives to achieve STEEEP care.

BACKGROUND AND FACILITIES

ICUs at each BHCS hospital provide critical medical and surgical care for a wide range of conditions including myocardial infarction, pneumonia, surgical

171

complications, premature birth, stroke, and trauma from accidents. The Critical Care Service Line is multidisciplinary and includes physicians and nurses with specialized critical care training, emergency and pharmacy personnel, respiratory therapists, radiology and laboratory specialists, and nutritionists.

In addition to general medical/surgical ICUs, the BHCS Critical Care Service Line includes cardiac ICUs, and units with specialized expertise and equipment for treating trauma, as well as critical pre- and postoperative transplant cases and critical neurologic cases.

ORGANIZATIONAL FRAMEWORK FOR IMPROVING CRITICAL CARE

Critical care saves lives, but is also associated with substantial risks. Due to the severity and complexity of their conditions, critical care patients are particularly vulnerable to infections and other adverse events. Mortality, adverse event rates, and costs of care, therefore, are all high.[2,3] To address these challenges, the Critical Care Service Line has created an infrastructure that enables rapid improvements to quality of patient care as well as cost reduction within each hospital and across BHCS.

ICU Breakthrough Quality Improvement Committee

In April 1997, the Baylor University Medical Center (BUMC) ICUs began identifying and implementing "breakthrough" projects that could quickly improve patient outcomes and reduce costs. The ICU Breakthrough Quality Improvement Committee—consisting of the director of the ICU, hospital administrators, ICU bedside nurses, nurse administrators, pharmacists, dieticians, and information system professionals—was created to initiate and oversee these efforts.[4] Improvement initiatives identified by the committee were implemented using the PDCA (Plan-Do-Check-Act) approach.

Critical Care Council

The Critical Care Council was established as one of nine Service Line Councils aligned with the STEEEP Governance Council (see Chapter 1). The Critical Care Council enables individual ICUs and other departments involved in critical care at each hospital to collaborate, sharing best practices and implementing improvement initiatives. Led jointly by a physician and nursing director, the council includes physician, nursing, and administrative representatives from each BHCS hospital; allied health team members

TABLE 22.1 Example goals set forth by the Critical Care Council

Domain	Goal
Safety	Reduce hospital-acquired infections including ventilator-associated pneumonia, central line–associated bloodstream infection, urinary tract infections, pressure ulcers, and *Clostridium difficile*
Timeliness	Decrease emergency department to ICU transfer time
Efficacy	Reduce hospital standardized ventilator mortality ratio
Efficiency	Reduce ICU costs, e.g., through assessment of medication ordering and use
Equity	Standardization of care across BHCS through implementation of standardized order sets, charges, ratios and documentation
Patient Centeredness	Improve patient satisfaction survey scores

with expertise in pharmacy and respiratory therapy; and an executive sponsor. According to its charter, the purpose of the council is to:

- Make decisions that advance critical care practice throughout BHCS by standardizing evidence-based practices and promoting research and quality improvement initiatives;
- Promote a healthy work environment within BHCS through interdisciplinary collaboration, effective decision making, and clinical leadership, resulting in critical care environments that are safe, healing, humane, and respectful of the rights, responsibilities, and needs of all people, including patients and their families; and
- Advance critical care practice outside BHCS through promotion of national certifications in critical care; active participation and leadership in local, state, and national critical care organizations; publications and presentations involving quality improvement, research, and evidence-based practices in critical care; and recognition for achieving the highest level of quality in critical care.

The specific goals of the Critical Care Council are set annually and aligned with the principles of STEEEP care. Ongoing goals include reducing the rate and overall number of hospital-acquired infections, implementing standardized procedures for common critical care practices, and reducing costs (Table 22.1).

MAJOR QUALITY IMPROVEMENT INITIATIVES

Over the past decade, numerous quality improvement initiatives have been implemented across the BHCS Critical Care Service Line; many of them in response to the Institute for Healthcare Improvement's (IHI) 100,000 Lives Campaign.[5]

100,000 Lives Campaign

BHCS was among the first 10 health care systems to implement the IHI's 100,000 Lives Campaign (see Chapter 1). During the campaign, BHCS's acute care hospitals averaged a greater than 12 percent reduction in inpatient risk-adjusted mortality, exceeding the 5 percent reduction needed nationally to achieve the overall goal of saving 100,000 lives.[6] Three of the six recommended interventions that are engaged in the Critical Care Service Line include deployment of Rapid Response Teams (RRTs), prevention of central line infections, and ventilator-associated pneumonia.

Intensivist Program

The quality of care in hospital ICUs is strongly impacted by the presence and involvement of "intensivists"—physicians with special training in critical care medicine who, thus, are better equipped to handle complications, use resources effectively, and minimize errors. Despite demonstrated advantages in mortality reduction,[7] substantial challenges exist to implementing the intensivist model of ICU care. First, there is an ongoing shortage of board-certified intensivists,[8] and, second, in hospitals with small ICUs, it may not be economically feasible to restrict the activities of intensivists to the ICU.

The Leapfrog ICU Physician Staffing Standard requires that, during daytime hours, intensivists be present to provide clinical care exclusively in the ICU.[9] At other times, physicians are expected to respond to pages within five minutes and may rely on in-hospital "physician extenders" (registered nurses and physician assistants) who can promptly attend to ICU patients when needed. BHCS currently has two hospitals with onsite intensivists 24 hours a day, 7 days a week, and is working toward system-wide adoption of a 12-hour (or greater) intensivist model in all of its hospitals with the patient volume to justify it. At hospitals with smaller ICUs (those with less then 12 beds), BHCS requires an intensivist consult (either in-person or using telemedicine), but each ICU case is not managed by a dedicated onsite intensivist.

ICU Open Visiting

As part of the transformation to a patient-centered model of care, BHCS has implemented specific changes designed to meet individual patient needs and improve the patient experience including that in the ICU. Understanding that visits from family and friends play an important part in patient healing, communication, and safety, BHCS lifted visiting restrictions at all of its ICUs beginning in 2010—a policy that required a major cultural shift, particularly with respect to nursing care. The Office of Patient Centeredness and ICU leadership were pivotal to addressing staff concerns by developing new family visiting guidelines, and developing plans to involve families in multidisciplinary rounds. These efforts have led to better understanding of the plan of care by patients' families as well as improved patient satisfaction scores.

Comprehensive Unit-Based Safety Program (CUSP)

The Comprehensive Unit-Based Safety Program (CUSP) is a strategic framework for safety improvement that embraces the principles of teamwork and learning from mistakes.[10] It was first adopted at BHCS by a cardiovascular ICU at BUMC in 2010, and is now spreading to other units within the Critical Care Service Line. The program is designed to educate and improve awareness about patient safety and quality of care, empower staff to take charge and improve safety in their workplace, create partnerships between units and hospital executives to improve organizational culture, and provide tools to investigate and learn from defects. CUSP has helped improve communication and teamwork among doctors, nurses, and other members of the ICU team. It also has resulted in specific patient safety improvements including the development of standard procedures for reporting patient histories and transferring vital patient information from the emergency room to the ICU. Demonstrated CUSP successes have spurred increased adoption of the program across BHCS.

LESSONS LEARNED

Timeliness, attention to detail, standardization, teamwork, and transparency have been essential to quality improvements across the Critical Care Service Line. Infection prevention measures and applications of evidence-based best practices and protocols greatly improve patient outcomes, but require strict attention to detail and a culture of teamwork to effect change. Transparency has also been an important driver of quality improvement across the Critical Care Service Line. Each ICU produces monthly "dashboards" that provide summarized clinical data related to central line infections, ventilator-associated pneumonia, mortality, and length of stay; patient experience data; as well as data on laboratory, radiology, and pharmacy expenses. These reports are reviewed by the Critical Care Council and inform new improvement initiatives. They are also included in the monthly STEEEP Care Reports that are shared with the Board of Trustees and all BHCS employees.

CONCLUSION

The BHCS Critical Care Service Line is dedicated to providing the most severely ill and injured patients with STEEEP care. These principles guide all of the service line's quality improvement initiatives and pervade all activities, from system-wide efforts to reduce hospital-acquired infections to the implementation of standardized protocols for drug administration and other common care practices in the ICU. The Critical Care Service Line is supported by an infrastructure that enables the rapid development and deployment of quality improvement measures and a culture that empowers staff at all levels to effect change.

REFERENCES

1. Society of Critical Care Medicine. Online at: http://www.sccm.org/Pages/default. aspx (accessed May 15, 2013).
2. Joint Commission Resources Staff. 2004. *Improving care in the ICU.* Oakbrook Terrace, IL: Joint Commission Resources.
3. Halpern, N. A., and S. M. Pastores. 2010. Critical care medicine in the United States 2000–2005: An analysis of bed numbers, occupancy rates, payer mix, and costs. *Critical Care Medicine* 38 (1): 65–71.
4. Baird, R. W. 2001. Quality improvement efforts in the intensive care unit: development of a new heparin protocol. *Proceedings (Baylor University Medical Center)* 14 (3): 294–296; discussion 296–298.
5. Berwick, D. M., D. R. Calkins, C. J. McCannon, and A. D. Hackbarth. 2006. The 100,000 lives campaign: Setting a goal and a deadline for improving health care quality. *JAMA* 295 (3): 324–327.
6. Baylor News: BHCS excels in national campaign to save 100,000 lives. 2006. *Proceedings (Baylor University Medical Center)* 19: 398–401.
7. Pronovost, P. J., D. C. Angus, T. Dorman, K. A. Robinson, T. T. Dremsizov, and T. L. Young. 2002. Physician staffing patterns and clinical outcomes in critically ill patients: A systematic review. *JAMA* 288 (17): 2151–2162.
8. Angus, D. C., M. A. Kelley, R. J. Schmitz, A. White, and J. Popovich, Jr. 2000. Caring for the critically ill patient. Current and projected workforce requirements for care of the critically ill and patients with pulmonary disease: can we meet the requirements of an aging population? *JAMA* 284 (21): 2762–2770.
9. The Leapfrog Group. 2008. Factsheet on ICU Physician Staffing. Online at: http://www.leapfroggroup.org/media/file/Leapfrog-ICU_Physician_Staffing_Fact_Sheet. pdf (accessed May 15, 2013).
10. Pronovost, P. J., B. Weast, B. Rosenstein, J. B. Sexton, C. G. Holzmueller, L. Paine, R. Davis, and H. R. Rubin. 2005. Implementing and validating a comprehensive unit-based safety program. *Journal of Patient Safety* 1: 33–40.

Chapter 23

Oncology Services

Alan M. Miller, Marvin J. Stone, and JaNeene L. Jones

CONTENTS

INTRODUCTION

Half of all men and one-third of all women in the United States will develop cancer during their lifetimes, and cancer remains the second most common cause of death in the United States.[1] The Baylor Charles A. Sammons Center at Dallas, the largest unit of the BHCS Oncology Service Line, was established more than 35 years ago with the vision of providing high-quality clinical care, outstanding research and education, and comprehensive support services for patients and families through multidisciplinary, cooperative interactions among diverse medical specialties and support staff. The center's organization and governance, including collaboration with one of the nation's largest oncology practice groups, were established to facilitate these goals.

Today, the Baylor Charles A. Sammons Cancer Center Network extends to six additional cancer programs throughout BHCS that are equally committed to advancing the science of cancer while providing the highest quality personalized, comprehensive, and compassionate patient care.

BRIEF HISTORY AND FACILITIES

The Baylor Charles A. Sammons Cancer Center at Dallas was established in 1976 in response to three driving factors: (1) an increasing number of cancer patients drawn to the medical center for its growing expertise in cancer-related care, (2) national support for basic and clinical cancer research,[2] and (3) designation of medical oncology as a new subspecialty of internal medicine.[3] Unlike freestanding cancer centers, it was conceived and implemented as an integral unit within Baylor University Medical Center (BUMC)—a "center without walls" encompassing oncology patient care, education, and research throughout the medical center. The Department of Oncology was simultaneously created and includes more than 125 members with primary appointments in the departments of surgery (and surgical specialties), internal medicine, radiology, obstetrics/gynecology, and pathology. The Cancer Center's mission is to provide high-quality clinical care through advanced screening, preventive, diagnostic and treatment services; outstanding research and education; and comprehensive support services for patients and families (Table 23.1).

The center's five disciplines (radiation oncology, medical oncology-hematology, surgical oncology, oncologic pathology, and gynecologic oncology) now treat more than 8,000 patients each year. The cancer program at BUMC has been continuously accredited by the American College of Surgeons Commission on Cancer (CoC) since 1962, a testament to the program's dedication to providing the highest level of care as measured against national standards and its continuing commitment to address each patient's needs while improving outcomes.[4]

Collaboration with Texas Oncology

In 1972, a small group of medical oncologists formed the Medical Oncology Group, beginning what would become one of the largest oncology practice groups in the country. The initial motivation was to provide coverage and assistance in attending to the burgeoning load of oncology consults at BUMC.[5] Community outreach to deliver sophisticated cancer care to underserved areas was seen as an important objective of the Cancer Center and this also relied on the Medical Oncology Group. Outreach activities began in 1979, with several group members making regular trips to Odessa, Texas, where the demand for comprehensive cancer care ultimately led to the establishment of an outreach clinic.[3] Clinics in

TABLE 23.1 Major programs and services at the Baylor Charles A. Sammons Cancer Center at Dallas

Center/Program	Description
Blood and Marrow Transplant Program	Offers a comprehensive range of services to treat hematologic (blood) cancers (leukemia, lymphomas, and myeloma), and is accredited by the Foundation for the Accreditation of Cellular Therapy
Hereditary Cancer Risk Program	Offers patient education, testing, interpretation of genetic testing results, and discussion of options for managing breast and ovarian cancer, colon cancer, and others.
Innovative Clinical Trials Center	Provides one location for patients to access phase I/II clinical trials including clinical examinations, infusions, sample collection, and lab work.
Integrative Medicine Program	Combines traditional medicine with complementary approaches including stress management, nutrition consultation, and acupuncture
Liver and Pancreas Disease Center	Provides comprehensive care to patients with hepatobiliary and pancreatic diseases
Oncology Outpatient Clinic	Includes specialty clinics for bone and soft tissue, cardiology services, dental services, head and neck cancer, lymphedema services, physical medicine and rehabilitation, skin cancer screening, and skull base tumors
Patient Navigation Program	Dedicated registered nurses to help patients and families gather medical records, coordinate appointments and referrals, answer questions about personal plans of care.
Virginia R. Cvetko Patient Education and Support Center	Services include a patient education library, disease-specific support groups, as well as guidance from nurse educators, chaplains, social workers, clinical psychologists, a music practitioner, and trained cancer survivor volunteers.
W. H. and Peggy Smith Breast Center	Offers education, early detection services, advanced treatment options and support services, and is accredited by the National Accreditation Program for Breast Centers

the Texas cities of Paris, Midland, and Corsicana soon followed, leading to the concept of a multicity practice and the development of Texas Oncology in 1986. Texas Oncology further contributes donations to the two-year medical oncology fellowship funded by the Baylor Health Care System Foundation, which accepts three fellows per year. As of 2013, 57 physicians have completed the fellowship program; about two-thirds have remained in the North Texas area.

Blood and Marrow Transplant Program

A major priority in the early years of the Cancer Center was the development of a bone marrow transplantation program, which was established in 1982 and became a major component of the Cancer Center's clinical and research efforts. The program engages transplant physicians as well as nurses, dieticians, case managers, social workers, patient education, and psychosocial support experts. It launched and continues research studies in the areas of hematopoietic cytokines (molecules that stimulate blood cell growth), prevention and management of infectious complications, and devising new methods for prevention and management of graft-versus-host disease. The program was also a founding member of the American Society of Blood and Marrow Transplantation and helped the society establish a journal for peer-reviewed manuscripts in clinical and laboratory transplantation science. Today it is one of only nine blood and marrow transplant programs in the United States, and the only Texas program to offer all four components of the National Marrow Donor Program: a donor center, transplant center, bone marrow collection center, and apheresis collection center.

Expansion of the Cancer Center Facilities and Brand

By 2005, BHCS leadership recognized that (1) cancer diagnosis was increasing across the country, (2) the need for cancer care in North Texas would be increasing dramatically in the coming decades, and (3) the Baylor Charles A. Sammons Cancer Center at Dallas should respond to this need through a major expansion of its facilities and patient services. A $350-million investment was made to create a new outpatient facility and inpatient hospital that opened their doors in 2011 and 2012, respectively. The 96-bed, in-patient facility includes a unique 24-hour oncology evaluation and treatment center, as well as an infusion center and an apheresis center. It and the outpatient center are fully integrated and were built to complement each other. They purposely share many of the same support services; hence, the transition from inpatient services to outpatient services is seamless.

In late 2012, the Charles A. Sammons Cancer Center Network was launched, adding cancer programs at six additional BHCS facilities that hold CoC accreditation. Patients are able to draw upon the strength of the entire network, in terms of access to nationally recognized experts in the treatment of various types of cancer and the availability of the most advanced techniques and equipment, while being treated close to home.

CANCER CENTER ORGANIZATION AND GOVERNANCE

The principal objective of the Baylor Charles A. Sammons Cancer Center at Dallas has been to facilitate multidisciplinary interaction among specialists from different fields to provide the most comprehensive, high-quality care for patients. This multidisciplinary approach has been implemented and coordinated through more than a dozen "site-specific tumor" committees, as well as a two-tiered organizational structure consisting of a medical and executive committee. At the system level, a BHCS Oncology Medical Committee and Administrative Panel, as well as an Oncology Nursing Forum, have been established to coordinate quality goals and initiatives and facilitate the sharing of best practices between oncology programs across BHCS.

Site-Specific Tumor Committees

When the Baylor Charles A. Sammons Cancer Center at Dallas opened in 1976, many physicians felt that the traditional concept of a "tumor board," in which a small group of physicians discussed patients with a variety of different types of cancer, was outdated. Therefore, the Center created separate committees for each of the major cancer sites, with each responsible for organizing and running a site conference at regular intervals and coordinating educational and research activities related to that site. Today, there are 13 site-specific committees and conferences for bone and soft tissue, breast, chest, endocrine, head and neck, liver, pancreas, hematologic malignancies, neuro-oncology, skin, skull base, stem cell transplant, and urology.

Other BHCS centers within the Charles A. Sammons Cancer Center Network have similarly organized multidisciplinary tumor committees and conferences following the Dallas model. These gatherings are not necessarily organized around individual tumor sites, but do meet regularly to discuss developments in research and patient care pertaining to a range of cancer types. They are an important source of continuing education for oncology clinicians across BHCS.

Medical and Executive Committees

Cancer Center leaders realized by the early 1980s that a distinct organizational structure was necessary if the Cancer Center as a whole was to function in an effective multidisciplinary fashion. A two-tiered committee system was instituted:

1. The Medical Committee oversees site-tumor committees, quality of care, and outreach activities, serving in an advisory capacity to the director of the Cancer Center. It includes representatives from every major discipline involved in cancer care, including medical oncology, radiation oncology, surgery, pathology, radiology, nursing, and social work.
2. The Executive Committee is responsible for overall policy and integration of Cancer Center programs into BUMC, and includes the chair of each major department involved in cancer care.

Both are standing committees of the medical staff and, thus, report to the medical board. Both have high-level administrative representatives as members in addition to physicians. This two-tiered committee system has proved valuable in providing broad-based input from the medical staff, which is both necessary and desirable for the multidisciplinary organization of the Cancer Center. It has also served to provide integrated implementation of Cancer Center activities into the medical center as a whole.

At the Charles A. Sammons Center at Dallas, medical and administrative leadership are physically located in the same office suite to facilitate the flow of information and ideas and collaborative problem solving. Monthly operations meetings of administrative leaders, as well as nursing leadership, nurse managers, nurse educators, and oncology pharmacists, facilitate information sharing and identify areas for quality improvement.

System-Level Oncology Infrastructure

As oncology services have expanded to include other cancer programs across BHCS, so have the challenges of standardizing care practices and quality initiatives. In 2010, the BHCS Oncology Administrative Panel and BHCS Oncology Medical Committee were established to help coordinate these efforts. The Administrative Panel includes Oncology Service Line leaders from each BHCS hospital with an oncology program; the Medical Committee includes the medical chairs of each hospital's cancer committee. These groups meet quarterly and facilitate sharing of information and best practices, and setting of system-wide oncology strategic plans and improvement initiatives according to overall BHCS priorities in the areas of quality, service, people, and finance. They also provide a forum in which new treatment protocols or patient outreach programs developed and refined at one center can be shared with other sites.

The Oncology Nursing Forum was also established in 2010 to provide an opportunity for oncology clinicians from across BHCS to confer on issues concerning the safety and health outcomes of oncology patients. The forum also improves patient care through sharing of evidence-based best practices. Oncology nurse managers and supervisors from nine BHCS hospitals with inpatient services currently participate. It is also open to nurse educators and pharmacists. The forum meets quarterly to develop and review standard policies, procedures, and practice guidelines at all facilities. The forum also plays an important role in the continuing education of oncology nurses through educational offerings and support of national certification. The Oncology Nursing Forum is currently working to increase the number of Oncology Certified Nurses (OCN®) across the Oncology Service Line.

RESEARCH AND CLINICAL TRIALS

The advanced care available for cancer patients at the Baylor Charles A. Sammons Cancer Center at Dallas is driven by an aggressive program in basic and translational research. This research is increasingly focused on personalized and precision medicine, using therapies targeted to specific patient characteristics and to specific pathways involved in the biology of individual cancers. The Cancer Center's Innovative Clinical Trials Center consolidates all phase I and phase II clinical trials in one location, simplifying patient participation by providing a common location for all clinical examinations, infusions, sample collection for lab work, and follow-up visits.

The Office of Clinical Oncology Research Coordination was established in 2009 as the central repository of clinical research activity across BHCS. The office maintains a list of active protocols, including trials that are open for patient enrollment, and tracks patient accrual. Trials are available for a broad range of oncologic diagnoses. This office also supports BHCS memberships in many cooperative research groups and consortia including the Southwest Oncology Group, Gynecologic Oncology Group, Multiple Myeloma Research Consortium, Brain Tumor Trials Collaborative, and Cancer Immunotherapy Trials Network. The clinical oncology research program now includes more than 100 clinical trials at any given time, with more than 1,000 patients participating annually.

INITIATIVES TO IMPROVE QUALITY OF CARE

Delivering comprehensive, efficient, patient-centered care is a core mission of the Charles A. Sammons Cancer Center at Dallas and its sister programs throughout BHCS. Among the center's major programs to improve quality of care are (1) a specialized evaluation and treatment center equipped to attend to time-sensitive patient needs and reduce pressure on the emergency department, (2) a Patient Navigation Program to assist patients through the complexities of their cancer journeys, and (3) efforts to improve end-of-life education and care.

Efficient Delivery of Continuous Quality Cancer Care: The Oncology Evaluation and Treatment Center and Infusion Center Model

Comprehensive and coordinated cancer care is necessary to promote favorable clinical outcomes, but is costly due to the high costs of treatment and the preventable utilization of resources. Interventions in the emergency and urgent care settings are an important avenue for reducing avoidable health care utilization and improving the timeliness and efficiency of care, and it was with these goals in mind that the Oncology Evaluation and Treatment Center (OETC) and the Infusion Center were incorporated into the Baylor Charles A. Sammons Cancer Center at Dallas to deliver urgent care and infusions 24 hours a day.[6]

The OETC provides urgent care after office hours as well as scheduled diagnostic and treatment procedures during office hours to adult oncology patients.[6] If necessary, OETC patients may be transferred to the nearby BUMC ED.

The Infusion Center is open 24 hours a day, 7 days a week to provide oncology patients access to blood product transfusions, as well as hydration, chemotherapy, and biological therapy infusions. Interruptions in cancer care can be prevented by administering infusions that are due on weekends and holidays in the Infusion Center.

To promote efficient patient care, physicians staffing the OETC are able to access both outpatient and inpatient clinical records that use separate electronic health record systems. Evidence-based medicine is used as a guide to deliver high-quality cancer supportive care. The most prevalent patient clinical problems evaluated and treated in the OETC are used to periodically select relevant quality measures derived from the National Comprehensive Cancer Network Guidelines for Cancer Supportive Care.[7] Adherence to clinical outcome-based quality of care measures is monitored on a quarterly basis, as are Press Ganey patient satisfaction scores, and the duration of time that patients spend in the OETC. Cost efficiency measures focus on revenue generated, as well as the staff, facility, and ancillary service costs required to evaluate and treat patients.[6]

During the first quarter of operation, 89 percent of oncology patients seen for urgent care at BUMC were referred by their oncologists to the OETC instead of to the BUMC ED. The average time spent in the OETC (3 hours, 54 minutes) was 46 percent lower than it was for the BUMC ED (7 hours, 38 minutes), and the hospital admission rate from the OETC was 36 percent, compared with 84 percent for the BUMC ED, which was attributed to the specialized clinicians and facilities available in the OETC being able address the majority of patient needs.

Patient Navigation Program

Research studies have shown that the one-on-one attention and assistance given to patients through patient navigation systems are associated with (1) a decrease in the time between initial presentation and definitive treatment, (2) increased treatment adherence, (3) shorter duration of hospitalization, and (4) fewer cancer-related problems.[8] The Baylor Charles A. Sammons Cancer Center at Dallas launched a Patient Navigation Program in 2008.

The Patient Navigation Program at Dallas is staffed by five full-time, specially trained registered nurses and provides personalized help with every aspect of cancer care, ranging from diagnosis to treatment and recovery. Patient navigators begin by collecting necessary patient records and other information. They then work with the patient's physician to determine what tests, specialists, and support teams will be needed to manage the disease while also helping to schedule these visits. The navigator can even attend physician visits if requested. In addition to these logistical needs, nurse navigators offer education and support so that patients and their caregivers understand their disease and their personalized plan of care. For newly diagnosed patients, patient navigators provide an invaluable service by reducing intimidation from a frightening and complex process. Patient navigators also help patients who may have exhausted standard treatment options and are seeking a clinical trial for a new investigational therapy. They can help find an appropriate trial, determine whether a patient qualifies, and gain access to the clinicians conducting the trial. Assistance navigating the cancer journey extends beyond clinic and hospital walls. The nurse navigator follows up with patients three months, six months, and one year following discharge from the hospital.

About 30 percent of patients at the Charles A. Sammons Center at Dallas are currently served by patient navigators, and the program has met with high levels of patient satisfaction, as evidenced by written and verbal feedback to Cancer Center staff and BHCS Board members, and a nearly 60 percent increase in navigator utilization from 2010 to 2012 (Figure 23.1). The program's goal is for at least one patient navigator to be dedicated to each site-specific cancer. More broadly, BHCS is working toward the ultimate goal that every patient diagnosed with cancer have access to a patient navigator.

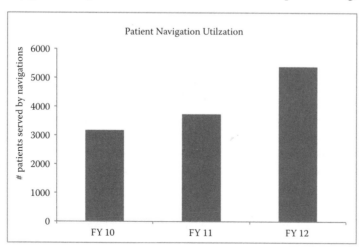

FIGURE 23.1 Increased patient navigator program utilization at the Charles A. Sammons Center at Dallas.

Improving End-of-Life Education and Care

The American Society of Clinical Oncology and other groups recommend that discussions about palliative and end-of-life care begin shortly after a patient has been diagnosed with advanced cancer.[9] Several studies have found that such discussions between physicians and patients lead to better patient and caregiver outcomes. These include improvement in symptoms, quality of life, patient satisfaction, and reduced caregiver burden. Earlier involvement of palliative care also leads to more appropriate referral to and use of hospice, which reduces use of costly and futile intensive care. Based on these findings, as well as a survey of hematology-oncology inpatient services at BUMC, the Charles A. Sammons Cancer Center at Dallas has implemented several initiatives to improve the frequency and timing of end-of-life discussions. These include (1) an education program to improve oncologists' communication skills, (2) addition of palliative care providers to the outpatient clinic, and (3) increased palliative care consults for patients with non-small cell lung cancer. In addition, an 11-bed inpatient hospice services program was opened on the BUMC campus in March 2013, to provide treatment and support for cancer and other ill patients with end-of-life care needs.

Approximately 30 oncologists so far have participated in the educational program to improve communication skills. The six-hour workshop covers issues in cancer communication from diagnosis to end of life including: (1) fundamental communication skills including giving bad news, (2) managing transitions to palliative care when appropriate, (3) talking about advance care plans and do-not-resuscitate orders, and (4) discussing treatment options and informed consent.

The Cancer Center plans to add a nurse specially trained in palliative care and advanced care planning to its outpatient clinic staff to facilitate end-of-life education, counseling, and care when necessary.

Finally, the Cancer Center is working to increase the percentage of patients with non-small cell lung cancer who receive palliative care consults. Metastatic non-small cell lung cancer is the leading cause of death from cancer worldwide, and is typically associated with a high burden of symptoms and poor quality of life. Research has shown that among these cancer patients, early palliative care led to significant improvements in both quality of life and mood. As compared with patients receiving standard care, patients receiving early palliative care had less aggressive care at the end of life, but longer survival.[10]

ACCREDITATION AND STANDARDIZED DATA COLLECTION

Accreditation and standardized data collection are important means by which health care organizations and their component clinical programs evaluate their performance and initiate improvements to ensure that patient care meets or exceeds the highest national standards. Quality improvement initiatives across the Oncology Service Line are guided by several national accreditations. Areas for improvement are also identified through use of oncology dashboards that track monthly metrics in the BHCS four areas of focus: people, service, quality, and finance.

National Accreditation

Individual Sammons Cancer Center facilities maintain several national accreditations that demonstrate their voluntary commitment to providing the highest quality comprehensive cancer care including:

- American College of Surgeons Commission on Cancer (CoC): http://www.facs.org/cancer/coc/whatis.html
- Foundation for the Accreditation of Cellular Therapy (FACT): http://www.factwebsite.org/
- National Accreditation Program for Breast Centers (NAPBC): http://napbc-breast.org/

Cancer Registry

BHCS maintains a cancer registry similar to those at other leading cancer centers across the nation. The registry has been in continuous operation since January 1960 and is essential to effective patient care, education, and research at BHCS. The primary duties of the registry include abstracting cancer data (including site, histology, stage, and treatment) on all reportable cancers, and providing a lifetime of reporting on patients. To ensure data quality, each cancer registrar works with the medical staff in completing quality reviews of more than 10 percent of annual abstracts. Casefinding is conducted monthly for inpatient and outpatient departments.

Cancer registry data are used to measure compliance with evidence-based clinical practice guidelines endorsed by the CoC and NAPBC. The data also enable the medical staff at BHCS to assess the quality of care delivered to its patients and identify areas for improvement. Cancer registry data are reported to the Texas Cancer Registry (required) and the National Cancer Data Base.

Oncology Dashboards

In addition to adhering to the standards of national accrediting bodies, quality of cancer care at BHCS is monitored and evaluated through monthly

TABLE 23.2 Example goals outlined in the Baylor Health Care System
Oncology Strategic Plan for FY2013–2015

Pillar of Patient Care	Goal
People	Increase the number of certified oncology nurses by 10%
Quality	Develop and implement BHCS Oncology Chemotherapy order sets
Service	Standardize core outpatient navigation program at each cancer center
Finance	Increase oncology contribution margin by 3%

oncology dashboards. These dashboards report general hospital metrics, such as infection rates and average risk of mortality, as well as metrics specific to oncology practice: oncology mortality rate, time to first dose of antibiotic for neutropenic patients, percentage of nurses who are OCN certified, number of patient navigator visits, and patient accrual to clinical trials. Additional dashboards, relating specifically to bone marrow transplants and breast imaging, are produced as well. All dashboard metrics are aligned with BHCS's four areas of focus—people, service, quality, and finance—and are used to help identify areas and goals for strategic quality improvement. Example goals outlined in the BHCS Oncology Strategic Plan for FY2013–2015 are listed in Table 23.2.

LESSONS LEARNED

The principal objective of the Baylor Charles A. Sammons Cancer Center at Dallas since it was founded has been to facilitate multidisciplinary interaction among specialists from different fields to provide the most effective care for patients. A two-tiered committee structure designed to support this vision has been integral to the growth and development of the center into the largest unit of the BHCS Oncology Service Line.

The launch of the Charles A. Sammons Cancer Center Network has not only extended the reach of high-quality cancer care to patients across North Texas, but provided new opportunities for learning, collaboration, and innovation among oncology researchers, clinicians, and other care providers across the health care system to improve the quality of cancer care. Lessons learned over nearly four decades at the first Charles A. Sammons Cancer Center in Dallas have helped guide the expansion of a network of centers whose personnel, resources, and experiences are affording additional opportunities for growth and improvement. A system-wide medical and administrative oncology infrastructure has played an important role in facilitating the sharing of resources and best practices, achieving national accreditations, and setting of strategic goals aligned with the BHCS goal of delivering STEEEP care.

CONCLUSION

The comprehensive and integrative approach to cancer care taken by the Baylor Charles A. Sammons Cancer Center at Dallas and its sister programs across BHCS strives to provide STEEEP care. The Oncology Service Line's ongoing dedication to cancer care, cancer education, research, and clinical trials is enabled by a clinical and administrative infrastructure that fosters multidisciplinary collaboration, a system-wide commitment to quality measurement and improvement, and a shared vision of providing help, hope, and healing to all patients and their loved ones.

REFERENCES

1. American Cancer Society. 2013. Cancer facts & figures 2013. Online at: http://www.cancer.org/research/cancerfactsfigures/cancerfactsfigures/cancer-facts-figures 2013 (accessed May 15, 2013).
2. The National Cancer Act. P.L. 92–218. 92nd Congress, 1971.
3. Stone, M. J., B. E. Aronoff, W. P. Evans, J. W. Fay, Z. H. Lieberman, C. M. Matthews, G. J. Race, R. P. Scruggs, and C. A. Stringer, Jr. 2003. History of the Baylor Charles A. Sammons Cancer Center. *Proceedings (Baylor University Medical Center)* 16 (1): 30–58.
4. American College of Surgeons. Cancer programs. Online at: http://www.facs.org/cancer/ (accessed May 15, 2013).
5. Winter, F. D., Jr. 2004. Group practice at Baylor University Medical Center. *Proceedings (Baylor University Medical Center)* 17 (1): 64–72.
6. Coyle, Y. M., A. M. Miller, and R. S. Paulson. 2013. Model for the cost-efficient delivery of continuous quality cancer care: A hospital and private-practice collaboration. *Proceedings (Baylor University Medical Center)* 26 (2): 95–99.
7. National Comprehensive Cancer Network. *Clinical practice guidelines in oncology.* Online at: http://www.nccn.org/professionals/physician_gls/f_guidelines.asp (accessed May 15, 2013).
8. Fillion, L., M. de Serres, S. Cook, R. L. Goupil, I. Bairati, and R. Doll. 2009. Professional patient navigation in head and neck cancer. *Seminars in Oncology Nursing* 25 (3): 212–221.
9. Smith, T. J., S. Temin, E. R. Alesi, A. P. Abernethy, T. A. Balboni, E. M. Basch, B. R. Ferrell, et al. 2012. American Society of Clinical Oncology provisional clinical opinion: The integration of palliative care into standard oncology care. *Journal of Clinical Oncology* 30 (8): 880–887.
10. Temel, J. S., J. A. Greer, A. Muzikansky, E. R. Gallagher, S. Admane, V. A. Jackson, C. M. Dahlin, et al. 2010. Early palliative care for patients with metastatic non-small-cell lung cancer. *New England Journal of Medicine* 363 (8): 733–742.

Chapter 24

Surgical Services

Ernest W. Franklin, IV

CONTENTS

INTRODUCTION

Over the past century, surgical care has evolved into a more standardized and evidence-based practice, with numerous national and international organizations, such as Centers for Medicare and Medicaid Services (CMS), The Joint Commission, World Health Organization (WHO), and the National Surgical Quality Improvement Program (NSQIP) providing guidelines to improve surgical quality. Surgical quality initiatives at BHCS are aligned with implementing the national and international initiatives, but numerous internal improvement initiatives have also been developed to drive quality across Surgical Services.

SURGICAL CARE IMPROVEMENT PROJECT

The publicly reported CMS Core Measures provide one means of comparing the quality of care that hospitals offer, as measured by their compliance with evidence-based recommendations for four priority conditions/areas of care.[1] Since 2003, the Core Measures have included a measure set for Surgical Infection Prevention (SIP). In 2006, this set was transitioned to the Surgical Care Improvement Project (SCIP) measures.[2]

TABLE 24.1 Surgical Care Improvement Project core measures, 2013

Measure	Process of Care
Core SCIP/SIP-Inf-1a	Antibiotic within one hour of incision
Core SCIP/SIP-Inf-2a	Antibiotic selection
Core SCIP/SIP-Inf-3a	Antibiotic discontinued within 24 hours
Core SCIP-Inf-4	Cardiac patients 6 a.m. postoperative serum glucose
Core SCIP-Inf-6	Appropriate hair removal
Core SCIP-Inf-9	Urinary catheter removed postoperative day 1 or postoperative day 2
Core SCIP-Inf-10	Surgery patients with perioperative temperature management
Core SCIP-CARD-2	Beta blocker prior to admission and perioperatively
Core SCIP-VTE-1	Venous thromboembolism prophylaxis ordered
Core SCIP-VTE-2	Venous thromboembolism prophylaxis timing

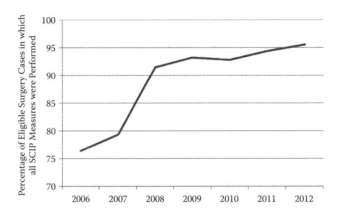

FIGURE 24.1 Baylor Health Care System performance on Surgical Care Improvement Project All-or-None Bundle (2006–2012).

SCIP is a national quality partnership of organizations interested in significantly reducing surgical complications, advised by technical expert panels with the expertise and resources to ensure the SCIP measures are fully supported by evidence-based research.[2] Current SCIP measures are presented in Table 24.1.

BHCS performance on the SCIP all-or-none bundle (i.e., the percent of eligible surgery cases in which all SCIP measures were performed and documented) from 2006 through 2012 is presented in Figure 24.1.

WORLD HEALTH ORGANIZATION (WHO) SAFE SURGERY SAVES LIVES INITIATIVE

The WHO launched the Safe Surgery Saves Lives (SSSL) initiative in January 2007 to reduce variation in surgical care.[3] BHCS piloted the SSSL checklist at eight hospitals and, in a sample of 3,733 surgical cases, demonstrated that this checklist reduced inpatient complications from 11.0 to 7.0 percent (p = 0.003) and 30-day mortality rates from 1.5 to 0.8 percent (p <0.001). As a result, BHCS adopted a resolution to fully implement the WHO SSSL checklist in 2009.

The SSSL checklist targets important safety issues, including effective surgical teamwork and communication, safe anesthesia practices, and prevention of surgical infections. Using the checklist requires team members to consistently follow critical steps to reduce risks to patients. Effective use requires the involvement and support of surgeons and anesthesia providers, as well as an understanding that all team members are expected to speak up if they see that the process is not being followed.

The BHCS SSSL checklist is displayed in Table 24.2.

NATIONAL SURGERY QUALITY IMPROVEMENT PROGRAM

BHCS is a member of the American College of Surgeons (ACS) NSQIP, a data-driven, risk-adjusted, outcomes-based surgical quality improvement program. It originated in the Veterans Health Administration and has been operational since 1991; implementation in the private sector began in 2001.[4]

NSQIP analyzes general and vascular surgery cases as well as cases from eight subspecialties (gynecologic, neurologic, orthopedic, otolaryngologic, plastic, cardiac, thoracic, and urologic surgery). Under NSQIP, hospitals provide data (abstracted by a dedicated clinical reviewer) on 135 pre-, intra-, and postoperative variables to ACS NAQIP for analysis. Data are reported back to hospitals, which then act on their data (designing and implementing quality improvement initiatives), and use data to monitor the success of the initiatives.

All outcomes are assessed 30 days after index surgery, and NSQIP constructs case-mix adjusted expected outcomes for comparison with the observed outcomes so that hospitals can see how they are performing relative to other participating hospitals.[4]

Participation in NSQIP facilitates the evaluation and monitoring of surgical quality improvement initiatives at BHCS hospitals, and dissemination of successful initiatives across the organization.

SURGICAL SERVICES GOVERNANCE

A system-wide Surgeons' Council and Operating Room Council lead surgical quality improvement efforts across BHCS. These councils work together to drive standardization of surgical processes and products, hold people accountable for metrics, and share best surgical practices across the organization.

TABLE 24.2 Baylor Health Care System
Safe Surgery Saves Lives checklist

SIGN IN (Before Induction of Anesthesia)

☐ Patient/designee has confirmed: identity, site, procedure, consent
☐ Site marked/not applicable
   ☐ Anesthesia safety check completed
   ☐ Anesthesia TIME OUT
Known allergy?
☐ Yes ☐ No
Difficult airway/aspiration risk?
☐ No ☐ Yes, and equipment/assistance available
Type & Crossmatch done?
☐ Yes ☐ No
☐ Need for Beta Blockers addressed

TIME OUT/PAUSE (Before Skin Incision)

☐ Confirm all team members have been introduced by name and role and actively participate
Briefing:
☐ Positioning
☐ Implants/special equipment/supplies
☐ Instrumentation
☐ Sterility (including indicator results) has been confirmed?
☐ TIME OUT–Surgical team verbally confirms correct patient, procedure, position, side and
   site; surgical site marking visible after patient prepped and draped; accurate consent form;
at _____ (time)
☐ TIME OUT–for new physician or new procedure
at _____ (time)
☐ Surgeon reviews: Critical or unexpected steps, operative duration, anticipated blood
   loss–risk of greater than 500 mL blood loss (7 mL/kg in children), need to administer
   antibiotics or fluids for irrigation
Antibiotic prophylaxis given within the last 60 minutes? (120 minutes for vancomycin
and fluoroquinilones)
☐ Yes _____ IV (medication) at _____ (time)
☐ Not applicable
Is essential imaging properly labeled and displayed?
☐ Yes ☐ Not applicable

SIGN OUT (Before patient leaves operating room)

RN verbally confirms with the team:
☐ The name of the procedure completed and wound classification
☐ Instrument, sponge, and needle counts are completed (or not applicable)
☐ All specimens appropriately labeled and sent (including patient name)
☐ Whether there are any equipment or other problems to be addressed
☐ Surgical team reviews the key concerns for recovery and management of this patient

RN Signature: _____ Date: _____ Time: _____

Surgeons' Council

The Surgeons' Council consists of surgeon and anesthesiologist members, and is chartered with providing advice and guidance, elevating issues, supporting operating room directors in making changes (to ensure facility-level surgeon support for controversial decisions), and influencing fellow operating room-based physicians to improve or standardize practices. To enable this work, the Council:

- Reviews clinical outcomes data on a scheduled basis and assists the hospitals' chief medical officer/vice president of medical affairs in addressing poor performance on quality, readmission, and complication rate measures with outlier surgeons and anesthesiologists;
- Reviews operational performance data for their hospital's operating room and leads/influences discussion about individual performance with physicians;
- Supports the Operating Room Council in surgical product selection, product comparisons, communications of results, and enforcement of product policies;
- Reviews mortality and other patient safety measures; and
- Suggests and implements improvement activities at the system and hospital level, based upon the above listed scheduled reviews.

Operating Room Council

The Operating Room Council is responsible for:

- Driving operational changes to improve efficiency in BHCS's operating rooms;
- Training the next generation of operating room nurses by attracting, retaining, and developing surgical nurse leaders;
- Standardizing practices and policies across BHCS to provide a consistent and high-quality surgical environment; and
- Improving perioperative nursing practice by implementing guidelines developed by the Association of Operating Room Nurses and American Society of Peri-Anesthesia Nurses.

The Operating Room Council also has oversight responsibilities that overlap significantly with the actions of the Surgeons' Council, reviewing the same performance measures, engaging in discussions with poor performers to get their practices into alignment with quality standards and procedures, supporting the Surgeons' Council in surgical product selection and enforcement of product policies, and suggesting and implementing improvement initiatives.

STANDARDIZATION OF SURGICAL QUALITY IMPROVEMENT INITIATIVES

Traditionally, standardizing surgical processes and improvement efforts has posed challenges because of the staffing model for surgeons and anesthesiologists. Surgeons who perform inpatient surgeries at BHCS may perform outpatient surgeries elsewhere, and anesthesiologists often travel between surgery sites. Overcoming these challenges to standardization is a specific area of focus for the Surgeons' and Operating Room Councils. Strategies BHCS has implemented include a standard preadmitting testing algorithm to improve effectiveness and efficiency, a standardized surgical consent process (using system-wide dynamic consent forms available in both English and Spanish), and deployment of standardized order sets.

ENHANCING SURGEON LEADERSHIP BEHAVIORS DURING TEAM FORMATION

Improving teamwork in the operating room can improve the safety and quality of surgery, and surgeon leadership plays an important role in establishing operating room teamwork.[5-7] The BHCS Office of Patient Safety recently examined surgeon leadership behaviors through observation of surgical procedures and unstructured interviews with surgeons and operating room staff to identify a set of ideal surgeon leadership behaviors. The four identified behaviors were engagement of team members, introduction of the patient, setting of a safety focus, and empowerment of team members. When surgeons and operating staff were surveyed regarding the importance of these behaviors and the consistency with which they were performed, there was strong agreement on importance (96–99% of surgeons and 92–100% of operating room staff rated each behavior as very or somewhat important), but staff were half as likely as surgeons (21 vs. 44%; p < 0.001) to report that these behaviors were performed consistently (8–10 times in the last 10 cases). BHCS is working to disseminate these results to promote the use of the four ideal leadership behaviors among surgeons. To further enhance teamwork, BHCS also, to the extent possible, assigns members of the surgical team based on the physicians' requests during the entire period that the surgeon is in the operating room for a given day.

LESSONS LEARNED

The first lesson BHCS has learned in its efforts to improve quality across Surgical Services is the importance of the right leadership. Effective leaders are both open to change and see the need to change. Physician leadership is also integral to quality improvement in Surgical Services. In the operating room environment, physician leaders are needed to champion the development of metrics and goals, and physician-to-physician discussions are needed both to create a culture that fosters quality improvement and to drive adoption of changes in practice.

The second lesson learned is that strong information technology support is a valuable quality improvement tool in Surgical Services because daily metrics are an effective means of driving improvement in this particular context.

CONCLUSION

BHCS uses numerous strategies to improve and sustain high-quality surgical care, including adherence to SCIP measures; use of a SSSL checklist; participation in NSQIP; system-wide Surgeons' and Operating Room Councils charged with driving standardization of surgical processes and implementation of improvement initiatives; and system-level efforts to identify and enhance surgeon leadership behaviors to foster teamwork in the operating room. BHCS is committed to providing consistent, accountable, high-quality surgical care.

REFERENCES

1. The Joint Commission. Core Measure sets. Online at: http://www.jointcommission.org/core_measure_sets.aspx (accessed January 30, 2013).
2. The Joint Commission. 2012. Surgical Care Improvement Project. August 15. Online at: http://www.jointcommission.org/surgical_care_improvement_project/ (accessed April 16, 2013).
3. Haynes, A. B., T. G. Weiser, W. R. Berry, S. R. Lipsitz, A. H. Breizat, E. P. Dellinger, T. Herbosa, et al. 2009. A surgical safety checklist to reduce morbidity and mortality in a global population. *New England Journal of Medicine* 360 (5): 491–499.
4. American College of Surgeons. National Surgical Quality Improvement Program (ACS NSQIP®). Online at: http://site.acsnsqip.org/ (accessed April 16, 2013).
5. Healy, G. B., J. Barker, and G. Madonna. 2006. Error reduction through team leadership: The surgeon as a leader. *Bulletin of the American College of Surgeons* 91 (11): 26–29.
6. Greenberg, C. C., S. E. Regenbogen, S. R. Lipsitz, R. Diaz-Flores, and A. A. Gawande,. 2008. The frequency and significance of discrepancies in the surgical count. *Annals of Surgery* 248 (2): 337–341.
7. Mazzocco, K., D. B. Petitti, K. T. Fong, D. Bonacum, J. Brookey, S. Graham, R. E. Lasky, J. B. Sexton, and E. J. Thomas. 2009. Surgical team behaviors and patient outcomes. *The American Journal of Surgery* 197 (5): 678–685.

Chapter 25

Orthopedic Services

Fabian E. Polo, Jay D. Mabrey, Alan Jones, and Jerri J. Garison

CONTENTS

INTRODUCTION

Musculoskeletal disorders and diseases are the leading cause of disability in the United States and account for more than half of all chronic conditions in people older than age 50 years in developed countries.[1] The BHCS Orthopedic Service Line is dedicated to caring for the myriad injuries and diseases that can affect the body's bones, joints, ligaments, tendons, muscles, and nerves. It encompasses orthopedics departments at 11 regional hospitals as well as the Baylor Orthopedic and Spine Hospital at Arlington, Texas.

SERVICE LINE STRUCTURE AND GOVERNANCE

The Orthopedic Service Line combines clinical care, research, and patient education to diagnose, treat, and provide follow-up care for orthopedic conditions ranging from arthritis and bone fractures to sports and spinal injuries. Depending on the diagnosis, treatments vary from conservative, nonsurgical options to high-tech, minimally invasive surgery or comprehensive joint replacement. Multidisciplinary care teams at each BHCS facility include expertise in sports medicine, trauma, rehabilitation, and total joint replacement, and are able to assess patient needs and work with patients to determine the appropriate course of treatment.

A system-wide Orthopedic Practice Council was established in 2012 to help standardize evidence-based, best-care practices and set quality improvement goals and action plans for the service line. The council is led by three co-chairs, an executive sponsor, and a physician champion, and includes a representative from the orthopedics department of each BHCS facility. The council meets monthly, and is tasked with developing standardized care paths so that patients receive similar treatment across facilities, identifying opportunities for continuing education of physicians and surgeons and effective physician recruitment strategies, and charting progress toward meeting specific quality improvement goals.

INITIATIVES TO IMPROVE ORTHOPEDIC CARE

System-wide initiatives to improve orthopedic care emphasize standardization of care procedures to reduce surgical complications and improve patient outcomes. Order sets have been developed and implemented for general orthopedic care and orthopedic outpatient surgery, as well as preoperative and postoperative care related to foot and ankle surgery, shoulder and elbow surgery, and joint replacement. These order sets incorporate best practices with respect to therapies that can improve surgical outcomes: venous thromboembolism prophylaxis, antibiotic prophylaxis, and glucose control. As shown in Table 25.1, recent quality improvement initiatives across the Orthopedic Service Line have focused on three areas of practice that account for the largest patient volumes: low back pain (LBP), hip fracture, and total joint replacement.

Improving Low Back Pain Care

About one quarter of adults in the United States reported having LBP in the past three months and 2 percent of all physician office visits are for low back complaints.[2] In 2005, total healthcare expenditures for LBP in the United States were estimated at $85.9 billion.[3] When used appropriately,[4] diagnostic imaging (radiographs, magnetic resonance imaging, computed tomography scans) is an important component of care for low back complaints. However, inappropriate imaging increases the risk of patient harm through unnecessary radiation exposure as well as surgery (and the inherent risks therein), and creates fear avoidance or other detrimental behaviors due to misconceptions about LBP that can predispose patients to chronic problems. Frequent and unnecessary imaging is also a major contributor to exorbitant health care costs without improving patient outcomes.[5]

TABLE 25.1 Example quality improvement initiatives
and goals outlined by the BHCS Orthopedic Practice Council

Quality Improvement Initiative	Goal
Low Back Pain	
Development of a low back pain protocol	Reduce unnecessary use of lumbar spine imaging
Hip Fracture	
Develop BHCS Hip Fracture Order Set	Reduce practice variations, errors, length of stay, and readmission rate
Standardized pre-op education	Improve management of patient expectations and outcomes
Improve osteoporosis diagnosis and treatment	Reduce potentially avoidable hospital admissions, reduce cost and resource utilization, address population health management
Total Joint Replacement	
Order set/care path development	Reduce complications and costs
Standardized pre-op education	Improve patient/family satisfaction and outcomes
Outcomes data collection	Evaluate comparative effectiveness of implants, surgical techniques, and treatment protocols
Blood use study	Reduce use of autologous blood use during surgery

Guided by recommendations from the American College of Physicians and the American Pain Society for the diagnosis and treatment of low back pain,[6] HealthTexas Provider Network (HTPN) (see Chapter 14) developed an LBP protocol to assist physicians in providing evidence-based treatment, while reducing costly and unnecessary imaging and/or diagnostic studies. The protocol directs clinicians to conduct a focused history and physical examination that includes assessment of psychosocial risk factors, which predict risk for chronic disabling back pain.[6] It also outlines procedures for three phases of treatment depending on the severity of the case/persistence of symptoms. The protocol was approved by the HTPN Best Care Committee in August 2012 and by the HTPN Board in September 2012.

Improving Hip Fracture Care

In fiscal year 2012, BHCS treated about 1,000 cases of hip fracture across eight facilities. This number is expected to climb as the U.S. population ages. In 2012, the average age of hip fracture patients was 78, the average length of stay was 5.4 days, and the 30-day readmission rate was 8.4 percent. The BHCS Orthopedic Practice Council, thus, has identified a number of goals related to improving patient outcomes and reducing the costs associated with hip fracture care.

Hip fractures in the elderly carry risk for all the potential medical complications that arise when aging patients are confined to a bed, including the development of pneumonia, pressure ulcers, deep vein thrombosis, urinary tract infection, and delirium. BHCS has implemented standardized order sets to address many of these complications, and is now developing a comprehensive Hip Fracture Order Set that will alert physicians to potential risks and guide them through evidence-based care paths to prevent these complications.

The best way to improve hip fracture care is to prevent the fractures from occurring in the first place. BHCS is working to identify patients at high risk for hip fracture, for example, through osteoporosis screening. Identifying patients at high risk of fragility fractures enables patient education and treatment to be initiated before a bone-damaging fall occurs.

To better manage patient expectations and outcomes related to those expectations, BHCS has developed a comprehensive patient guide to hip fracture treatment as part of the Joint Wellness Program that has been adopted by all BHCS facilities.[7] This guide educates patients and their caregivers about the types of hip fractures, the surgical treatment options (and potential complications), and physical and occupational therapy and other rehabilitation options. It also provides instructions for everyday maneuvers, such as climbing stairs, getting in and out of the car, dressing, and getting into and out of bed as well as strategies for preventing future falls.

Improving Total Joint Care

Total joint arthroplasty (reconstruction or replacement) remains the definitive treatment for advanced, symptomatic joint destruction regardless of the underlying cause.[1] Joint replacement surgeries are expected to increase as these procedures become safer and the implants more durable, expanding the population likely to benefit from surgery to both older and younger patients. The BHCS Orthopedic Service Line performs more than 3,000 joint replacements annually, and is committed to improving the quality of these procedures as well as patient outcomes. Goals include developing order sets and standard care paths to reduce practice variation, length of stay, and surgical complications; developing a staffing structure that provides greater consistency between surgical teams; improving preoperative education; and enhancing outcomes data collection for comparative effectiveness studies.

Improved Safety and Efficiency through Reduction in Total Joint Blood Use

In the 1980s, preoperative autologous blood donation (PABD) became a common practice for patients undergoing total joint replacement due to concerns about transmission of viral diseases through the allogeneic blood supply.

Twenty years later, it was still common practice at BHCS hospitals for patients to predonate one to two units of blood, and for those units to be transfused after surgery, regardless of the patient's need for them. However, a growing number of studies were revealing some of the drawbacks of PABD as a standard practice, such as greater incidence of preoperative and postoperative anemia (increasing the likelihood of a patient needing a transfusion during and/or after surgery), general risks of bacterial contamination and clerical errors that are associated with all stored blood; poor cost-effectiveness due to special handling and storage requirements, inconvenience to the patient, and substantial waste in terms of unused and discarded blood units.[8,9] BHCS examined its own blood use practices with respect to total joint replacements and determined a need to reduce autologous blood use.

Reducing routine autologous blood use required convincing surgeons to change their standard practice. To facilitate this change, each surgeon received a profile of his blood use compared to his peers every six months. Blood use was also monitored and reported at the hospital level, showing a declining trend over the years to which individual surgeon performance was compared. These efforts decreased the percentage of primary unilateral knee or hip replacement patients who received blood by one third from 2001 to 2007, as did the average amount of blood used per case (Figure 25.1). Importantly, the volume of allogeneic blood used did not go up to compensate for the reduction in autologous blood use. The reduction in blood use in hip and knee surgery since 2001 is estimated to have reduced hospital expenditures by about $250,000 per year.

Joint Wellness Program

People who have joint replacement surgery are not "ill." The Joint Wellness Program was designed to make sure patients know that and to help them quickly return to their normal lives. Patients who have joint replacement surgery at BHCS are automatically enrolled in the Joint Wellness Program. Each BHCS hospital has a designated unit with private rooms, dedicated staff trained to work with joint replacement patients, group exercise classes and education sessions, and postdischarge care coordination. Patients are encouraged to dress in clothes from home, rather than hospital gowns, as soon as possible. They also are encouraged to stay up in specially designed reclining chairs for most of the day and in bed only when they need to rest. The program also includes optional, but highly recommended, preoperative education. This pre-op education and the coordinated care that patients receive after surgery enables them to leave the hospital sooner and better prepared to continue their rehabilitation at home. During postsurgical care, patients participate in physical therapy sessions with others who had surgery the same day, adding an element of camaraderie to the healing process. Family or friends also are encouraged to participate and act as coaches.

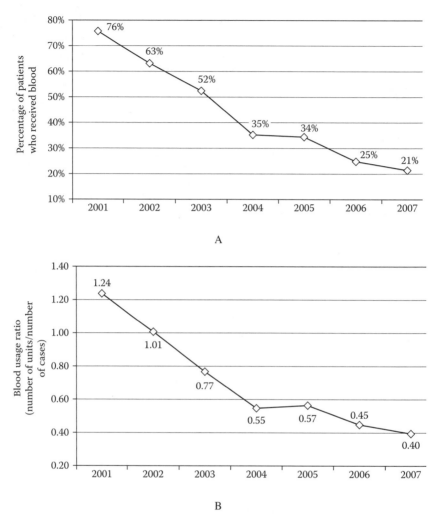

FIGURE 25.1 (A) Percentage of primary unilateral knee or hip replacement patients who received blood and (B) rate of blood usage (no. of units/no. of cases) knee or hip replacement cases, 2001 to 2007.

National Data Collaboratives and Registries

Clinical data registries and collaboratives play an important role in improving patient outcomes and ensuring patient safety by providing large data sets that cover a wide range of care providers and procedures and driving informed research studies. The BHCS Orthopedic Service Line has committed to two such efforts that address total joint care quality and outcomes: the American Joint Replacement Registry (AJRR)[10] and the High Value HealthCare Collaborative (HVHC).[11]

The AJRR is a collaborative effort supported by more than 100 hospitals, several national societies (including the American Academy of Orthopedic Surgeons), health insurers, consumers, and government agencies, such as the Centers for Medicare and Medicaid Services and Agency for Healthcare Research and Quality. More than a data repository, the AJRR provides a wide range of actionable information and reporting that can be used to evaluate the comparative effectiveness of implants, surgical techniques and treatment protocols, and improve care quality and patient outcomes.

HVHC is a consortium of health care systems formed in 2011 to improve health care quality, lower costs, and move best practices out to the national provider community. Participating health care systems are committed to sharing care pathways and cost and outcomes data with each other and the public as they adopt best practices and new, expanded standards of measurement. The collaborative is focusing on nine increasingly prevalent condition/disease-specific areas that have wide variation in rates, costs, and outcomes nationally: total knee replacement, diabetes, asthma, hip surgery, heart failure, perinatal care, depression, spine surgery, and weight loss surgery.

An HVHC analysis of total knee replacement delivery revealed substantial variations across the participating health care organizations in surgery times, length of stay, discharge dispositions, and in-hospital complication rates.[12] The study also revealed that higher surgeon caseloads were associated with shorter length of stay and operating time as well as fewer in-hospital complications. HVHC participants are now testing the effects of coordinated management for medically complex patients, use of dedicated teams, and a process to improve the management of patients' expectations.

LESSONS LEARNED

The Orthopedic Service Line comprises a number of individual group practices and independent physicians, many of whom also work in ambulatory surgery centers, physical therapy/rehabilitation centers, and other entities not affiliated with BHCS. This posed challenges to establishing a system-wide quality improvement infrastructure and standardizing care paths, supplies, and surgical protocols. The creation of the BHCS Orthopedic Council is helping to address these challenges by bringing together stakeholders from across the health care system, facilitating physician/surgeon buy-in. BHCS's commitment to national initiatives such as the HVHC and AJRR have also proved useful in providing a framework for collecting data, sharing best practices, and implementing initiatives to enhance care quality, improve patient outcomes and reduce costs. Transparent reporting of performance measures and clinical outcomes data has been another important motivator for improvement as it appeals to a physician's competitive nature.

CONCLUSION

The Orthopedic Service Line at BHCS is dedicated to improving the quality of life for people with musculoskeletal conditions and injuries, chronic or acute. Standardizing care paths, reducing surgical complications, collaborative data collection, and improving patient education are common themes underlying quality improvement initiatives across the service line, particularly in the areas of low back pain, hip fracture, and total joint replacement. These endeavors are all aimed at facilitating better informed decision making, more timely and effective patient follow-up and intervention, and enhanced quality control. Physician leadership and a culture supporting the practice of evidenced-based care and quality improvement are essential to the success of these and other service line efforts.

REFERENCES

1. United States Bone and Joint Initiative. 2011. *The burden of musculoskeletal diseases in the United States*. Rosemont, IL: American Academy of Orthopaedic Surgeons.
2. Deyo, R. A., S. K. Mirza, and B. I. Martin. 2006. Back pain prevalence and visit rates: Estimates from U.S. national surveys, 2002. *Spine* (Philadelphia, PA 1976) 31 (23): 2724–2727.
3. Martin, B. I., R. A. Deyo, S. K. Mirza, J. A. Turner, B. A. Comstock, W. Hollingworth, and S. D. Sullivan. 2008. Expenditures and health status among adults with back and neck problems. *JAMA* 299 (6): 656–664.
4. Fitch, K., S. J. Bernstein, M. S. Aguilar, B. Burnand, J. R. LaCalle, P. Lazaro, M. van het Loo, et al. 2001. *The RAND/UCLA Appropriateness Method User's Manual*. Arlington, VA: RAND.
6. Flynn, T. W., B. Smith, and R. Chou. 2011. Appropriate use of diagnostic imaging in low back pain: A reminder that unnecessary imaging may do as much harm as good. *Journal of Orthopaedic & Sports Physical Therapy* 41 (11): 838–846.
6. Chou, R., A. Qaseem, V. Snow, D. Casey, J. T. Cross, Jr., P. Shekelle, and D. K. Owens. 2007. Diagnosis and treatment of low back pain: A joint clinical practice guideline from the American College of Physicians and the American Pain Society. *Annals of Internal Medicine* 147 (7): 478–491.
7. Joint Wellness Program at Baylor University Medical Center. 2009. Patient guide to hip fracture treatment. Online at: http://www.baylorhealth.com/PhysiciansLocations/Dallas/SpecialtiesServices/Orthopaedics/Documents/Hip%20Fractures%20Guide_Web.pdf (accessed April 14, 2013).
8. Rosencher, N., and A. Shander. 2006. Preoperative autologous blood donation. *Transfusion Alternatives in Transfusion Medicine* 8 (1): 29–34.
9. Spence, R. K. 2004. Current concepts and issues in blood management. *Orthopedics* 27 (6 Suppl): s643–s651.
10. American Joint Replacement Registry. Online at: http://teamwork.aaos.org/ajrr/default.aspx (accessed May 15, 2013).

11. High Value HealthCare Collaborative. Online at: http://www.dartmouth-hitchcock. org/about_dh/hvhc_collaborative.html (accessed May 15, 2013).
12. Tomek, I. M., A. L. Sabel, M. I. Froimson, G. Muschler, D. S. Jevsevar, K. M. Koenig, D. G. Lewallen, et al. 2012. A collaborative of leading health systems finds wide variations in total knee replacement delivery and takes steps to improve value. *Health Affairs* (Millwood) 31 (6): 1329–1338.

Chapter 26

Driving STEEEP Care through an Owned and Operated Health Plan

J. Paul Dieckert and J. James Rohack

CONTENTS

INTRODUCTION

Scott & White Healthcare is a nonprofit collaborative integrated health care system founded in 1897 in Temple, Texas, that is currently one of the nation's largest multispecialty group practices (see Chapter 9).[1] Recently, Scott & White and BHCS announced their intent to merge, creating the largest not-for-profit health system in the state of Texas. Scott & White owns and operates the Scott & White Health Plan, which serves more than 215,000 members in group, individual, and Medicare coverage programs and contracts, with care provided by both Scott & White and independent providers.[2] This chapter describes Scott & White's history, successes, and lessons learned regarding its efforts to drive quality improvement that results in STEEEP care through a health care delivery system owned and operated health care plan.

DEVELOPMENT OF SCOTT & WHITE HEALTH PLAN

Scott & White was originally organized as three distinct legal entities: the clinic, the hospital and foundation, and the health plan. Each entity had its own physician leader and chief administrative officer, all of whom met weekly to coordinate leadership efforts. In 2000, the hospital and clinic merged and a single chief executive was appointed to lead the entire system. The health plan remains a separate nonprofit legal entity under this leadership.[2]

Scott & White functioned much like a group model health maintenance organization (HMO) until recently. In response to increasing market competition and purchaser preference, it evolved from a closed, capitated model to an open fee-for-service network model. The clinic and hospitals began pursuing contracts with national health insurance providers while the health plan began to contract with independent providers. Salary-based compensation for Scott & White–employed physicians began to include productivity expectations in addition to patient care, teaching, research, and community service. Scott & White physicians currently provide about 75 percent of services provided under the Scott & White Health Plan.[2]

According to the National Committee for Quality Assurance (NCQA) Private Health Insurance Plan and Medicare Health Insurance Plan Rankings (based on evaluations of 474 private health insurance plans and 395 Medicare health insurance plans nationally), in 2012–2013, the Scott & White Health Plan was the highest-ranked Medicare and private HMO in Texas, with national ranks of 44 and 161, respectively, in these areas.[3]

ATTRIBUTES OF A HIGH-PERFORMANCE HEALTH CARE DELIVERY SYSTEM

The Commonwealth Fund Commission on a High Performance Health System identified six attributes of an ideal health care delivery system: information continuity, care coordination and transitions, system accountability, peer review and teamwork for high-value care, continuous innovation, and easy access to appropriate care.[4] Examples of the six attributes from Scott & White are displayed in Table 26.1.

STEEEP CARE IN THE SCOTT & WHITE HEALTH PLAN

As an owned and operated health care delivery system plan, the Scott & White Health Plan has several unique features that enable it to provide STEEEP care. Because it has access to claims data, Scott & White has a rich data source that allows it to follow patients as they enter, leave, and pass through different parts of the health care system. In addition, Scott & White owns its own pharmacies and employs its own pharmacy benefits manager, which facilitates a true partnership between pharmacists and the organization with the capability to capture pharmacy fill-rate data. While health care providers know what

TABLE 26.1 Examples from Scott & White of six attributes of a high-performing health care delivery system[2]

Attribute	Examples from Scott & White Healthcare
Information Continuity	• An electronic health record links main hospital and community clinics, facilitating communication across the care continuum. • Hospital nurses use mobile computers for electronic medication administration at the bedside. • Primary care physicians receive e-mail notifications of specialist consultations for their patients and e-mails to reconcile medication following hospital discharge. • An online portal allows patients to find a doctor, schedule appointments, request prescription refills, make payments, and learn about health topics.
Care Coordination and Transitions; System Accountability*	• Nurse care managers are embedded in two large clinics to work with primary care physicians on patient chronic disease management. • Health plan-sponsored nurse care managers provide telephonic support for chronic disease education, monitoring, and follow-up after hospital discharge, and refer patients for clinic appointments as needed. • New mothers receive phone follow-up and transitional support following birth. • Anticoagulation clinics staffed by pharmacists or nurses monitor patients outside the hospital using standardized protocols.
Peer Review and Teamwork for High-Value Care	• Physicians are evaluated through annual credentialing and performance reviews including patient care, teaching, research, and community service. • The electronic health record facilitates informal peer review and feedback. Some departments perform formal blinded peer review with feedback to physicians. • Divisions/departments can earn a 20 percent bonus by scoring 90 percent or higher on quality targets and goals. • The Patient Panels program invites patients to share personal stories of negative experiences; lessons learned are shared across the organization to improve quality and service.
Continuous Innovation	• Every major facility has a director of quality and a Quality and Patient Safety Council; the System Quality and Patient Safety Council monitors system-wide quality measures; any Core Measure not achieving a 90 percent score becomes an organization-wide quality improvement initiative with a formally chartered team led by a physician and an operational leader. • The Clinical Simulation Center designs and tests new processes and promotes continuous learning for human error prevention.

Continued

TABLE 26.1 *(Continued)* Examples from Scott & White
of six attributes of a high-performing health care delivery system[2]

Attribute	Examples from Scott & White Healthcare
Easy Access to Appropriate Care	• Clinic "ambassadors" greet patients at the door, direct them to appointments, and generally facilitate patient comfort and access. • The Office of International Affairs serves non-English-speaking patients (primarily from Mexico and Korea) with 24-hour interpretation and bilingual providers. • A telemedicine program for select specialties reduces geographic barriers for patients in remote areas. • HealthExpress clinic offers walk-in, urgent-care access seven days a week. • Group visits are offered for chronic disease education.

* System accountability is grouped with Care Coordination and Transitions, since one supports the other. *Source:* McCarthy, D., and K. Mueller. 2010. Scott & White Healthcare: Opening up and embracing change to improve performance. *Commonwealth Fund.* 1365, 37, January.

medications are prescribed, they typically do not have any way of knowing whether patients are filling those orders.

Examples of Scott & White Health Plan initiatives and practices to drive STEEEP care include:

• Every new Scott & White Health Plan member is offered counseling with a pharmacist about his or her medications. In addition to promoting patient safety, these counseling sessions allow pharmacists to check on the availability of equivalent generic medications that could save money for both the patient and the organization without compromising the quality of care; (*Safe, Efficient*).
• Scott & White Health Plan recently examined NCQA Healthcare Effectiveness Data and Information Set (HEDIS) measures for its members and recognized that some patients were not getting the right preventive or chronic care for diabetes. To address this issue, the health plan held "Diabetes Day," when various diabetes care providers gathered to see patients. To reduce the number of patients who would need to take time off work to attend Diabetes Day, Scott & White held the event on a Saturday; (*Timely, Effective, Equitable, Patient Centered*).
• Scott & White Health Plan has low administrative overhead costs. One reason for these low costs is that the plan has no employees; instead, Scott & White Healthcare employees are assigned, or "loaned," to the health plan and many services are shared with Scott & White (e.g., legal, Human Resources); (*Efficient*).
• Scott & White Health Plan supplies practice guidelines to practitioners to facilitate the provision of evidence-based, clinically appropriate care. In the late 1990s, a Scott & White eye specialist noticed he

was performing an increased number of corneal transplants in patients wearing extended-wear contacts. The health plan examined the reasons for this increase and found that many patients were rarely removing the contacts. Subsequently, the health plan provided a guideline to ophthalmologists and optometrists about patient education regarding use of extended-wear contacts. Corneal transplantations due to misuse of extended-wear contacts decreased so dramatically as a result of the guideline that the health plan was eventually able to retire the guideline; (*Safe, Effective*).

- Each new Scott & White Health Plan member is assigned to a primary care physician. The health plan has eliminated many barriers to referral. For example, in some geographic areas, a patient has no requirement to visit a primary care physician before seeing a specialist. This attention to patients' individual needs aligns with Scott & White's mission to provide personalized, comprehensive, high-quality health care; (*Efficient, Equitable, Patient Centered*).

SCOTT & WHITE HEALTH PLAN MANAGEMENT OF CHRONIC DISEASE

The Scott & White Health Plan approach to chronic disease is multifaceted and includes the following initiatives:

- Education and engagement of the member through various programs, including nurse line, disease management of 65 different conditions, nurse coaching, and shared decision making. These programs are available 24/7. Member self-management is encouraged and supported.
- Engagement and provision to clinicians, especially within Scott & White, with regular and accurate data on evidence-based goals and any gaps in those goals on a specific patient basis for common diseases, such as heart diseases, chronic obstructive pulmonary disorder, and diabetes.
- Provision of special, innovative interventions for specific chronic diseases. These programs are designed to make management of chronic disease easier, more comprehensive, and more collaborative for both members and their doctors.
- Complex Case Managers who reach out to members with multiple chronic conditions and assist them optimize their health after identifying specific health care or functional goals.
- Measurement and continuous improvement: Through the Scott & White Health Plan Quality Improvement and Analytics Departments, chronic disease management data are tallied, goals are analyzed, and barriers to improving care are identified so they can be overcome. The quality

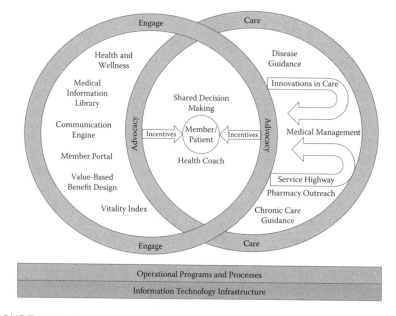

FIGURE 26.1 Scott & White health plan VitalCare Member Enablement Model. (McCarthy, D., and K Muller. 2010. Scott & White healthcare: Opening up and embracing change to improve performance. *Commonwealth Fund* 1365, 37, January. With permission.)

improvement team members meet with Scott & White Health Plan medical directors and practicing Scott & White clinicians who champion interventions to improve care for those with chronic diseases. Examples include the "All Things Respiratory" and "All Things Cardiac" groups made up of clinicians and quality improvement staff who implement projects to improve compliance with care plans and improve outcomes in members with chronic disease.

The Scott & White Health Plan has developed a number of innovative programs to help members with management of chronic disease. The plan has integrated its tools and programs for members under the title of VitalCare (Figure 26.1).

LESSONS LEARNED

Operating its own health plan has situated Scott & White well for the imminent shift from volume-based to population-based health care. Because of its long-standing focus on population-based care with attention to managing health care delivery and administrative costs through the patients enrolled in its health plan, Scott & White is uniquely positioned to achieve the Triple Aim,[5] as it has already embraced these principles on an ongoing basis.

Population-based care requires clinicians to embrace the stewardship role they play in health care finance and for financial leaders to embrace the stewardship role they play in delivery of effective clinical care. They must work together to ensure that care is neither under- nor overutilized. Because Scott & White operates its own health plan, clinical and financial interests have a longstanding history of and capacity to continue working together effectively to promote the delivery of STEEEP care.

CONCLUSION

Scott & White owns and operates its own health plan, which has given it valuable experience in managing the health of a population of patients. Scott & White has driven STEEEP care through its health care plan in a variety of ways, including medication counseling for all new members, a "Diabetes Day" to improve chronic care management, maintaining low administrative costs, providing evidence-based practice guidelines to clinicians, and eliminating many barriers to referral. Driving STEEEP care through its health care plan is aligned with Scott & White's continued commitment to the principles of the Triple Aim of improving the patient experience, improving the health of populations, and reducing the per capita cost of health care.

REFERENCES

1. Scott & White Health Care Fact Sheet. January 2013. Online at: www.sw.org (accessed April 9, 2013).
2. McCarthy, D., and K. Mueller. 2010. Scott & White healthcare: Opening up and embracing change to improve performance. *Commonwealth Fund* 1365, 37, January.
3. Scott & White Health Plan. SWHP—Texas and regional leader in NCQA health insurance plan rankings. Online at: http://www.swhp.org/news/ncqa12-13 (accessed April 10, 2013).
4. Shih, A., K. Davis, S. Schoenbaum, A. Gauthier, R. Nuzum, and D. McCarthy. 2008. Organizing the U.S. Health Care Delivery System for high performance. Online at: http://www.commonwealthfund.org/usr_doc/Shih_organizingushltcaredelivery-sys_1155.pdf (accessed May 15, 2013).
5. Berwick, D. M., T. W. Nolan, and J. Whittington, The triple aim: care, health, and cost. *Health Affairs* (Millwood) 27 (3): 759–769.

Chapter 27

Engaging STEEEP Care in an Accountable Care Organization

Carl E. Couch, F. David Winter, and William L. Roberts

CONTENTS

INTRODUCTION

Health care reform efforts that emphasize value, as opposed to the volume, of care are gaining momentum nationwide, including the formation of local clinically integrated organizations that are assuming accountability for both quality and cost.[1,2] The Patient Protection and Affordable Care Act provides incentives for the creation of these accountable care organizations (ACOs), including establishment of a federal shared savings program that rewards organizations that meet quality benchmarks while reducing health care spending.[3] Baylor Quality Alliance (BQA) is a clinically integrated ACO comprising of physicians, hospitals, and other providers of care whose mission is to achieve the highest quality, cost-effective care possible for the patients and communities served by BHCS.[4] BQA is pursuing this mission through an emphasis on primary care and better population health, improved coordination of patient care, and the creation of new payment models that reward high-quality, low-cost care.

ACOs offer potential advantages for patients, clinicians, hospitals, and payers. These advantages include (1) better coordinated and more cost-effective care to a growing number of chronically ill patients whose poor health outcomes are often attributable to fragmented care; (2) a strong foundation for implementing electronic health records and electronic patient communications to improve care management processes and encourage greater patient involvement in their own care; (3) use of performance measures that provide external accountability to payers and the public, and internal metrics to facilitate quality improvements; (4) reduction of the shortage of primary care clinicians currently facing the country by fostering primary care practices to care for larger numbers of patients through team-based practice; and (5) financial incentives that provide rewards for keeping patients well by bringing clinicians together into teams that take responsibility for all aspects of care across the spectrum of medical conditions and facilities.[5]

BHCS'S APPROACH TO ACCOUNTABLE CARE

In 2009, BHCS charted a roadmap for the future of its health care improvement journey, outlining seven pathways to achieving the Triple Aim of better care for individuals, better health for the population, and high-quality, low-cost care for all (Figure 27.1):[6]

1. Influence health care reform through patient-centered models of care
2. Fully implement clinical transformation to create an ideal experience for patients, physicians, nurses, and other caregivers
3. Continue to be a leader in medical education and research
4. Continue to develop existing and build new clinical centers of excellence to serve all people and improve the health of the communities we serve
5. Demonstrate financial stewardship by maintaining a top bond rating (AA)
6. Become an accountable care organization
7. Be routinely listed as one of the "top 5" health care systems in the nation

The BHCS commitment to creating a clinically integrated ACO is a testament to its belief that proactive, evidence-based, and value-driven care offers the best solution to the country's simultaneous needs to improve quality, reduce costs, and increase access to health care.

Baylor Quality Alliance

In the Dallas–Fort Worth metroplex, physicians and hospitals have a long history of success in a strong fee-for-service environment. The area is nationally recognized as one of the higher health care cost areas of the nation, with overall clinical outcomes no better than areas that deliver care at lower cost.[7] The opportunity therefore exists for physicians and hospitals to produce better value, where value is defined as the health outcomes achieved per dollar spent and measured over the patient's entire care cycle.[8–10] If value can be properly

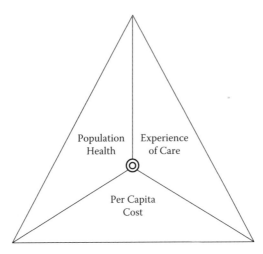

FIGURE 27.1 The Triple Aim. The Triple Aim framework was developed by the Institute for Healthcare Improvement and involves the simultaneous pursuit of improving the patient experience of care, improving the health of populations, and reducing the per capita cost of health care.

measured, reimbursement can be connected to the health care value provided, which "rewards providers for efficiency in achieving good outcomes while creating accountability for substandard care."[8] BHCS established BQA, a clinically integrated ACO, in 2011 with the expressed mission of delivering the highest quality, cost-effective, and coordinated care possible to the patients and communities served by BHCS.[4]

BQA is owned by BHCS and as of July 2013, includes 600 HealthTexas Provider Network (HTPN) physicians, 1,450 independent physicians, and 17 owned and operated BHCS hospitals. Its aim to improve patient care and population health while reducing overall cost is predicated on five interconnected approaches:

1. Redesigning health care entry points with an emphasis on patient-centered medical homes (PCMHs)
2. Connecting primary and specialty care physicians using health information technology to improve coordination across the continuum of care
3. Creating care coordination infrastructure to ensure that appropriate resources and services are able to meet the needs of the highest acuity patients
4. Establishing new health care payment models, such as shared savings and bundling, that reward value and performance rather than volume of service
5. Using sophisticated analytics tools to measure, improve, and predictively model care for the populations served

TABLE 27.1 Baylor Quality Alliance (BQA) committee structure

BQA Committee	Committee Function
Membership and Standards	Create standards of membership and manage performance of all participants; NCQA-accepted credentialing of physicians and other providers, and standards for alliance with postacute care providers and facilities.
Best Care/Clinical Integration	Multidisciplinary creation and monitoring of quality and efficiency of care paths across continuum of care; chronic disease management; transitional care management. This committee has almost 25 specialty subcommittees, each responsible for specialty-specific processes.
Compliance	Organizational adherence to regulatory requirements; assurance of rights and ethical care for patients served.
Finance/Contracting	Monitor financial performance of organization; create and adjudicate reward distribution; approve managed care contracts.
Information Technology	Ensure electronic connectivity to support clinical integration and measure both quality and cost performance.

BQA Structure and Governance

BQA is a limited liability corporation wholly owned by BHCS with a board, committee structure, and management team focused on patient-centered clinical integration across all points of care. The physician-led Board of Managers includes 15 practicing physicians, 3 BHCS executives, a community representative, and a member of the BHCS Board of Trustees. The BQA Board chairman is a practicing physician, and the physician Board members were selected from multiple medical staff communities to represent all parts of BHCS. An extensive physician-led committee structure is responsible for creating policies, establishing and evaluating membership criteria, monitoring regulatory compliance and financial performance, and creating disease management and population management care delivery protocols and pathways (Table 27.1). The designation of these committees reflects BQA's commitment to cultural transformation to become a clinically integrated organization that emphasizes collaboration. Committee participation affords interested physicians the opportunity to help shape the direction, operations, and success of the organization.

BQA Membership

Subject to meeting participation criteria, BQA membership is open to any qualified, board-certified physician who wishes to join with BHCS and its clinical partners in an accountable alliance to improve quality, reduce costs, and clinically integrate patient care. Members must agree to pay an initial fee to cover costs of credentialing and basic organization, submit quality and cost data, acquire an electronic health record, and log onto a secure Web site to view their quality and efficiency data no less than 8 out of every 12 months.[11] They also must agree to integrate clinical care, with primary care and specialist physicians jointly treating patients using agreed-upon, evidence-based care paths and protocols. In return, BQA physicians can expect (1) leadership commitment to a strong clinical integration infrastructure including robust information technology resources, (2) data to assist them in delivering high-quality, cost-effective care, (3) access to clinical decision support tools and other practice management resources to improve care and patient satisfaction and reduce practice costs, (4) better coordination of care for patients in all care settings, (5) a clinically integrated referral network devoted to a common mission, and (6) eligibility for quality and efficiency rewards that may become available.

A Foundation of Patient-Centered Medical Homes

The mission of an ACO is to manage the full continuum of care and be accountable for the overall costs and quality of care for a defined patient population. It is widely recognized that better primary care and care coordination organized around the patient offer the potential for improved outcomes at lower costs through improved prevention and management of chronic diseases, such as diabetes, coronary artery disease, and respiratory illnesses. As such, health care delivery models like the PCMH are rapidly gaining support across the health care industry to make health care more effective and efficient. BQA is committed to a strong primary care foundation and has redesigned its primary care sites to align with the PCMH model.

The foundation of the PCMH model is that each patient has a relationship with a primary care clinician who leads a team that takes collective responsibility for patient care, providing for the patient's health care needs, and arranging for appropriate care with other qualified clinicians. The model also emphasizes coordination of care facilitated by health information technologies; quality and safety, including use of evidence-based medicine; enhanced access to care; and reimbursement structured to recognize the value added by the medical home.[12]

BQA believes it is essential that every patient have a patient-centered medical home and expects all of its primary care physician members to achieve National Committee for Quality Assurance (NCQA) PCMH recognition within 24 months of joining the alliance. BQA's belief in the PCMH model has been strengthened by the HTPN experience with requiring its primary care practices to achieve PCMH recognition (see Chapter 14).

Achieving ACO Accreditation

BQA plans to strengthen its standing as an ACO by applying for NCQA ACO accreditation, a program that provides a roadmap for provider

TABLE 27.2 NCQA ACO accreditation standards

Standard	Requirement
ACO Structure and Operations	The organization clearly defines its organizational structure, demonstrates its capability to manage resources, and aligns provider incentives through payment arrangements and other mechanisms to promote the delivery of efficient and effective care.
Access to Needed Providers	The organization has sufficient numbers and types of practitioners to provide timely and culturally competent primary care, specialty care, urgent/emergency/inpatient/long-term care, and community and home-based services.
Patient-Centered Primary Care	The primary care practices in the organization's network act as medical homes for patients and offer patient-centered care.
Care Management	The organization collects, integrates, and uses data from various sources for care management, performance reporting, and identification of patients for population health programs. The organization provides resources to patients and practitioners to support care management activities.
Care Coordination and Transitions	The organization facilitates timely exchange of information between providers, patients, and caregivers to promote safe transitions.
Patient Rights and Responsibilities	The organization informs patients about the role of the ACO and its services. It is transparent about its clinical performance and any performance-based financial incentives it offers to practitioners.
Performance Reporting and Quality Improvement	The organization measures and publicly reports performance on clinical quality of care, patient experience, and cost measures. It identifies opportunities for improvement and helps providers and stakeholders collaborate on improvement initiatives.

organizations to demonstrate their ability to coordinate the high-quality, efficient, patient-centered care expected of ACOs.[13] As a voluntary program, NCQA accreditation signals an organization's intent to be transparent about its capabilities and performance, and can be used by payers seeking to distinguish among organizations offering to be accountable providers. Table 27.2 shows the standards applied by NCQA for ACO accreditation.

CHALLENGES AND OPPORTUNITIES

Few ideas for transforming health care delivery over the past several years have received as much attention as ACOs. There is growing consensus that without payment reform and aligned incentives, the goal of providing high-quality, affordable care and better health for all Americans will not be achievable. BQA leadership expects that transitioning from a volume-based, fee-for-service health care environment to a delivery system that rewards performance and value will pose both opportunities and challenges.

BQA already encountered practical barriers to applying for Medicare Shared Savings Program designation. The program currently requires that patient attribution be based on the physician's tax identification (ID) number, which is problematic for BQA because many of its physicians practice in groups that include physicians who do not practice within BHCS and are not participating in BQA, with the entire group sharing a single tax ID for billing purposes. As such, patient attribution by tax ID would capture all of that group's patients rather than those cared for by the individual participating physician, putting the ACO at risk for patients mostly seeing a physician who is not participating in the ACO's clinical integration activities, risks, and rewards.[11,14]

BQA is nevertheless committed to the goals of higher quality and lower overall cost of care through effective clinical integration and, so far, has identified three areas of opportunity for shared savings: (1) improving utilization of generic drugs, (2) minimizing avoidable hospital readmissions, and (3) reducing advanced imaging procedures for common low back pain. BQA formalized its first contract in 2013 with the BHCS Employee Benefit Plan. It is also actively engaged in discussion with Medicare Advantage plans and several commercial plans, looking primarily at shared savings models and PCMH fees.

Another significant challenge for BQA has been finding a secure and feasible means to share and report necessary clinical and performance data across multiple electronic health record (EHR) systems. Although all HTPN physicians share a common EHR system, many of BQA's independent physicians use different systems. To overcome this obstacle, BQA is in the process of implementing a Health Information Exchange (HIE) that will enable all participating providers to electronically share health information about their patients, such as test results, medications, allergies, immunizations, radiology images, and consents. It is also implementing a health–population analytics software system that will link inpatient electronic medical records, HTPN records, the HIE, claims data from BHCS's contracted commercial insurers, and BHCS financial records. Such electronic connectivity is needed to produce "actionable" data on health care quality and cost at the population level.

The financial logistics of the ACO's shared savings is another uncertainty facing BQA and other developing ACOs. Whether each participant will share equally in the savings, or whether savings will be proportional to how much each provider invests in forming the ACO remains to be determined. There also may be internal disagreement regarding what are considered appropriate uses of potential shared savings; hospitals may want to use savings to offset expenditures related to operations costs, while physicians may want to purchase medical equipment or care management tools. Likewise, it has not yet been determined how potential losses will be distributed across the ACO, or even whether a shared savings program alone will remain financially viable over the long term. These issues will continue to be modeled, debated, and formalized at multiple levels of health care governance as the accountable care model is adopted and implemented.

Physician recruitment and referral sources, especially among specialist providers, also pose challenges. Although the PCMH and Medicare ACO models place a clear emphasis on primary care, formal organization with specialists is essential to coordinating patient care across the entire care continuum. Although the incentive for specialists to join an ACO are less clear than for primary care physicians, a specialist who is not recognized as a "preferred" provider could potentially lose a substantial number of referrals. Ancillary care providers and suppliers may lose referral sources as well if they do not choose to join the ACO. Conversely ACOs need sufficient numbers of primary and specialty physicians serving a wide geographic area to ensure that they are able to deliver high-quality care to the patient population they serve across the continuum of care. Therefore, depending on factors such as the group's market share and relative negotiating power, some specialty groups will be more motivated than others to join the ACO. BQA encountered this situation as it began putting together its network of providers. While BQA has now assembled a network that includes the specialists considered adequate to care for the population it serves, it is continuing to recruit in specialties and geographic areas where access to care can still be substantially improved. Currently, the focus is on adding pediatric physicians as well as providers and facilities that specialize in postacute care.

CONCLUSION

The ACO concept has been embraced, both nationally and privately, as a promising framework for achieving the Triple Aim of improving population health, improving the patient experience of care, and reducing per capita cost. The establishment of BQA signifies BHCS's continuing commitment to provide STEEEP care for the patients and communities it serves. BQA's structure and governance are organized around the belief that accountable, evidence-based, collective, proactive, value-driven efforts will lead to a better health care system because it is truly patient centered. Its strength lies in a foundation of strong hospital-physician alignment, and a long history of quality improvement and dedication to the delivery of STEEEP care.

REFERENCES

1. Shortell, S. M., and L. P. Casalino. 2008. Health care reform requires accountable care systems. *JAMA* 300 (1): 95–97.
2. Fisher, E. S., M. B. McClellan, J. Bertko, S. M. Lieberman, J. J. Lee, J. L. Lewis, and J. S. Skinner. 2009. Fostering accountable health care: Moving forward in medicare. *Health Affairs* (Millwood) 28 (2): w219–w231.
3. Patient Protection and Affordable Care Act. P.L. 111–148. §4205, 2010.

4. Baylor Quality Alliance. Online at: http://www.baylorqualityalliance.com/Pages/home.aspx (accessed May 15, 2013).

5. Shortell, S. M., L. P. Casalino, and E. S. Fisher. 2010. How the center for Medicare and Medicaid innovation should test accountable care organizations. *Health Affairs* (Millwood) 29 (7): 1293–1298.

6. Berwick, D. M., T. W. Nolan, and J. Whittington, The triple aim: care, health, and cost. *Health Affairs* (Millwood) 27 (3): 759–769.

7. Agency for Healthcare Research and Quality. 2011. State snapshots. Online at: http://statesnapshots.ahrq.gov/snaps11/ (accessed May 15, 2013).

8. Porter, M. E. 2010. What is value in health care? *New England Journal of Medicine* 363 (26): 2477–2481.

9. Porter, M. E., and E. O. Teisberg. 2006. *Redefining health care: Creating value-based competition on results.* Boston, MA: Harvard Business Press.

10. Kaplan, R. S., and M. E. Porter. 2011. The big idea: How to solve the cost crisis in health care. *Harvard Business Review* 89 (9): 46–52, 54, 56–61.

11. Couch, C. E. 2012. Why Baylor Health Care System would like to file for Medicare Shared Savings accountable care organization designation but cannot. *Mayo Clinic Proceedings* 87 (8): 723–726.

12. Patient-Centered Primary Care Collaborative. Joint Principles of the Patient-Centered Medical Home. Online at: http://www.pcpcc.net/content/joint-principles-patient-centered-medical-home (accessed May 15, 2013).

13. National Committee for Quality Assurance. *Accountable Care Organization Accreditation.* Online at: http://www.ncqa.org/Programs/Accreditation/AccountableCare-OrganizationACO.aspx (accessed May 15, 2013).

14. ABIM Foundation. Choosing wisely®. Online at: http://www.choosingwisely.org/ (accessed May 15, 2013).

Chapter 28

Diabetes Health and Wellness Institute
An Escape Fire Model for STEEEP Care

John B. McWhorter, III, Paul Convery, and Charles E. Bell

CONTENTS

INTRODUCTION

The Diabetes Health and Wellness Institute (DHWI) at Juanita J. Craft Recreation Center in the southern sector of Dallas was developed as a holistic health equity model of care, aiming to not only meet the clinical needs of a medically underserved population, but to provide targeted interventions that promote wellness and behavior modification with the ultimate goal of improving disease management, health, and quality of life. DHWI is a collaborative partnership between BHCS, the City of Dallas, and a local community (comprising schools, churches, community leaders, and local businesses). It represents an unconventional solution to a crisis that cannot be solved using traditional approaches—an "escape fire," such as some experts have called for to deal with the crises of a health care system beset by medical errors, confusing and inconsistent information, a lack of personal attention, and fragmented care.[1]

In firefighting terms, an "escape fire" is a swath of land deliberately ignited to provide refuge from an oncoming blaze. This technique gained fame following the 1949 Mann Gulch wildfire in Helena National Forest, Montana, when smokejumper foreman R. Wagner "Wag" Dodge, unable to control or outrun the blazing wildfire, had to devise a life-saving solution: He lit a match and set fire to the grass in front of him, creating a makeshift buffer zone within which he was able to wait safely while the main fire burned around him. He survived the crisis virtually unharmed, but his crew, either unable to hear his instructions or unwilling to trust their lives to the burnt-out zone, largely perished—13 of the 15-man team were overtaken by the raging fire and died. Descriptions of the escape fire technique date at least as far back as James Fennimore Cooper's 1827 novel *The Prairie*, and it has most recently become the metaphor for the type of solution needed to solve the health care crisis in the United States in the 2012 documentary *Escape Fire: The Fight to Rescue American Healthcare*.[2] As envisioned in this documentary, the escape fire for health care consists of unfettered access to care, reliance on the best available science, and a focus on healing relationships.[1]

IMPROVING EQUITY IN DIABETES CARE: THE SOUTHERN SECTOR HEALTH INITIATIVE

BHCS's commitment to improving health equity includes efforts to eliminate variation in health care access, delivery, and outcomes. The Southern Sector Health Initiative (SSHI) was approved by the BHCS Board of Trustees in 2006 as the system's first health equity improvement project.[3]

Dallas County is the second largest county in Texas, with a population of 2.4 million, and has a high prevalence of diabetes, exceeding both state and national rates (11.4%, compared with 9.6% in Texas, and 8.3% nationwide[4]). Significant economic, social, and health disparities exist within the county, with the southern half containing areas that are significantly disadvantaged. Southern Dallas has the lowest per capita income ($13,400) and highest unemployment rate (13.1%) in the county.[4] Dallas County's high diabetes burden is disproportionately borne by communities in southern Dallas County. They lack adequate access to health services, safe environments, and healthy foods, and have the highest rates of short- and long-term diabetes complications, lower extremity amputations, and uncontrolled diabetes. Thirty percent of hospital admissions and emergency department (ED) visits at Baylor University Medical Center (BUMC) are due to diabetes or diabetes-related conditions; Southern Dallas residents make up the largest proportion of these visits.

An SSHI task force identified the Frazier neighborhood of southern Dallas as the community having the greatest need for health-equity improvement. The task force also determined that implementing a new model of care focused on diabetes management would have the greatest impact on improving the overall health and wellness of the community. The task force outlined a holistic health equity model that would not only meet residents' clinical needs related to diabetes, but also apply health education and evidence-based strategies to improve population health.[5] The centerpiece would be a center of excellence in diabetes treatment and prevention that would work in concert with community partners to promote education, public health, economic development, and faith-based health initiatives within this vulnerable community.

THE DIABETES HEALTH AND WELLNESS INSTITUTE: A NEW MODEL OF DISEASE PREVENTION AND MANAGEMENT

Following the SSHI proposal to establish a local center of excellence in diabetes care, BHCS and the City of Dallas formed a partnership to transform an existing recreation center into the area's first and only facility dedicated to diabetes health and wellness. In June 2010, the DHWI opened its doors. Its mission is to improve the care and save the lives of people with diabetes by creating a new care model focused on health care, education, and research. Named for a beloved community activist, the Juanita J. Craft Recreation Center served the neighborhood for decades prior as a trusted place for individuals and families. It provided a practical foundation for the new institute's efforts to promote collaboration among community stakeholders and improve individual, family, and community health outcomes.

DHWI provides a comprehensive approach to diabetes prevention and management by providing access to clinical health care services, a recreation facility, health education, and an array of wellness programs. The first part of the DHWI model (Figure 28.1) represents the concept of a center of excellence for diabetes care driven by three core competencies: (1) primary prevention focused on the identification and removal of barriers to health and wellness, (2) secondary prevention focused on individuals diagnosed with the disease and the prevention of diabetes-related complications as well as other chronic diseases, and (3) tertiary prevention interventions designed to provide treatment for individuals with established diabetes and related co-morbidities.[6] DHWI aims to deliver on these prevention and treatment goals through its commitment to four fundamental principles: (1) collective mission and collaborative financial support; (2) integration of social, cultural, political, and economic initiatives; (3) innovative approaches to the care of diabetes and related conditions; and (4) incorporation of multidisciplinary, community-based research to understand the needs of the community.

The second part of the DHWI model details the collaboration between DHWI and community partners to promote and implement education, public health, economic, and faith-based initiatives that support health and wellness as well as clinical interventions. An important focus of these community partnerships is empowering individuals and families that have or at risk for

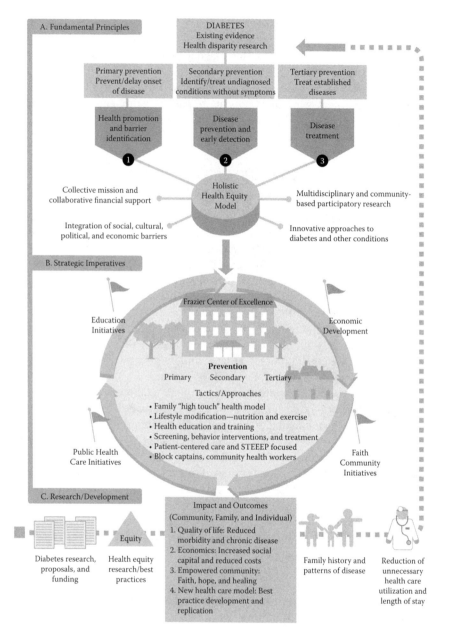

FIGURE 28.1 The Diabetes Health and Wellness Institute (DHWI) model of diabetes/chronic disease care.

diabetes with the education, training, and resources necessary to make decisions and engage in behaviors that positively affect their health. Effective self-management is a key step in improving diabetes-related health outcomes and quality of life.[7]

The third part of the model identifies development and research opportunities generated by outcomes that impact the community, families, and individuals. Not only can this holistic model of diabetes care improve health promotion and disease prevention, it also can improve the economy, community empowerment, and quality of life of families and individuals. A proactive approach to diagnosis and disease management that includes increased utilization of screening tests for early detection and treatment can reduce unnecessary health care utilization and length of hospital stays. Outcomes of the DHWI model will also contribute to the body of knowledge needed to guide future diabetes research, submit proposals for external funding, substantiate best practices for equity research, and promote the detection of patterns of disease. This information will contribute to health disparity research and enable innovative approaches in primary, secondary, and tertiary prevention to be developed and utilized in the future to detect and treat diabetes and other disabling conditions.[6]

DHWI ORGANIZATION AND FACILITIES

BHCS invested $15 million in DHWI, with an additional $2 million provided by the city of Dallas. DHWI includes a state-of-the-art health clinic staffed by a family practice physician and nurse practitioner, medical assistants, and a referral coordinator for specialty and ancillary care. In addition, certified diabetes educators, an exercise physiologist, and health educators are employed to promote individual and community wellness and health education. To round out the care team by addressing the mental and spiritual health of our members, the services of a licensed clinical social worker and a fulltime clergy member are engaged as well. Together the team helps weave diabetes prevention into the neighborhood's social fabric so that it is an integral part of community life. DHWI also assists members in obtaining affordable medications, and hosts nutrition and healthy cooking classes delivered in English and Spanish, exercise programs (including running and walking clinics and weight training), and a variety of youth and adult recreation programs administered by the Dallas Park and Recreation Department.

DHWI's daily health and wellness activities are overseen by a president and three key executives: a medical director, vice president of educational programs, and vice president of business development and finance. A DHWI Board of Directors, a Community Advisory Board, and a Ministerial Advisory Board have been established to ensure that initiatives are aligned with the community's social, economic, and spiritual needs and values.

INITIATIVES TO IMPROVE HEALTH, WELLNESS, AND THE PATIENT CARE EXPERIENCE

The Frazier community and southern Dallas face a number of barriers to the diagnosis and effective control of diabetes. A community needs assessment based on a survey methodology revealed that more than 57 percent of respondents believe their family history of diabetes makes developing the disease "inevitable." Dealing with diabetes for many of these residents means waiting until a crisis occurs and then entering BUMC through the emergency department. Residents of the community also lack awareness and knowledge about preventing and managing diabetes. DHWI has implemented a number of initiatives to increase access to primary care and to promote overall health and wellness with a heavy emphasis on community partnerships to help provide needed education and support.

Engaging Community Health Workers: The Diabetes PEERS in Faith Program

Successful programs to close the gap in diabetes-related health disparities in various racial and ethnic populations are built on strengthening the links between health care providers and the community members they serve. An emerging body of literature appears to support the unique role of community health workers (CHWs)—also known as community health advocates, lay health workers, *promotores* (promoters), and peer health educators—in strengthening existing community networks for care, providing community members with social support and education, and facilitating access to care.[8] Engaging and training CHWs has been integral to the DHWI mission to reduce diabetes disparities and improve population health since its inception.

In developing a CHW model to deploy in the Frazier community, DHWI capitalized on BHCS's experience engaging CHWs as part of the Diabetes Equity Project (see Chapter 18). This experience was combined with knowledge that the predominantly African American and Hispanic residents served by DHWI view churches as pillars in the community and trusted sources of information, leading to development of the Diabetes PEERS (Prevention, Empowerment, Education, Resources, Support) in Faith Program. This program engages church members as CHWs to provide the community with education and support in the prevention and management of diabetes. In FY2010, it helped 38 local church members in southern Dallas complete the state-approved CHW Certification Training program and obtain certification from the Texas Department of State Health Services.[9] These PEERS are now providing education and awareness activities and programs in their churches. They refer members of their congregations, who are seeking to improve their health and diabetes self-management, to DHWI.

Coordinated Care around the Whole Patient

The DHWI model of chronic disease management is a holistic approach that aims to address the emotional, behavioral, and spiritual needs of patients, as well as their physical health needs. Personalized care is coordinated by a diabetes care team that includes a primary care physician, nurses, diabetes educators, community health workers, pastors, social workers, and exercise specialists. Patients living in a targeted geographic area are assigned to a health partner, a trained diabetes educator, to guide them through their journey toward good health. Patients complete a health risk assessment and receive point-of-care testing to assess levels of glycemic control, hypertension, lipids, and obesity. This assessment provides a triage mechanism to assign individuals to the appropriate care providers based on their level of diabetes risk. Patients at high risk are referred to the DHWI primary care physician, or their own primary care physician if they have one. The health partner helps the patient select and enroll in DHWI education, counseling, and exercise programs designed to improve overall health and wellness. These programs teach skills related to the American Association of Diabetes Educators' seven health care behaviors (AADE7™): healthy eating, being active, monitoring, taking medication, problem solving, reducing risks, and healthy coping.[10]

The use of patient data management systems that provide timely access to information about individuals and aggregate patient populations is key to providing coordinated chronic disease care and management and demonstrating the effectiveness of the care model.[11] DHWI uses DiaWEB,[12] a web-based diabetes and chronic disease management tool, to collect and track information about patients' health risk, health behaviors, clinical outcomes, and quality of life. The system also provides the ability to set and manage behavioral change goals around diabetes self-management as defined by AADE7. It promotes the consistency of care patients receive from any member of the care team and helps the patient to achieve improved health outcomes.

Improving Access to Healthy Food Options
through a Weekly Farm Stand

Poor food access is a major contributor to health disparities and health problems in low-income communities.[13] People who live in a neighborhood without access to grocery stores, who live in "food deserts," are less likely to have healthy diets, thus increasing their risk of diet-related diseases including high blood pressure, cancer, and diabetes. Many areas of southern Dallas fit this profile. Since opening in June 2010, DHWI has held a weekly farm stand offering fresh fruits and vegetables at low-cost to residents to address the lack of access to healthy food options. Most items are prebagged and sell for $1. Nearly 100 people from adjacent communities and businesses visit the farm stand each week; data are captured related to what is being purchased by individuals. Sales total about $500 per week accounting for nearly half a ton of produce sold. As an extension of its nutritional and cooking classes, DHWI develops and prepares healthy recipes and provides the recipes along with tasting samples to farm stand patrons.

Partnerships and Collaborations

DHWI's community and ministerial advisory groups, as well as a variety of partnerships and strategic alliances, have been instrumental to the development of programs designed to engage community members in their own health care and overall well being. DHWI's partnership with the City of Dallas provides participants with access to recreational programs and activities at low or no cost. DHWI also has partnered with the YMCA of Metropolitan Dallas and their water aerobics program, expanding the physical activity options available to community members.

In 2011, DHWI teamed up with AMERIGROUP Community Care, a Medicaid managed care program, and other community partners to conduct Project F.U.N (Families Understanding Nutrition) to improve the health and health behaviors of children aged 6 to 11 years.

CHALLENGES AND OPPORTUNITIES

Data collected through March 31, 2013 on DHWI participants diagnosed with diabetes indicate that these individuals have experienced modest improvements in meeting recommended standards for diabetes care (see Table 28.1).[14]

DHWI currently provides health care services and wellness programs to nearly 1,500 active participants. Of those participants, 64 percent are at risk for developing diabetes if therapeutic lifestyle changes are not adopted. The other 36 percent currently have diabetes. A tremendous opportunity exists to introduce health and wellness interventions that can reduce or eliminate the burden of disease for many previously underserved community residents. Yet challenges also exist.

On the benefits side, the concept of patients being aware of and accountable for their own health is central to DHWI's mission of improving health through engagement and empowerment. However, this concept is at odds with how health care is perceived and delivered in many parts of the country, including southern Dallas. Getting individuals to commit to their health and a health care model that emphasizes many points of care, self-management of chronic disease, and prevention over quick fixes is extremely difficult. It requires a shift in cultural attitudes, particularly in historically underserved

TABLE 28.1 Active DHWI participants achieving guidelines
for diabetes care, June 2010 through March 2013

Hemoglobin A1c (<7.0%) n = 742

	Meets	Does Not Meet
Baseline	12%	88%
Follow-Up	30%	70%

Blood Pressure (<130/80 mmHg) n = 742

	Meets	Does Not Meet
Baseline	13%	87%
Follow-Up	16%	84%

LDL Cholesterol (<100 mg/dl) n = 742

	Meets	Does Not Meet
Baseline	10%	90%
Follow-Up	11%	89%

Note: Participants shown have been diagnosed with type 2 diabetes and enrolled in DHWI treatment programs for ≥1 year. The mean length of time between baseline and follow-up measurements was 9 months.

communities. Continued engagement with the local faith community and other community partners is essential to DHWI's efforts to address this challenge.

Difficulty with enrollment procedures and a high population of uninsured residents pose additional challenges to the DHWI mission and efforts to increase participation. Individuals who join DHWI are required to fill out a health questionnaire, a disclosure form required by care providers affiliated with HTPN, and other documents. Residents often lack awareness about their eligibility for Medicaid and other government services. Patients with medical needs that fall outside the scope of DHWI, such as dental care, are referred to specialized clinics, where fees and documentation can pose additional barriers. Many do not qualify for Medicaid, struggle to pay their medical bills, and thus are unwilling or apprehensive about seeking care. DHWI has engaged an eligibility consulting group to assist community members in navigating these complexities. One day per week, consultants are available onsite to help patients apply for various government assistance programs that may help provide for their care.

Although the challenges are clear, the potential benefits of the DHWI approach are great. DHWI provides a practical working model for how community partnerships, education, interdisciplinary care teams, and holistic care practices can be put to work to improve chronic disease management and population health, and provides opportunities for research pertaining to health equity and best practices.

Through its ongoing data collection and evaluation efforts, DHWI will be able to assess the effectiveness of its interventions and provide instructive lessons to communities across the county, the state, and the nation striving to reduce health disparities and improve health outcomes. DHWI embodies the BHCS commitment to equitable and accountable care and improving the health of the community beyond the walls of the hospital.[15] At a time of soaring health care costs, eroding access to care, and frequent devaluation of patient needs, the DHWI model offers a possible solution to an intractable problem—an escape fire and a veritable lifeline.

REFERENCES

1. Berwick, D. M. 2002. Escape Fire: Lessons for the Future of Health Care. *The Commonwealth Fund.*
2. *Escape fire: The fight to rescue American healthcare.* DVD, directed by Matthew Heineman and Susan Froemke (2012; Aisle C Productions & Our Time Projects, 2013).
3. Baylor Health Care System. Diabetes Health and Wellness Institute. [Online at: http://www.baylorhealth.edu/COMMUNITYOUTREACH/Pages/DiabetesHealthand-WellnessInstitute.aspx (accessed May 15, 2013).
4. Edwards, J., Pickens, S., Schultz, L., Erickson, N., Dykstra, D. 2012. Horizons:The Dallas County Community Health Needs Assessment.Online at: http://www.dallas-county.org/department/hhs/documents/FINALCHNA.pdf (accessed April 10, 2013).
5. Rice, D., T. M. Bain, A. Collinsworth, K. Boyer, N. S. Fleming, and E. Miller. 2012. Effective strategies to improve the management of diabetes: Case illustration from the diabetes health and wellness institute. *Primary Care* 39 (2): 363–379.
6. Rice, D., B. Kocurek, and C. A. Snead. 2010. Chronic disease management for diabetes: Baylor Health Care System's coordinated efforts and the opening of the Diabetes Health and Wellness Institute. *Proceedings (Baylor University Medical Center)* 23 (3): 230–234.
7. Centers for Disease Control and Prevention. 2005. *National diabetes fact sheet: General information and national estimates on diabetes in the United States.* Atlanta: CDC.
8. Centers for Disease Control and Prevention (Division of Diabetes Translation). Community health workers/promotores de salud: Critical connections in the communities. Online at: http://www.cdc.gov/diabetes/projects/pdfs/comm.pdf (accessed April 10, 2013).
9. Texas Department of State Health Services. Community Health Worker Training and Certification Program. Online at: http://www.dshs.state.tx.us/mch/chw.shtm (accessed April 10, 2013).
10. American Association of Diabetes Educators. AADE7™ self care behaviors. Online at: http://www.diabeteseducator.org/ProfessionalResources/AADE7/ (accessed April 10, 2013).
11. Improving Chronic Illness Care. The Chronic Care Model. Online at: http://improving-chroniccare.org/index.php?p =The_Chronic_Care_Model&s = 2 (accessed November 18, 2010).
12. Chiron Data System Inc. 2010. DiaWEB Chronic Disease Management software summary. Online at: http://www.chirondata.com/documents/DiaWEB%20Summary_6_2010.pdf (accessed May 15, 2013).

13. Satia, J. A. 2009. Diet-related disparities: Understanding the problem and accelerating solutions. *Journal of the American Dietetic Association* 109 (4): 610–615.

14. Standards of medical care in diabetes—2012. *Diabetes Care* 35 (Suppl 1): S11–S63.

15. Baylor Quality Alliance. Online at: http://www.baylorqualityalliance.com/Pages/home.aspx (accessed January 8, 2013).

Chapter 29

Conclusion

Neil S. Fleming and David J. Ballard

The BHCS mission is "to be trusted as the best place to give and receive safe, quality, compassionate health care." This is a difficult objective to achieve and, in some sense, can never be counted as completed and checked off the "to do list." Instead, as new developments in health care delivery, medical technology, and health care policy arise, it is a constantly receding goalpost, which is, ironically, only reached by its continued pursuit. While BHCS has made strides toward closing the gap between its performance and its mission, the STEEEP quality journey will never end, simply because tomorrow's "best" is never the same as today's in a constantly changing environment.

That being said, BHCS has gained valuable experience in its STEEEP quality journey. It has positioned itself well to continue moving closer to achieving the ideal of health care delivery that it has set for itself. Critical aspects of its success to date, and that will contribute to its ongoing success, include:

1. The commitment to quality improvement from the highest levels of leadership
2. The investments made in training leaders in quality improvement techniques and clinicians in leadership skills, and supporting their application of those skills
3. The creation and maintenance of the infrastructure needed to support large-scale, in-depth data collection, analysis, and reporting of performance data
4. The application of the STEEEP framework, both to clearly communicate goals and priorities throughout the organization and to guide the organizational management framework

5. The close structural alignment with the HealthTexas Provider Network (HTPN) physician network
6. Remaining vigilant of changing conditions in the health care environment through participation in national organizations and implementing new strategies, tactics, and tools when these indicate a new need to be met

Essential to BHCS's success has been unwavering commitment by the Board of Trustees, as well as administrative and clinical leaders, to quality improvement. The alignment of this leadership triad has facilitated all the other changes instituted at BHCS in pursuit of becoming the "best place to give and receive safe, quality, compassionate health care." The first deliberate step taken on the BHCS STEEEP quality journey was the quality resolution passed by the Board of Trustees in 2000, establishing the conviction that maintaining the status quo in health care delivery would no longer be acceptable, and setting the stage for the strategic deployment of resources needed to build a quality infrastructure. This early commitment to quality set BHCS ahead of the pack when the Institute of Medicine (IOM) issued its seminal report, *Crossing the Quality Chasm,* the following year,[1] but BHCS did not yet have the infrastructure in place to attain its lofty vision. Establishing that infrastructure, and training the necessary leadership in its application to health care improvement has been the work of the decade that followed.

One of the first key steps in this process was the training that 40 BHCS clinical and nonclinical leaders received in 2002 in the Intermountain Healthcare Advanced Training Program. Quality expert Brent James introduced them to the fundamental concepts of culture, processes, and tools for improving health care. Through this training, BHCS leaders began to understand the principles of rapid-cycle improvement and its application to health care, and they returned to Dallas with a newly stoked passion for quality and an understanding that improvement would require a steady pursuit that would build upon itself as it gained momentum. Moreover, these leaders had a common understanding that BHCS needed to build its capacity for improvement to realize its vision.

A direct outgrowth of the BHCS leaders' participation in the Advanced Training Program was the creation of a BHCS-tailored version of this rapid-cycle improvement training that was taught locally, educating BHCS employees in quality improvement principles and applications. This training course, originally known as ABC Baylor, but now offered as part of the STEEEP Academy, has graduated more than 1,500 BHCS clinical and nonclinical leaders since it was first offered in 2004. An essential aspect of this rapid-cycle quality improvement training is the PDCA (Plan-Do-Check-Act) cycle, which has become embedded in the BHCS quality improvement culture. Under this ethos, BHCS has learned the value of piloting its quality improvement initiatives to determine whether—and how—they work before bringing them to scale. This model relies heavily on the organization's capacity to conduct analytic evaluations in terms of the employee skill sets, software tools, and data infrastructure that are in place. The STEEEP Academy also incorporates Lean thinking principles—which provides common ground for the integration of the organizations' respective care delivery models following the BHCS–Scott & White merger.

BHCS invested heavily in establishing the necessary analytic infrastructure to support its improvement efforts. Many transactional data applications have rudimentary reporting capabilities, but BHCS has extended its analytic capabilities by hiring individuals with sophisticated data management and analytic skills who are able to extract, transform, load, and merge the necessary data from disparate sources for complex evaluations of multiple dimensions of STEEEP care. This work, performed by the STEEEP Analytics group, requires powerful database management software, business intelligence tools, and statistical programming, but enables the creation of reports for BHCS leaders and clinicians that both "drill down" to the physician or patient level to examine the clinician's performance or the patient's experience, and "aggregate up" to enable population management. The fragmentation of data information systems that is endemic to health care within the United States makes a properly equipped resource, such as STEEEP Analytics, essential to a health care organization that recognizes the critical need to evaluate its performance and the effects of its quality improvement interventions.

A further important tool that this analytic infrastructure and pilot testing of initiatives offers is the creation of local evidence of an intervention's effectiveness. When positive benefits are demonstrated (e.g., the mortality and costs savings described in this book with the use of standardized order sets for pneumonia and heart failure care), clinical leadership can present these results and challenge clinicians or administrators to adopt the tool or practice as "the right thing to do." Local data have been found to be particularly useful in this context, as it is immediately obvious that they are relevant to the particular setting in which the individuals being asked to make the change work. As BHCS clinical leaders often point out, "Physicians are trained first and foremost as scientists so they understand the concept of hypothesis testing, and will be more likely to accept the results after seeing the evidence." BHCS has engrained this data-driven perspective in both its clinical and nonclinical leaders, supported by advanced graduate training of physician and nursing leaders so they understand how to interpret findings for decision-making purposes.

Looking more broadly than the capacity to evaluate individual quality improvement initiatives and create the local evidence to drive their adoption, BHCS's capacity for collection, analysis, and reporting of extensive performance data related to the processes and outcomes of care for specific populations enables internal comparisons between BHCS facilities (which can motivate improvement through friendly competition) as well as external comparisons with national, regional, and local benchmarking data. BHCS has intentionally dedicated resources to data collection within its hospitals and the HTPN physician practices to provide transparent feedback to various stakeholders. In addition to the quality improvement benefits such performance feedback has supported, these investments have paid off more broadly as requirements for public performance reporting have grown and, more recently, been linked to reimbursement. Rather than having to "scramble" to meet the new requirements, BHCS had the infrastructure in place to smooth the transition to the increased focus on performance data in the broader U.S. health care system.

In addition to training its leaders in quality improvement techniques and data interpretation, BHCS recognized the importance of training clinical leaders in effective leadership skills to create success on its STEEEP quality journey, and of developing these leaders within the organization to ensure successors are in place to maintain the quality improvement momentum as earlier leaders transition elsewhere or retire.[2] BHCS has made significant investments in developing nursing and physician leaders to help move the organization along its quality journey. This has taken the form of both formal programs, such as those developed in collaboration with the Southern Methodist University Cox School of Business, and less formal mechanisms within a culture that supports very strong mentoring of future leaders by current leaders. In the quality leadership space, the Institute for Health Care Research and Improvement's Clinical Scholar program has served to identify and develop future physician leaders, with the added benefit of selecting for individuals with advanced training and experience in research methods that cross over well to data-driven quality improvement. These formal and informal development approaches communicate that continuous improvement is imperative at the individual as well as the organizational level.

A running theme throughout the factors contributing to BHCS's success on its quality journey is the adoption and implementation of the STEEEP framework, guiding all the initiatives undertaken and the requisite infrastructure established. This framework provides a common language for communicating to individuals throughout BHCS the specific aspects of "quality" that needed to be considered and met: safety, timeliness, effectiveness, efficiency, equity, and patient centeredness. The clear definition of quality this provides has become endemic to BHCS's culture as the lens through which health care delivery must be viewed. Coupled with the basic quality principle of improving care through standardization of evidence-based best practices, the STEEEP framework has laid the foundation for the BHCS-wide improvement efforts.

STEEEP also has become the guiding principle according to which the management framework of clinical and nonclinical leaders is organized. This was implemented through the STEEEP Governance Council (SGC), which connects corporate areas, hospitals, and service lines for the purpose of setting and prioritizing system-wide goals and related activities. Subcommittees are organized around the domains of STEEEP to facilitate the development of specific initiatives based on needed leadership and resources, subject to approval by the SGC. At the same time, the involvement of clinical service line leaders supports efforts to bring a system-wide approach to the delivery of care across multiple hospitals. Leadership and resource support along the dimensions of STEEEP is also being implemented to standardize the delivery of evidence-based care across service lines at each hospital, with requisite feedback of process and outcomes performance data.

A second structural aspect of BHCS that has been essential to its quality achievements is the alignment between the hospital system and physicians created through the formation of HTPN—the entity through which physicians are employed. Physician involvement is critical to the success of most health care improvement activities,[3] and the close integration of BHCS and HTPN enables physician involvement and leadership of hospital-based quality initiatives. It also provides a larger perspective of the health care delivery system for both BHCS and HTPN, and opportunities to align quality improvement efforts across in-hospital and ambulatory care settings.

A final aspect of BHCS's approach to the STEEEP quality journey that is critical to both its past and continued success is the strong anticipatory approach it has adopted, being "on the lookout" for changing conditions in the current environment, through participation in leadership activities at the national level. This approach is particularly important in the dynamic environment of health care reform. BHCS engages with organizations such as The Joint Commission; the National Quality Forum, which sets the agenda for metrics that the Centers for Medicare and Medicaid Services will consider for reimbursement related to quality; and the Leadership Institute, which convenes national clinical and nonclinical leaders to share best practices. BHCS also participates in groups such as the High Value Healthcare Collaborative, which enables it to share best practices with other leading health care systems by pooling data and resources to examine and respond to current policy questions. As changes are detected in the health care environment that indicate new approaches will be needed to maintain the STEEEP quality journey, BHCS identifies and implements the necessary strategies and tools. For example, as the Patient Protection and Affordable Care Act and the accountable care movement have shifted the focus in health care to emphasize adding value from the patient's perspective, BHCS has begun applying Lean thinking to improving throughput across BHCS. This approach emphasizes efficiency and timeliness of care that is patient centered, using techniques such as value stream mapping to identify activities that do not benefit patients. Reducing time in the delivery of care can create benefits for patients as well as for clinicians. This approach enhances BHCS's traditional perspective along the lines of standardizing the delivery of evidence-based care and the integration of BHCS's experience implementing STEEEP care with Scott & White's experience applying Lean thinking to health care is anticipated to lead to substantial further gains in quality across all components of the newly formed entity following the merger. As the emphasis in health care shifts toward under-standing the value created for the patient, over the entire continuum of care,[4,5] the relevant question for health care organizations and providers is becom-ing: "What health outcomes are achieved, and what resources are expended in achieving them?" This question shifts the focus away from the volume of services delivered, which is the centerpiece of the current fee-for-service reimbursement system. It rewards providers based on results over a given duration of care for the patient so that efficiency and effectiveness become paramount for all stakeholders. This patient-centered, value-based approach coupled with patient contributions to their own well being is the next genera-tion of health and health care, recognizing that individuals need to *produce* their own health rather than *consume* health care.[6]

BHCS has made significant strides on its STEEEP quality journey, and its approach to quality continues to gain strength, having reached the "flywheel" stage of achieving perpetuating momentum necessary to improve and "break through" from "incremental" to "exponential" gains in performance.[2] The health care delivery system in the twenty-first century has become increas-ingly dynamic and uncertain, but the capacity for improvement BHCS has established over the past decades also makes it resilient in the face of this uncertainty. At the core of BHCS's efforts is a focus on achieving STEEEP care and the infrastructure needed to take a data-driven approach in doing so. The same tools that enabled BHCS to recognize and address challenges to pro-viding high quality care in previous years can be adapted to identify and meet those that emerge in the increasingly dynamic health care sector. Applying this approach to its unwavering commitment to "be trusted as the best place to give and receive safe, quality, and compassionate health care" positions BHCS well for continued success along its STEEEP quality journey, and to collabo-rate with other health care delivery organizations with similar aspirations.

REFERENCES

1. Corrigan, J. M., M. S. Donaldson, L. T. Kohn, S. K. Maguire, and K. C. Pike. 2001. *Crossing the quality chasm: A new health system for the 21st century.* Washington, DC: National Academy Press.
2. Collins, J. 2001. *Good to great.* New York: HarperCollins.
3. Berwick, D., A. Godfrey, and J. Roessner. 1990. *Curing health care.* San Francisco: Josey-Bass.
4. Porter, M. E. 2010. What is value in health care? *New England Journal of Medicine* 363 (26): 2477–2481.
5. Kaplan, R. S., and M. E. Porter. 2011. The big idea: How to solve the cost crisis in health care. *Harvard Business Review* 89 (9): 46–52, 54, 56–61.
6. Fuchs, V. R. 1975. *Who shall live? Health, economics, and social choice.* New York: Basic Books.

Index